TRACK AND FIELD
Coaching Manual

- Coaching techniques and guidelines formulated by **The Athletics Congress'** Olympic Development Committee

edited by

Vern Gambetta
University of California, Berkeley

LEISURE PRESS

CHAMPAIGN, ILLINOIS

Published by Leisure Press
A division of Human Kinetics Publishers, Inc.
Copyright © 1981 Leisure Press
All rights reserved. Printed in the U.S.A.

ISBN - 0918438 - 73 - X
Library of Congress Number: 81-81394

Printed in the United States

PERMISSION CREDIT:
Championship Books for permission to reprint material from their publications in the chapters on the pole vault and the long jump.

PHOTOGRAPHIC CREDITS:

Athletic Journal: sequential photos for the chapters on the hammer throw and sprinting.

Scholastic Coach: sequential photos for the chapters on the high jump, hurdling, javelin, long jump, pole vault, and shot put. Photos by Toni Nett, Helmar Hommel, and Bruce Weber.

University of California Sports Information Office: 10,100 (David Gradeur)

Stanford University Sports Information Office: 104 (Robert Beyers), 116 (James A. Spirakis), and 132 (Jim Lanahan).

USMA Army Information Office: 200

Don Gosney: 4, 8, 16, 19, 38, 40, 43, 47, 50, 52, 53, 57, 59, 62, 67, 71, 78, 86, 97, 98, 103, 105, 113, 165, 176, 177.

Stan Pantovic: 201

CONTENTS

INTRODUCTION

The Olympic Development Coaches' Manual stands as a unique effort on the part of the American track coaching community.

It presents the combined views of both the Men's and Women's Development Committees of the Athletics Congress which met in Gainesville, Florida to prepare a text on the most recent trends in training and technique for each of the track and field events.

Over fifty of American's top collegiate, club, and high school coaches have contributed. The Manual also contains chapters by other top experts in some of the specialized areas of knowledge with which the modern-day track coach must be familiar in the quest to meet the needs of the young athlete.

This Coaching Manual focuses on practical drills, teaching points, and training schedules. It is intended to serve as a blue print for "grass roots" coaches to follow in seeking to optimally develop their charges in the build-up years leading to the Los Angeles Games.

This first-ever Manual is being distributed free to every high school sponsoring a track program and to all TAC member clubs across America as a service of the Athletics Congress.

We hope that it proves to be a valuable tool in our nation's development effort in the great sport of track and field.

John Randolph
Chairman
Men's Olympic Development
Committee of The Athletics Congress

Democracy is the key word—The Athletics Congress is run by people involved in track and field, long distance running, and race walking.

INTRODUCING THE ATHLETICS CONGRESS (TAC)

By Jimmy Carnes
President
Athletics Congress

As President of the Athletics Congress, it gives me a great deal of pride and pleasure to be a part of the production of this coaches' manual. Throughout the United States we have a vast amount of knowledge that has long needed to be condensed into a manual and provided to the coaches throughout this nation. The Olympic Development Committee has now made this possible and I congratulate each and every coach who has played an important role in this production.

In October, 1978, Congress enacted into law the Amateur Sports Act, which required full autonomy for all United States governing bodies for sports on either the Olympic or Pan American Games programs. The first of the Olympic program disciplines to become independent of the AAU was athletics (track and field, distance running and race walking). Since August, 1979 the Athletics Congress of the United States has been working as the national governing body for athletics and as the United States member of the International Amateur Athletic Federation. This change has given us the opportunity to bring together an effective, unified body in the United States.

The Athletics Congress of the USA is a national organization of Americans, junior and senior, male and female, who work voluntarily to promote and encourage amateur athletics throughout the United States. Through its membership of athletics clubs, schools, colleges and countless other organizations, TAC/USA promotes opportunities for participation nationwide.

There are 60 local associations which constitute the national organization of the Athletics Congress. Interested individuals may join the local organizations and in turn have direct representation on the national level. TAC/USA membership includes over 2000 athletics clubs, high schools, colleges and universities with over 100,000 registered members.

Registration is the back bone of the Athletics Congress, providing a means of identification and control of all competing athletes. Registration fees are established by each of the Athletics Congress' local associations. They cover the administrative costs of the local and national program and include an insurance program that provides coverage against accidents which occur in the course of participation in sanctioned events and organized practice.

Democracy is the key word and the essential fact is that the Athletics Congress is run by people involved in track and field, long distance running and race walking. Members of the Congress are elected by each of the TAC/USA associations and its member national organizations with athletes comprising at least 20% of the delegate role. TAC/USA national officers are elevated by the Congress. A board of directors establishes and carries out policy.

The Athletics Congress now has the duty of developing outstanding representation for the United States in Olympic and Pan American Games as well as responsibility for raising funds necessary for American athletic participation in national and international competition. Every individual in America interested in this great sport has an opportunity and a duty to become involved and I encourage you to join with us in developing a strong, unified organization which can keep our sport at the top of all international competition.

Part A
Coaching
Principles

All training responses are the result of stress and adaption by the athlete to that stress.

1
Basic Exercise Physiology

by
Phil Henson, Ph.D.
Indiana University

In coaching track and field, one must constantly be concerned with the physical response taking place in the athlete as a result of the prescribed training or exercise. The desired response is the objective of all training and must be kept firmly in mind during the construction and application of workouts.

Stress and Adaptation

All training responses are the result of stress and adaptation. A stress is placed on the system, and the body adapts. If the stress is not too intense, the adaptation will result in the body being stronger than before. Several important factors should be kept in mind:
1. The adaptation will be specific to the stress.
2. All adaptation takes place during recovery.
3. If the stress is too intense or too frequent, adaptation is not possible. This is often called "failing adaptation", and results in negative improvement in performance.

Training Principles

The physical responses desired in track and field are improved strength, speed, and endurance. Regardless of the type of workout, the following important training principles influence these responses:

Specificity

The training must be specific to the requirements of the event. If the event requires strength, then strength training must be an integral part of the overall program. It does little good to have a shot putter run 10 miles each morning. Although strength is important to all athletes, a distance runner should not spend the same amount of time in strength training that a thrower or jumper would. The endurance athlete must spend the majority of his/her training time in endurance activities.

Intensity

Intensity of training must be individualized and relative to the requirements of the event and the fitness of the athlete. A warm-up for one athlete may be a very intense workout for another. The intensity must not be so great that recovery cannot take place before the next workout period.

Frequency and Duration

More is not always better. As with the intensity, the frequency and duration of workouts must match the capabilities of the athlete. Some very intense workouts such as strength training or intense running may require more than 24 hours of recovery time. Thus, alternating workouts, or mixing hard-easy days are important factors in proper recovery.

11

Genetic Limitations

Each individual is born with inherent limits of strength, speed, and endurance. With proper training the athlete may reach the upper limit of his/her abilities. It is the coach's responsibility to see that the athlete is placed in the event in which his/her abilities best meet the requirements of the event.

Physiological Effects of Strength Training

In general, the greater the muscular strength, the faster the speed of movement against a given resistance. This principal is important in all areas of track and field but is most critical in the throws, the jumps, and the sprints.

Types of Muscle Contraction

Eccentric -	Muscle contraction while lengthening. Walking down steps is an example.
Concentric -	Muscle contraction while shortening. Most common type of contraction used in strength training.
Isotonic -	Contraction with constant resistance. Limited by the weakest point in the range of motion.
Isometric -	Contraction with constant length or without movement. Strength gains occur only at a single point in the range of motion.
Isokinetic -	Accomodating resistance. Resistance is maximum throughout the range of motion. Provides ''best of both worlds'' in terms of isotonic and isometric.
Plyometric -	Involves rapid eccentric-concentric while involving strength reflex. Found in depth jumping and other bounding activities.

Repetitions and Overload

Strength training can be used to develop strength, endurance, or a combination of the two, depending on the number of repetitions.

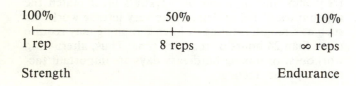

100%	50%	10%
1 rep	8 reps	∞ reps
Strength		Endurance

One repetition at maximum resistance would result in some increase in muscular strength, but virtually no change in muscular endurance. Likewise one hundred or more repetitions would result in almost pure endurance training, with little or no strength gains. It appears that working with weights which can be handled for a maximum of eight repetitions results in approximately equal increases in strength and endurance.

The overload principle is important in strength training. Resistance against which the muscle works should be increased throughout the course of the program as the muscle gains in strength and endurance. Work loads should be above those normally encountered in the performance of the event.

Body Composition

The desired goal in strength training is an increase in muscular strength along with a decrease in the amount of fat tissue contained in the body. This is often accomplished with little change in the total body weight.

It is important to keep careful records of strength and body weight changes and to monitor body composition through determination of the percentage of body fat. Body fat can be estimated by a determination of body density through underwater weighing techniques or through the measurement of skin fold thickness. Included are the instructions and formulae for the estimation of body composition by skin folds.

Procedure for Skinfold Determinations

1. The thumb and forefinger of the left hand should be placed far enough apart so that a full fold can be pinched up firmly and clearly from the underlying tissue.
2. The fold is then held firmly between the fingers while the measurement is being made.
3. The calipers are applied to the fold below the fingers so that the pressure at the point measured is exerted by the caliper faces, not by the fingers. Readings to the nearest ½ mm are adequate.
4. Skinfolds are measured on the male at the midpoint of the thigh on the front of the leg, and at the lower tip of the scapula on the back.
5. Female skinfold measurements should be taken at the tip of the iliac crest on the side and at the midpoint of the triceps on the back of the arm.

Body Density (Male) = 1.1043 - (0.001327 x thigh) -(0.00131 x scapula)

Body Density (Female) = 1.0764 - (0.0081 x Iliac Crest - (0.0081 x triceps)

Calculation of Body Fat Percentage

$$\% \text{ Fat (Male)} = \frac{4.570}{\text{Body D.}} - 4.142 \times 100$$

$$\% \text{ Fat (Female)} = \frac{4.201}{\text{Body D.}} - 3.813 \times 100$$

Total body fat = % Fat X Body Weight

Lean body weight = Body weight - total body fat
Average values for a 20 year old individual.
Male 15%
Female 20%
Ideal values for track and field athletes should be near these norms:

	Male	Female
Distance	7%	10%
Sprints, Jumps	8%	12%
Throws	15%	20%

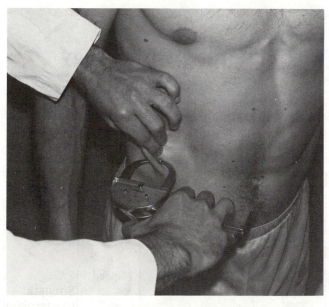

Body fat can be estimated by determining body density through measuring skin fold thickness.

Physiological Effects of Speed Training

It has often been written that sprinters are "born, not made". Although training effects may be less pronounced in the sprints when compared to other events, there is no doubt that sprinting can be increased through proper training.

Sprint speed is the product of stride length (SL) and stride frequency (SF): (Speed = SL x SF). In order to increase speed, one or both of these variables must be changed.

Stride Length

The stride length is probably the most easily affected through training. Improvements in efficiency through better movement mechanics can result in a more fluid motion with a greater range of motions of the limbs. This more efficient movement can add several inches to each stride taken.

Stride length may also be increased through increases in muscular strength. Greater strength in the extensor muscles can result in a more vigorous push-off against the running surface, which then results in a greater velocity and distance traveled between strides.

Stride Frequency

Stride frequency is less easily affected through training and is probably more related to genetic limitations. It appears that the ability to oscillate the limbs is largely inherited and is related to factors which are not easily affected by training. The muscle fiber ratios, which are fixed at birth, correlate closely with speed. Also, recent research indicates that speed of nerve conduction is also related to speed and is affected little by training.

Improvements in movement efficiency probably provide the best means of increasing the stride frequency. This may be effected by having the athlete perform the proper movements over and over until they become so ingrained that they occur automatically and efficiently at high speeds.

Physiological Effects of Endurance Training

Maximal Oxygen Uptake

Maximal oxygen uptake, expressed in ml. of oxygen, consumed in a minute's time, for each kg. of body weight. ml/kg min is probably the best predictor available for endurance capabilities. For runners the test is usually conducted on a motor-driven treadmill, and the amount of oxygen consumed is indirectly measured by determining the difference between the total amount of oxygen inhaled and the amount exhaled.

Average Values of Oxygen Uptake		
	Male	Female
20 year old	45	40
H.S. Distance Runner	60 +	55 +
College Dist. Runner	70 +	60 +
World Class Athlete	75 +	70 +

Since most coaches do not have available a treadmill and equipment for analysis, a simplified test for estimating maximal oxygen uptake is the 12 min. run for distance. This test can be administered to a large group in a short period of time and an estimated maximum oxygen uptake value calculated for each individual. The formulae for this calculation and an example are provided.

The estimated maximal oxygen consumption is derived from running as far as possible in a 12 minute period. By knowing the distance covered, the average velocity can be determined. To compute average velocity multiply distance covered by 5. To convert average velocity in miles per hour to meters per minute, multiply average velocity by 1609 and divide the result by 60. The resultant figure will be average velocity expressed in meters per minute.

Example:

Distance covered in 12 minutes = 1.25 miles

1.25 x 5 = 6.25 MPH

$$6.25 \text{MPH} = \frac{6.25 \times 1609}{60} = \frac{10056.25}{60}$$

= 167.6 Meters/minute

= 168 Meters/minute

An average velocity of 150 meters requires 33.3 milliliters of oxygen per kilogram of body weight per minute. Each additional meter above or below this velocity requires an additional +0.178 milliliters of oxygen. In the above example the average velocity of 168 meters per minute is 18 meters above the 150 meters and would require 18 x 0.178 or +3.20, which results in an estimated maximal oxygen consumption of 36.50 milliliters of oxygen per kilogram of body weight per minute.

Fitness Categories for Men

Under 30

I. Very Poor	less than 25.0
II. Poor	25.0 - 33.7
III. Fair	33.8 - 42.5
IV. Good	42.6 - 51.5
V. Excellent	51.6

What Max VO² Does Not Show

● Anaerobic Ability

The Max VO₂ test measures oxygen uptake only, which is an indirect indication of aerobic capacity. What is not shown, but which does play a key role in competitive situations, is anaerobic capacity or the ability to work without oxygen. Anaerobic work results in a buildup of lactic acid in the system. Some individuals are capable of tolerating much higher levels of this substance without substantial reductions in performance. This ability is often referred to as "guts" in competitive situations and is many times the difference between winning and losing when individuals have similar capabilities.

● Ability to Exercise at High % of Max

An average individual begins to accumulate acid when exercising at little more than 50% of maximum value. However, highly trained individuals have been known to exercise at 80-90% of max uptake without difficulty. This ability, which is partly innate, but largely aquired through training and competition, gives the trained athlete a tremendous advantage in distance events.

● Mechanical Efficiency

The greater mechanical efficiency that most exceptional runners have allows them to run at the same velocity while consuming less oxygen. In a competitive situation this allows the trained individual to run at a greater velocity without exceeding his/her aerobic capacities. This may allow an individual to defeat an opponent who has a greater oxygen uptake, but is less efficient mechanically.

Training Physiology

The following table represents an approximate breakdown of aerobic and anaerobic components of the most common distance training methods:

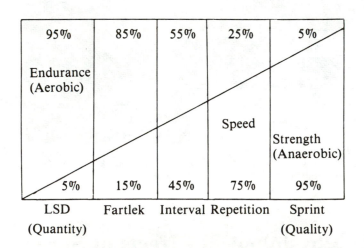

LSD (Quantity)	Fartlek	Interval	Repetition	Sprint (Quality)
95%	85%	55%	25%	5%
5%	15%	45%	75%	95%

From this table it can be shown that aerobic capacity is most affected by LSD, fartlek, and interval training methods. On the other hand, anaerobic capacity is most affected by sprint, repetition, and interval methods. Since an endurance athlete utilizes both aerobic and anaerobic capacities in competition, this explains why a variety of training methods is valuable in developing the fullest abilities of the athlete. For the remaining discussions of the physiological effects of training refer to this aerobic-anaerobic relationship.

Biochemical Effects of Training

● Aerobic Changes

1. Increased levels of myoglobin found in the muscle tissue. Myoglobin stores small amounts of oxygen at the tissue level similar to hemoglobin, which is found in the blood.
2. Increased ability to store and oxidize carbohydrates. Carbohydrates provide the primary energy source for running distances up to 12-14 miles.
3. Increased ability to oxidize fats. Fat is used as an energy source when running distances beyond 10 miles.

● Anaerobic Changes

1. Increased capacity of the ATP-PC system. This system provides enough energy for very short explosive types of exercise lasting only a few seconds.
2. Increased ability to oxidize glycogen without oxygen. This ability is most important in middle distance events. Energy can be provided in this manner for up to 45 seconds and plays a particular role at the start and finish of each race.

Circulatory Effects

Most circulatory changes which are a result of training contribute to improvements in aerobic capacity. The circulatory system is the most important link in providing oxygen to the muscle tissue. The most important component in this system is cardiac output (CO) which is the product of stroke volume (SV) and heart rate (HR). (CO = SV x HR)

Indications are that cardiac output is improved through increases in stroke volume and that these changes are often a result of interval training. The training effect takes place during the recovery interval, and this is the single most important aspect of training for circulatory improvement.

● Changes Apparent at Rest

1. An increase in heart size occurs as a result of heart muscle hypertrophy.
2. An increased stroke volume is directly related to the increased heart size but is also a result of improved circulation; (i.e., aortic compliance, increased capillary beds, venous return).
3. Little change in cardiac output occurs since the tissue needs at rest are not appreciably changed with training.
4. There is a significant reduction in heart rate with training. Since CO is unchanged, an increase in SV will be accompanied by a decrease in HR.
5. Trained individuals appear to have an increase in blood volume and amount of hemoglobin.
6. There may be a slight decrease in hematocrit (blood thickness) which may be an attempt by the system to enable the blood to flow more easily.

Most circulatory changes which are a result of training contribute to improvements in aerobic capacity.

The body is a dynamic system capable of making enormous adjustments to physiological stress.

● Changes Apparent at Easy Work Loads

1. A slight decrease in O_2 consumption occurs because of improved efficiency of movement. Improved coordination and elimination of wasted muscle contractions cause less demand for oxygen.
2. A slight decrease in lactate production occurs as more of the work is accomplished aerobically with less need for anaerobic work.
3. A slight increase in cardiac output supplies most of the oxygen needed.
4. Increased stroke volumes and slightly decreased heart rates accompany the increased cardiac output.

● Changes Apparent at Maximum Output

1. Increased oxygen uptake is apparent due to other improvements in the supply chain.
2. Increased cardiac output.
3. Increased stroke volume.
4. A slight decrease in heart rate likely occurs. Since the greatest heart efficiency is at about 150 beats per min., increases beyond this rate actually result in a decreased stroke volume due to a lack of filling time. At heart rates beyond 180-190, the cardiac output actually declines, resulting in a point of diminishing return.
5. An increased lactate production occurs as the athlete is better able to tolerate and continue running with high levels of lactic acid in his system.
6. Some changes occur in the distribution of blood flow, primarily through greater restriction of blood to non-working areas and greater supply to muscles directly involved in running.
7. An increase in the number of open capillaries in the working muscles seems to occur. It is not clear if this results from the creation of new capillaries or merely from greater use of existing vessels. This increase seems to be most effected by LSD and Fartlek training.
8. An increase in the Arterial-Venous O_2 difference occurs. This is an indication that a greater amount of oxygen is being extracted from the blood as it passes through the muscle tissue. Since all blood leaving the lungs is about 98% saturated with oxygen, the increased A-V O_2 difference is primarily a result of lower oxygen levels in the venous return.

Additional Effects of Endurance Training

1. Although the respiratory system is seldom the limiting factor in endurance exercise at sea level, some changes do occur with training. Increase would be found in the tidal volume, the maximal ventilation, and the diffusion capacity.
2. Training in warm environments enables the body to become better acclimatized to heat. Acclimatization to heat is related to improvements in blood circulation, since the cooling mechanism is closely dependent on greater skin blood flow. Hot environments will nearly always produce slower performances in distance events, due to the added need for blood flow for cooling purposes.

In summary, the body is a dynamic system capable of making enormous adjustments to physiological stress. Nearly every adaptation which occurs can be explained, and these explanations can be used in adjusting training programs for optimum improvement.

2
Basic Biomechanics*

by
Tom Ecker
Cedar Rapids, Iowa,
Public Schools

> **BIOMECHANICS** is the science that examines the external forces which act on inanimate objects and on the human body, and the effects produced by those factors. Other terms, such as **MECHANICS** and **DYNAMICS** have been used interchangeably with biomechanics but the latter term has gained wider acceptance than any other in recent years. The following definitions relate to specific aspects of biomechanics as they apply to track and field. A comprehensive overview of how biomechanics affects the technique for running, throwing, and jumping appears as the introductory chapter to each of these sections in this text.

BIOMECHANICS is the science that examines the external forces which act on inanimate objects and on the human body, and the effects produced by those factors. Other terms, such as **MECHANICS** and **DYNAMICS** have been used interchangeably with biomechanics but the latter term has gained wider acceptance than any other in recent years. The following definitions relate to specific aspects of biomechanics as they apply to track and field. A comprehensive overview of how biomechanics affects the techniques for running, throwing, and jumping appears as the introductory chapter to each of these sections in this text.

MOTION (continuous change of position) is of two types—linear and rotary.

LINEAR MOTION is motion along a generally straight line, such as the path of the long jumper during the approach run.

ROTARY MOTION is turning or rotating around an axis, such as the motion of the high jumper going over the crossbar, the turning of the discus thrower, before the throw, or the movement of a runner's arms and legs.

VELOCITY is a distance traveled in a specific direction, divided by time. In running, velocity may be computed by multiplying stride length times stride frequency.

ACCELERATION is a positive rate of change of velocity (speeding up).

DECELERATION is a negative rate of change of velocity (slowing down).

ACCELERATION DUE TO GRAVITY is acceleration of a freely falling body, with an increasing velocity of approximately 32 feet per second every second that it falls.

HORIZONTAL VELOCITY is velocity in a horizontal direction (straight ahead).

VERTICAL VELOCITY is velocity in a vertical direction (straight up).

A PARABOLIC CURVE is the regular flight curve followed by an object's (or person's) center of mass when projected into the air. The flight trajectory is determined by the combination of the horizontal and vertical velocities at take-off. While the object is in the

*Reprinted from **Track and Field: Technique Through Dynamics** by Tom Ecker. Publisher: Tafnews Press, Box 296, Los Altos, California 94022.

air, its horizontal component is unaffected by outside forces (except for some air resistance), but gravity gradually slows the vertical component to zero and then reverses the process, with the object gaining in velocity as it falls. The result is a perfect regular curve of flight. The size and shape of a parabolic curve is determined by the horizontal and vertical velocities at release (or at take-off). A long jumper's horizontal velocity at take-off is much greater than his or her vertical velocity, creating a long, low parabolic curve. A high jumper's vertical velocity at take-off is greater than his or her horizontal velocity, creating a short, high parabolic curve. It is important to remember that it is the center of mass that follows the parabolic curve, and that nothing can alter that curve once the athlete (or object) is free in the air.

An **AERODYNAMIC CURVE** is the irregular flight curve followed by objects that are affected by air resistance, such as the discus and javelin.

FORCE is any physical cause that modifies the motion of a body, such as the force the shot putter exerts against the shot, the force the high jumper exerts against the ground, etc.

RESULTANT (or EFFECTIVE) FORCE is the sum of all the forces acting on a body.

ACTION-REACTION IN THE AIR (Newton's third law of motion) occurs in the same plane, or in planes that are parallel, around an axis which passes through the body's center of mass. Any movement initiated by the athlete while free in the air must bring about an equal and opposite reaction on the opposite side of the center of mass.

GROUND REACTION is the equal and opposite force that the ground returns when a force is applied against the ground. When a shot putter lifts the shot prior to release or a high jumper is in position for take-off, the forces applied to the ground are returned to the athletes in the form of upward lift. The greater the effective force against the ground, the greater the lift.

IMPULSE is force times time. A change of velocity (e.g., of a shot or of the human body) is dependent upon the force itself and upon the time during which the force is applied. An increase in the force or in the time of the force will increase impulse.

MASS is the amount of matter in an object (or person), measured in pounds or grams.

The **CENTER OF MASS** of an object (or person) is the point where all of the object's mass is considered to be concentrated. In the human body, the center of mass is not a fixed point in a specific part of the body. As body positions change, the center of mass changes its position within the body.

CONCENTRIC THRUST is the application of force along a line that passes directly through the object's (or person's) center of mass. The result is no rotation of the object and maximum potential for projection of the object's center of mass through the air.

VERTICAL ECCENTRIC THRUST is the application of force along a generally vertical line that does not pass directly through the object's (or person's) center of mass. The result is rotation of the object and a reduc-tion in the potential projection of the object through the air. The more eccentric the thrust, the more the rotation, and the less the projection.

High jumping is a compromise. Obviously there must be enough eccentric thrust for the jumper to be able to achieve an efficient layout position, but not so much as to reduce the height of the jump more than is absolutely necessary.

HORIZONTAL ECCENTRIC THRUST (which creates a "hinged moment") brings about a continuation of motion by the upper body after the linear motion of the lower body has been stopped momentarily. When the athlete's foot is grounded, the upper body continues forward at an increased velocity, and forward rotation of the body is begun. The javelin thrower at release and the long jumper at take-off experience horizontal eccentric thrust.

An **AXIS** is a straight line about which a body—either animate or inanimate—rotates.

GROUND AXES are those axes which an athlete's body rotates around when in contact with the ground. A ground axis may be generally vertical, with the axis running from the point of contact with the ground on up through the athlete's center of mass; it may be horizontal, running through the point where the athlete's body touches the ground, or it may be a combination of the two. A discus thrower turns about a vertical axis prior to the release of the discus; a javelin thrower rotates over a horizontal axis during the release of the javelin.

PRIMARY AXES are those axes which pass through the athlete's center of mass after the athlete leaves the ground and is free in the air. Any rotation of the entire body must be around one or more of the three primary axes—the longitudinal (head to toe), the transverse (side to side), and the frontal (front to back).

NUTATION is rotation around more than one of the primary axes at the same time, creating a "wobble" in the air. The "wobble" can be in the human body, such as during the rotation of the high jumper during the flight path over the crossbar, or it can be in an inanimate object, such as in an eccentrically-thrown discus.

An **AXIS OF MOMENTUM** is one around which continued turning takes place. Rotation that begins on the ground continues in the air around an axis of momentum.

An **AXIS OF MOVEMENT** is one around which action and reaction take place in the air. Any action initiated by an athlete who is free in the air brings about a simultaneous equal and opposite reaction on the opposite side of the athlete's center of mass. Both the action and the reaction are around an axis of movement.

SECONDARY AXES are those which pass through a part of the athlete's body, but do not pass through the center of mass. The rotation around a secondary axis is not the rotation of the entire body; in general, it is rotation involving only the limbs. Athletes create secondary axes to reduce or reverse unwanted body rotation (or to correct body position) while in the air. The most obvious example is the hitch-kick in long jumping.

MOMENTUM is mass times velocity.

Transference of momentum is the process through which momentum may be transferred from the entire body to one part or from one part of the body to the entire body.

TRANSFERENCE OF MOMENTUM is the process through which momentum may be transferred from the entire body to one part, as in discus throwing, or from one part of the body to the entire body, as in the high jump and long jump take-offs.

INERTIA is a body's resistance to change in motion. A body at rest tends to stay at rest; a body in motion tends to stay in motion.

ROTARY VELOCITY is the turning velocity of a body as it rotates around an axis. It is measured by the angle through which the rotating body turns in one second (degrees or revolutions per second).

ROTARY INERTIA is resistance to change in rotary motion. Before an object begins to rotate about an axis, it is the object's rotary inertia which acts as a resistance to the turning; after the object begins turning, the object's rotary inertia acts as a resistance to its stopping. Two factors contribute to the rotary inertia of a turning object—the amount of mass (m) which lies outside the axis of rotation, and the radius (r) of rotation. Written as mr^2, rotary inertia can be decreased or increased, without increasing the amount of mass itself, by altering the distribution of mass around the axis of rotation. The closer the mass is to the axis (which means a shortening of the radius), the less the resistance to speeding up or slowing down of rotation; the farther the mass from the axis, the greater the resistance.

ROTARY MOMENTUM is rotary velocity (the velocity of turning) times the turning object's rotary inertia (resistance to turning). Any turning object (or person), free in the air, has unchanging rotary momentum. This momentum begins on the ground and cannot be added to or subtracted from during the time in the air, remaining constant until the object returns to the ground.

CONSERVATION OF ROTARY MOMENTUM is a means of increasing or decreasing rotary velocity by decreasing or increasing rotary inertia. Since the product of rotary velocity and rotary inertia is rotary momentum, which must remain constant once the turning object is in the air, reducing one of the two factors must increase the other. In other words, increasing rotary inertia (mr^2) by increasing the radius (the distance the body's mass is from the axis of rotation) decreases rotary velocity. Conversely, decreasing the radius increases rotary velocity.

3
Flexibility for Track and Field

by
Bob Lawson
University of Wisconsin—Parkside

Flexibility or **Suppleness** is the component to physical fitness that pertains to the functional capacity of the joint to move through a normal range of motion. It involves the muscular system as well as the bones, joints and connective tissue. Merely adequate flexibility can be increased to some extent by stretching, but those with limited range of motion or the tight person is restricted to some degree and subject to a higher risk of injuries, than is the very supple person.

All active persons need three components for total fitness before they can use their natural inherited abilities:

1. **Strength**: Best gained through weight training (artificial weight used against gravity - the overload principle).
2. **Stamina or Cardio-Respiratory Fitness**: The ability to handle oxygen. Gained through aerobic running of 30 plus minutes in a continuous rhythmic motion - with a control pulse rate of 120 to 155 beats/minute for training effort.
3. **Suppleness or Flexibility**: The capacity of being easily flexed or bent without damage.

- Strength
- Stamina   BEFORE
- Suppleness
- Speed
- Skill

You need the first three components of fitness before skill can be applied or before you can use your inherited speed.

Two Types of Flexibility Exercises

1. **Ballistic Movement**. Tissue is moved to its maximum range with such force that the momentum may continue beyond the normal range of that joint. Sudden or violent stretching (ballistic) may cause a reflex contraction of the exercising muscles to prevent those tissues from over stretching. This may cause the opposite reaction, or shortening. This is the body's in-built self-protecting mechanism or the

Static stretching is the best method of stretching.

stretch reflex that protects you from injury. So, stretching by jerking, bobbing, or bouncing should be eliminated from your program. If you do movement type stretching, control the stretch and then relax - don't bounce.

2. **Static Stretching.** (isostatic) The joint is held briefly in a position that stretches the tissue to its maximum controlable length without undue stress and is held for a period of 10 to 30 seconds (or more). Isostatic stretching is safer than ballistic methods because it doesn't impose sudden stress upon the involved tissue, yet does the work intended.

Guidelines for Static Stretching
1. **Never force** a stretching exercise. Don't over stretch. Do it by feel.
2. Be patient; work within your limits.
3. Stay relaxed in all areas of the body.
4. Maintain good posture and body alignment at all times.
5. Don't hold your breath - breathe normally.
6. Never force to a level of discomfort or pain.
7. Always warm-up before stretching.
8. Afer all long distance running and weight training, stretch the muscles being used that day. Even better, stretch the muscles used in weight training between sets for 10 seconds.
9. Being over weight leads to a decrease in range of motion.
10. Unbalanced training or muscle groups will also restrict range of motion.
11. Proper stretching will aid in relieving tension from daily stress.
12. Use equal time between exercises to let the muscles relax (10-30 seconds rest).
13. It should be done daily.

Training Environment
1. Comfortable area about 68°F-72° and clean.
2. Gymnastics or wrestling mat or grass area.
3. Lighting not too bright.
4. Quiet area so athlete may concentrate on relaxation and body alignment.
5. Soft music or tape recording of exercise program is best. Each athlete may make his own tape to exercise by.

How to Teach Exercise
1. Always work right side of body first, then left side. This will help keep you in sequence and proper order.
2. First **name exercise** - and say "**position**" - **begin** number **one**; second rep say **two**; third rep say **three**, etc.
3. If doing exercises that use both sides of body - do right side then say "**switch**" to left side - then **two**, **three**, etc.

4. End of interval of time - say "**okay**" - rest, repeat.
   Example: a. to start new exercise: **Positions - Begin** (number 1)
   b. end of 10 seconds - **Okay**; rest equal interval
   c. **Two**; start second rep, etc.
5. Use stop watch for time control or tape recording with the above commands and time controled intervals with music.

Exercises

If you have had any serious injuries, check with your physician before doing any of these exercises.

A. Standing Passive Hang
1. Standing Position - feet 6 inches apart; legs slightly flexed in a straight log position.
2. Bend from the upper thighs and let the body and arms hang passively - like touching your toes. Drop all tensions of your total body. Stay relaxed & let gravity take over.
3. Value: stretches lower back, hamstrings. Feel yourself settling down with gravity.
4. 2-3 x 30 seconds.
5. Bend knees before standing up.

Passive Hang

"J" Stretch

B. The "J" Stretch
1. Lying on your back, hands out to sides or over head.
2. From a tucked position, roll hips over head - then straighten your legs with a slight flex at the knees. Reverse this position to a tuck between set.
3. Hold position 2-3 x 30 to 60 seconds.
4. If you get tight or feel discomfort, flex the knees toward the head, then return legs to proper position.
5. Value: stretches the upper and lower back, hamstring and neck.

C. The Pretzel

1. Sit with right leg straight.
2. Bend your left leg, foot crossed over right leg to the outside of right knee.
3. Right elbow bent and placed on outside of left thigh.
4. Look over left shoulder with left hand behind you.
5. Hold 2-3 x 10-15 seconds.
6. Value: lower back and side of hip.

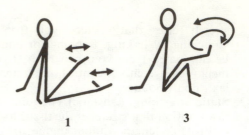

1   3

Ankle flexion and extension   **Circumductions**

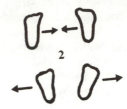

Inversion and eversion

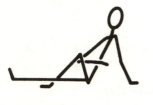

Pretzel    **"V" Set**

D. "V" Set

1. Sit on the floor both legs slightly forward and extended.
2. Bend over from the hips with the head in line with the back bone (don't round the shoulders). Grab the legs, ankles or toes. Keep the toes in line with the legs & bring the toes back toward the head.
3. Hold 10 x 10 seconds.
4. Value: hamstrings, lower back and lower hips.

E. Ankle Drills - Shin Splint Drills

(to help prevent shin splints & lower leg injuries you need. . .flexibility to the ankle joint)

1. Sit on the floor, legs extended - body erect.
   a) In a slow steady movement, extend foot in a **plantar** or down position (keep toe in line with the leg segments). Move slowly to full range of motion to dorsi flexed position: do the first five with pressure on the big toe side, number 6-10 pressure on little toe side.
   b) Do next set of 10 fast: repeat a.
   c) Repeat a, but do super slow or hold position about 10 seconds.
2. Next **invert** foot with toe pointed upward, then **evert**, do 5 sets.
3. **Circumductions** of both feet 10 times each direction - do complete very slow circles (or do number 4).
4. **Tucker Crunch** - grab foot and push and pull foot in all positions.
5. **Calf Stretch** against the wall. 3-5 x 10 seconds or both feet down and do 1 set toes pointed in, 1 set toes pointed out, 1 set toes straight ahead. Pressure - toes out big toe side, toes in little toe side; straight - balance pressure. Do #5 here if you haven't done it earlier.

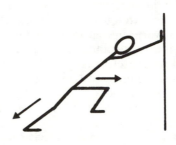

Calf Stretch

F. Trail Leg Stretch - (ground hurdle position)

1. Lying on your back and hips flat on the floor - foot pointed to the sky. Opposite leg bent (trail leg) and gently push knee towards the floor - hold at tolerable position for 10 seconds x 5 sets. Alternate legs.
2. Value: stretches groin area, hips, quadriceps and lower back.

Trail Leg Stretch

Lower Back Press

G. Lower Back Press (hook lying position)

1. To counteract #6 in the lumbar area or lordosis.
2. Tighten or suck in abdomen muscles and tilt the pelvis downward and push lower back into the floor. Hold 5 x 10 seconds.
3. Stretches and strengthens the lower back muscles and abdomen.

H. Yoga

1. Sit erect-back straight-head up-soles of feet together.
2. Draw heels as close to the body as possible without stress.
3. Push knees towards the floor - hold 10 x 10 seconds or for 2 minutes, releasing pressure when needed. Stretch and relax at your own pace.
4. Value: groin hip area and lower back.

Optional Exercises

K. Static Ground Hurdle

1. Get into ground hurdle position one leg straight with opposite leg bent to the side at right angles to the body.
2. Bend forward from the hips and keep upper body squared. The lead leg foot is pointed skyward.
3. Head is in line with the backbone.
4. Pull toe back towards the head.
5. Hold for 10 seconds x 3-5 each leg.
6. Remain relaxed and don't force or bounce.
7. Value: lower back, hips, hamstring and lower leg.

Yoga

Sideknee Tuck

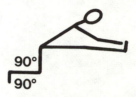

Static Ground Hurdle

I. Sideknee Tuck

1. Roll knees to side in a tight tuck position. Shoulders flat to floor. Knees and feet together.
2. Hold 10 seconds. Reverse 3-5 x 10 seconds.
   Push knees into the floor and push opposite.
   shoulder down and reach out with opposite arm and place other arm across the knees and gently push down.
4. Value: lower back, hips - rotators on lower back.

Hurdle Stretching

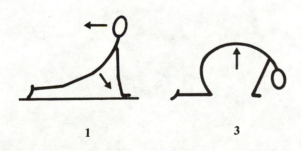

1   3

Cobra and Cat Stretch

L. Hurdle Stretching

1. Place lead leg (knee & toe facing upward) on hurdle while standing on one leg. Lean forward from the hips - hold 10 seconds x 3-5.
2. Value: same as K. Do both legs.

J. Cobra and Cat Stretch

1. Front resting position. Push hips forward - arms straight and hold head and shoulders up. Do 5 x 10 seconds alternating - cat and catch stretch.
2. Value: stretches lower back, lumbar area, abdomen and lower rib cage.
3. In between reps of the cobra: get into hand/knee position and do a cat stretch by rounding and pushing your back skyward - hold 6-10 seconds x 5. This counter balances the cobra stretch.

The Mind Must Control The Body

You can invent your own exercises by placing the body in any position you need for your event and follow these general guidelines:
- Align body
- Relax
- Good posture
- Breathe normally
- Don't force to point of discomfort

A stronger athlete is a better athlete.

4
Strength Development*

Weight Training

by
Dr. Paul Ward

A Year-Round Training Program

A rational approach to strength development assumes that there be a year-round weight training program. The year-round concept separates into three divisions: (1) the conditioning period, (2) the training period, and (3) the in-season period. The total scheme may be illustrated by a pyramid. (Figure #1) The first step of the pyramid is called the conditioning period. It consists of large volumes of exercise done at low intensity. High intensity and large volumes of exercise represent the train-

ing period which makes up the second. The top of the pyramid is analogous to quality training. It consists of high intensity exercises of small volumes for strength maintenance during the competitive season.

Each division in the pyramid is differentiated in terms of load, sets and repetitions mainly, and to a small degree by exercises. The principle followed is that there is a design or pattern for strength training as there must be design in all training programs.

Figure #1

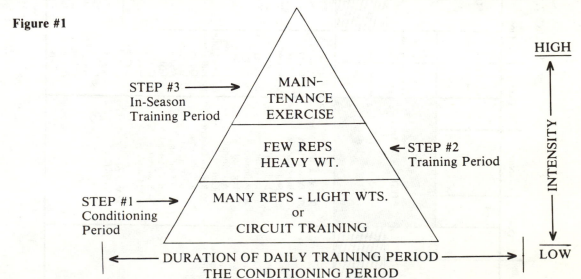

*This chapter consists of two articles: (1) "Weight Training" and (2) "Plyometric Training."

FIGURE 2. Example of a Yearly Training Cycle: Strength Training

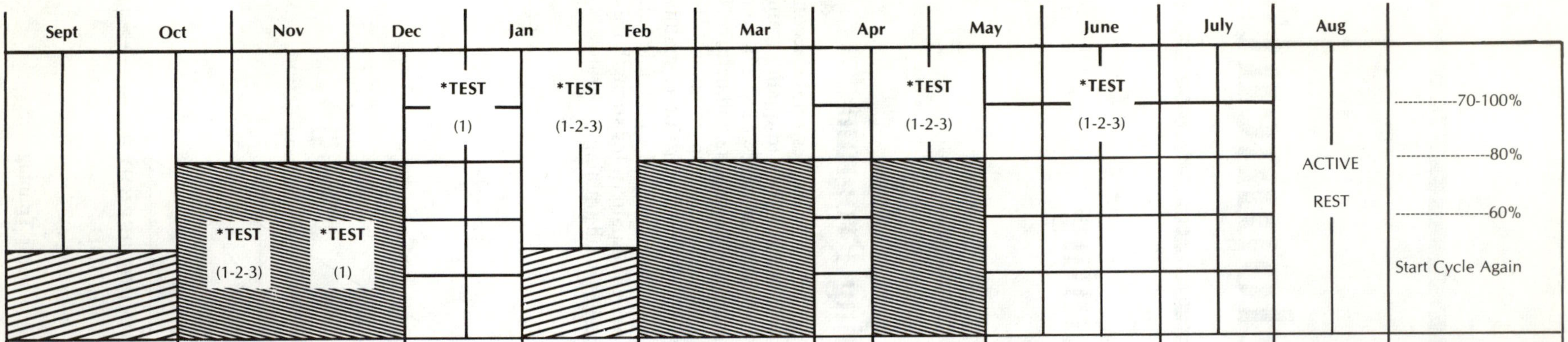

Legend:
— 70-100%
— 80%
— 60%
Start Cycle Again

Timeline (Sept – Aug):

Tests:
- Nov: *TEST (1-2-3)
- Dec: *TEST (1)
- Dec: *TEST (1)
- Jan: *TEST (1)
- Feb: *TEST (1-2-3)
- Apr/May: *TEST (1-2-3)
- June: *TEST (1-2-3)
- Aug: ACTIVE REST

(A) — Sept
1. 3 × 10 × 60% Max.
or
2. CWT
   a. 40-60%
   b. 12-15 Rep 30 sec-work 15 sec-work
   c. 1-3 laps
36 weeks inc 18 training sessions
M-W-F or T-TH-SAT

(B) — Nov
4 × 5 × 80% Max.
1. Power clean
2. Bench press
3. Squats
4. Incline Pr
5. Dead lifts
6. Pulldown
7. Leg Curl
8. Abdominal
9. Curl
10. Special Exercise
    a. Pullover
    b. Ft. Squat
    c. Snatch
    d. Clean/jerk
11. 8 weeks/ 24 sessions
M-W-F or T-TH-SAT

(C) — Dec
Pyramid 70-100% Max
1. Power cleans
2. Bench Press
3. Squat
4. Inc Press
5. Dead Lifts
6. Pull-Down
7. Leg curl
8. Abdominal
9. Curl
10. Spec exercise
    a. Pull-over
    b. Ft. Squat
    c. Snatch
    d. Clean/jerk
11. 4 wks- 12 sess.
12. M-W-F or T-TH-SAT

(A) — Jan/Feb
Same
1. 4 Wks 12 Sess.
2. M-W-F or T-TH-SAT

(B) — Mar
Same
16 weeks 18 sessions
M-W-F or T-TH-SAT

(C) — Apr
Same
1. 2 wks 6 session M-W-F or T-TH-SAT

(B) — Apr/May
Same
1. 4 Wks 12 Sess.
2. M-W-F or T-TH-SAT

(C) — May/June
Same
1. 10 weeks 30 sess.
2. M-W-F or T-TH-SAT
3. Use until competition is over
4. Can use the following
   a. heavy-light-medium
   b. heavy-light-heavy

(D) — Aug
1. 4 wks.
2. low intensity fun
3. Games

Comments: Testing AT*
1. IRM
   P.C., B.P., P.D./Chins, Squats, Snatch, Incl. P. C + 3, Leg Curls Dead Lift
2. Motor Performance
   VJ, SLJ, 50 Dash RTA-RTV
3. Body Composition
   a. Circumference
   b. Skinfold
   c. Underwater weighing
   d. Girths

The Conditioning Period

During the conditioning period the intensity is low, with large volumes of work. The primary purpose of this period is to learn proper lifting techniques and to condition the muscle, tendons, ligaments, and the connective tissue for high intensity work. The amount of weight used is low or moderate and the repetitions are many. Circuit training may be employed here if weight exercises are used in the circuit. The duration of the daily workout may be of considerable length. This regimen is usually followed for three to four weeks, but can be extended if desired. As soon as the base of good local muscle endurance is developed, the program shifts gears for work of higher intensity.

Circuit Training

Definition: Circuit Training is interval training striving to obtain strength, CVR endurance and LME by timed control of submaximal exercise.

Concept: A series of 10 exercise stations working every major muscle group is laid out. A person would normally execute 2 to 3 laps around the circuit in each training session. It is important to plan the sequence of exercise so that different muscle groups are exercised at succeeding exercise stations. A person can use 30 second work intervals followed by 15 second rest intervals or a pre-planned rep/weight prescription for time.

It can be biased for any physical fitness component; used with equipment or without; group or individually directed; and can be used effectively with running.

Purpose: The purpose of circuit weight training is fourfold:
1. To condition the muscles, tendons, ligaments and connective tissue in preparation for heavier lifting.
2. To develop to a high degree LME & CVR endurance.
3. To assist in reducing body fat.
4. To break out of a plateau.

Selection of Exercise:
1. Work every major muscle group in body.
2. Strenuous.
3. Simple.
4. Standardized performance and sequence.
5. Sequence of Exercises needs attention.

Duration: 15 minutes to 30 minutes.

Intensity: 40-60% maximum or approximately 15 reps per 30 second period. Training Heart rate can range from 130-170 B.P.M.

Frequency: Three times per week with a day of rest between.

Miscellaneous:
1. Exercise heart rate should be used as an indicator of intensity.
2. If using 30 second work intervals, 15 repetitions should be the goal for each station. As soon as 15 reps is reached one can increase the weight and reduce the reps to 10. Progression is accomplished by increasing the reps to 15 with the new weight.
3. Research has shown that Circuit Weight Training will increase:
   A. Strength (Not maximally though)
   B. LME-Local muscular endurance.
   C. CVR Endurance
   D. Flexibility
   E. Body fat loss
4. Circuit Weight Training is basically low in muscular intensity and high in metabolic intensity; therefore it will not develop maximal strength.
5. The duration of using Circuit Training can run for 4 weeks or longer.
6. Maintain record of Training.

Conditioning Period Weight Training (3X10X60%)

Definition: Sets and Reps is a system of progressive resistance exercise that requires 3 sets of 10 repetitions with approximately 40-60% of one repetition maximum.

Concept: A series of exercises are selected working every major muscle group in the body for 3 sets of 10 repetitions for each exercise. All three sets are executed before going to the next exercise. Two minutes of rest are used between sets.

Purpose: The purpose of conditioning weight training.
1. To condition the muscles, tendons, ligaments, and connective tissue in preparation for heavier lifting.
2. To develop to a high degree strength, LME, & CVR Endurance.
3. To assist in reducing body fat.
4. To break out of a plateau.

Selection of Exercise:
1. Work every major muscle group.
2. Alternate muscle groups in exercise sequence.
3. Use the basic standard exercises. Do not introduce unusual exercises at this time.

Duration: 1 hour and 1½ hours depending upon state of conditioning.

Intensity: 40-60% maximum. With squats and/or power cleans the intensity may be less until the execution of the movement is perfected and strength is improved.

Frequency: Three times per week with a day of rest between.

Miscellaneous:
1. Weight increases should occur once a week usually on Mondays. (5 lbs. upper body, and 10 lbs. lower body).
2. The use of this program can extend for two weeks or longer.

The "training period" emphasizes exercising the large muscle groups with heavy loads and performing few repetitions.

The Training Period

This is the time to concentrate all energies upon strength development. This period emphasizes exercising the large muscle groups with heavy loads and performing few repetitions. The power lifts, olympic lifts, and related exercises are given preference during this time. The duration of daily training periods is long, with high intensity exercise and in large volumes. This period may extend well ito the competitive season. On the off days there should be fundamental work on basic movement skills of all types and cardiovascular conditioning.

Training Period Weight Training

Definition: This technique involves determining one's maximum strength on a variety of lifts. Then eighty percent of the maximum is performed for each exercise for 4 sets of 5 repetitions.

Concept: A series of exercises are selected in which all the major muscle groups are used. The following is a typical example of the exercise list:
1. Power cleans
2. Inclines
3. Squats
4. Bench Presses
5. Pull downs
6. Dead lifts
7. Curls
8. Leg Curls

A warmup set or two is executed, then 4 sets of 5 reps x 80% maximum is executed. Rest periods of two minutes between sets are adequate.

Purpose: The purpose of this technique is to develop maximum strength and size.

Selection of Exercises:
1. Work all major muscle groups.
2. Concentrate on large muscle groups.
3. Alternate muscle groups in the exercise sequence.

Duration: 1½ to 2½ hours depending upon state of conditioning.

Intensity: 80% maximum

Frequency: Three times per week with a day of rest between.

Miscellaneous:
1. Weight increase should occur once a week, usually on Monday (5 lbs. upper body, 10-20 lbs. lower body).
2. This program can extend through most of a season.
3. Maintain Record.

Example:	Squats	Bench Press
	135x10	135x10
	205x10	185x10
	205x10	185x10
	205x10	185x10

The In-Season Period

The in-season training program is an extension of the training period. The main objective is to maintain the strength that has been developed during earlier training. At this time the routine is altered to implement only those exercises that are absolutely necessary. In other words, there must be specificity of training. The time devoted to weight training during this period is necessarily short; however, the intensity of the work is high. It is obvious that priorities of specific skills must be honored. Because weight training can be integrated with some sport activities more readily than others, there can be a sacrifice of performance in the early season for additional benefits by actually extending the training period into the competitive season. This is done knowing that at the end of the season, during the championships, strength will be higher and performance will be better.

It is interesting to note that many coaches and athletes do not employ the in-season weight training. Consequently, many hours of diligent and arduous training are wasted and are paralleled by poor performances. In the absence of strength training during the season, the incidence of injuries is greater and performances are reduced. There must be an effort to maintain strength at the desired level without consuming vast quantities of time and energy. Obviously, the duration and intensity cannot be, and indeed, need not be, the same as used in the off-season training period.

There is no reason to believe and little evidence to indicate that there is any negative effect upon performance as a result of participating in weight training during the season. In fact, performance is enhanced by reduction of injuries and maintaining the strength at high levels, insuring maximum performance of skills.

Selection of Exercises:
1. Work all major muscle groups.
2. Concentrate on large muscle groups.
3. Alternate muscle groups in the exercise sequence.

Duration: 2 to 3 hours depending upon state of conditioning.

Intensity: Varies up to 100% maximum. Various intensities can be used in succeeding training sessions.

Frequency: Three times per week with a day of rest between training sessions. **Note:** When lifting extremely heavy poundages (high percentages of maximum) two days of rest may be required between training sessions.

Miscellaneous:
1. It is very difficult for the body to accomodate this procedure for long periods of time. The recommended length for application of this technique is 2-4 weeks. If used for longer periods the athletes begin to plateau.
2. This program should be used in the tapering process.
3. Maintain record.

Pyramiding

Definition: The pyramiding technique involves executing a decreasing number of repetitions with corresponding increases in load (weight) for each selected exercise. It corresponds somewhat to determining ones' 1 RM.

Concept: A series of exercises are selected using all major muscle groups. The following is a typical list:
1. Power cleans
2. Inclines
3. Squats
4. Bench presses
5. Pulldowns
6. Dead lifts
7. Curls
8. Leg curls

A warmup set or two is executed, then the procedure is implemented. Rest periods of two minutes between sets are adequate, normally.

Examples:

Power Cleans	Inclines
135x5	135x10
155x5	185x8
185x4	205x6
205x3	225x5
225x2	245x4
255x1	265x3
	275x2
	285x1

Power Cleans	Bench Presses
135x5	135x5
175x5	185x5
205x5	225x5
205x5	225x5
205x5	225x5
205x5	225x5

SUMMARY

The foregoing is an overview of the scientific approach to year-round weight training. More specific information relating to the physiology of weight training and training principles is presented in the following sections.

SCIENTIFIC AND EMPIRICAL PRINCIPLES OF STRENGTH (POWER) TRAINING

Quite often, coaches and athletes get mesmerized by new concepts and consequently stray from tried and true principles of training. When this happens and success is experienced, there is something added to the body of knowledge. However, in many of these experimentations, success is not forthcoming, and the coach and athlete are forced to return to the scientifically established methods of training.

An approach to training is doomed to failure if it is not based on sound physiological principles. Many athletes have had their progress impeded by following an unsound training program. The following physiological principles have been gleaned from research relative to progressive resistance training. They are presented to assist the coach and athlete in planning their strength (power) training programs. Every program will be reflective of local conditions, facilities, equipment, objectives, and motivations. Nevertheless, the adherence to scientific principles is imperative for maximizing the benefits of training.

Selected Physiological Principles Related to Strength

1. Weight training has proven to be the quickest way to develop strength in athletes. Strength, local (muscle) endurance, flexibility and power increase as a result of regular training with weights.
2. To increase muscle strength, there has to be an overloading of the muscle or muscle groups beyond that which is normal for them. The muscle adapts to this overloading. To get further increases, additional stress must be applied. This process continues as long as the athlete continues to train. This is known as the "overload principle".

3. Muscle fibers grow larger with increased strength, but there is no increase in the number of fibers. There is also coincidental growth of connective tissue. There may be an increase in strength without an increase in size of the muscles. The increase in strength, in this case, appears to be due to a change in the central nervous system.
4. Capillarization occurs with increased strength. This is in concert with the increased demand for nutrients and removal of waste products from the muscle.
5. Muscle protein increases while muscle fat decreases.
6. Strength of males increases rapidly from 12 to 19 years of age. This indicates that the ideal physiological time to start weight training is around the seventh grade. Empirical evidence indicates that it can be started earlier.
7. It is not wise to distort the muscle balance by concentrating only on a single muscle or muscle group. This increases the chance of muscle strain, tear, and faulty body mechanics. A general program with emphasis on deficient areas is prudent practice.
8. De Lorme's principles:
   a. Increase in muscle strength can be accomplished by a few repetitions against heavy resistance.
   b. Increase in muscular (local) endurance can be accomplished by many repetitions with light resistance.
   c. These two methods are not interchangeable; one cannot replace the other.

Note: There is some empirical evidence to suggest that an improvement in strength may be accomplished by an increase in local endurance. On the other hand, improvement of local endurance does not seem to affect muscular strength in a positive direction. This subject is indeed in need of more extensive study.

9. The training stimulus for increasing strength is muscle tension and not the duration of exercise. This statement gives further insight into De Lorme's first principle.

10. The amount of work done per unit of time is the critical variable upon which improvement in performance depends. This is associated with high muscle tension which seems to be the stimulus to growth. The work rate may be intensified by increasing the speed of movement (this is efficient) or by increasing the load. Rapidly contracting muscles exhibit a loss in strength and involve an uneconomical expenditure of energy, making increases in speed of exercise unacceptable. An increase in work load is more advantageous. With the increase in load, the speed of movement is slow, but the muscle tension remains high. Consequently, a greater improvement in strength and hypertrophy. A. V. Hill states that ". . .the mechanical efficiency (work/total energy) of muscle is greatest at about 1/5 of maximum speed." When executing exercises, a moderate rhythm should be used.

11. The trainability of muscles is high during summer and autumn months and low in the winter (December, January, and February).

12. Ultra-violet radiation, natural and artificial, increases strength development.

13. A training stimulus of as low as 1/3 has demonstrated increases in strength. Empirical evidence indicates that the training stimulus should be between 70 and 80 percent of maximum.

14. There appear to be changes in the central nervous system as a result of training. Strength may depend not only on the increase in contractile strength and size of muscle fibers, but also on neuromuscular changes. The ability to develop maximal tension appears to be dependent on the proprioceptive facilitation with which overloading is associated.

15. Strength of muscle contraction depends upon: (1) number of stimuli, and (2) number of motor units called upon. From empirical observations it seems more advantageous to encourage heavy weight exercises executed at a moderate rhythm, rather than light weight done very rapidly. It is interesting to note that increases in rate of muscle contraction increases the ability to produce high tensions. Heavy weight produces the ability to activate maximum number of motor units.

16. There is a strong relationship between gain in speed and gain in strength. Speed of movement has been significantly increased by both isometric and isotonic programs. Isotonic programs are preferred as indicated by research. It should be emphasized that simply training muscle groups alone, part from a specific speed movement, increases speed of that specific movement.

17. For increasing strength, four sets of five repetitions is the method that seems to be most effective. An

THEORETICAL FACTORS INFLUENCING FORCE OF MUSCULAR CONTRACTION

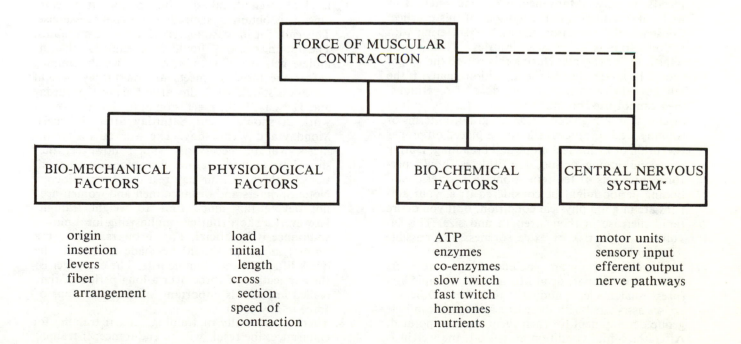

*CNS influence over-rides all other factors.

alternative program design might include a Pyramiding (progressive increasing) of weight, decreasing of weight and decreasing of repetitions. This is not as effective as the former; however, it is a good change-up for two or three workout periods. Then an athlete should return to four sets of five repetitions.

18. Strength gains are specific to the angle in the range of motion at which the resistance is met in training.

19. The rate of strength gain is most rapid when a muscle has achieved only a small proportion of its possible maximal end strength. The rate of gain slows down as muscle strength approaches its maximal end strength.

20. The rate of strength loss after training ends is a very much slower process than strength gain. Retention of strength can probably be brought about by as little as one maximal contraction per week.

TRAINING PRINCIPLES

One must have more than a knowledge of the physiological principles of strength (power) training. They must be able to implement and adapt those principles to a program and local situation. The following training principles are presented as guidelines to assist the coach and athlete in deriving the optimum benefits of training.

1. All heavy lifting programs should be proceeded by a three to four week conditioning program. This conditioning period is necessary to strengthen the muscles, tendons, connective tissue, and ligaments to withstand the stress of heavy training. Another reason is to learn the correct technique for each specific exercise. Many neophytes and veterans as well fail to understand the wisdom of this practice. Consequently, they find themselves suffering with various joint and muscle injuries. This greatly retards their progress. During this period the weight should be moderate and the repetitions many. If the athletes adhere to the training dose of repetitions, they cannot use too much weight. There is built-in discipline in a high repetition program, in terms of training load. Emphasis should be placed on proper execution of lifting technique and breathing. During this conditioning period, the athletes should perform three sets of ten repetitions. A shorter conditioning period might be considered if: a. your athletes are in good physical condition. b. if you desire rapid increase in their strength and size. This involves a slight risk of extra soreness and possible joint problems.

2. The training program includes the power lifts (bench press, squat, dead lift) and the olympic lifts (press, snatch, clean, and jerk) as the core. Other exercises associated with these lifts and specific muscle group development for each event are incorporated. After the initial conditioning period, the weight is increased and the repetitions are reduced. The recommended dosage of sets and repetitions is four sets of five repetitions. It should be noted that exercises are designed for development of large muscle groups. Antagonistic muscles are also developed.

3. Consistency in workouts is paramount and insures improvements. The loss of a workout period per se is not the problem; what does cause trouble is the fact that once the athlete misses a workout, it becomes progressively easier to miss others. Soon the athlete is training irregularly, if at all. Satisfactory gains cannot be expected unless there is training regularity.

4. Training sessions should occur every other day, i.e., Monday, Wednesday, and Friday; or, Tuesday, Thursday, and Saturday. The length of the training sessions should extend from one and a half hours to two hours. Shorter periods, although beneficial, are not sufficiently long enough for maximum results. Off days can be used for skill development and recreation.

5. If time is short, a split routine technique can be used. In this technique, one works the upper body one day, and the lower body the next. This means the workout week is extended to six days. However, the workout sessions are shorter. The same exercises can be used as with the regular technique. One will retrogress before he/she improves. This will discourage some, especially those who insist on using heavy weights without a conditioning period. Persist with training, and results will be forthcoming.

6. Warm-up before training. The Europeans, especially the Russians, spend up to 1/2 hour in warm-up before touching the weights. This makes good sense in terms of preventing injury and increasing performance during the workout.

7. For the average person, the achievement of a high level of strength takes a long period to develop. Once it is obtained, it needs maintenance exercise. This calls for in-season strength training programs. The training sessions should be scheduled so that the athlete gets two days of rest from weight training before the meet. If meets are on Friday, weight workouts should be Friday after the meet, Saturday and Tuesday. If the meet is on Saturday, the weight workout should occur Saturday after the meet, Monday and Wednesday. The workouts after the meets will be necessarily short; however, they should be intense. Before championship competitions, a three or four day rest can be considered. Note: Sprinters and distance men and women need not devote this much time to weight training. However, a short routine emphasizing local muscle endurance is beneficial. For throwers, during the season, an effort should be made to include the quick lifts, i.e., the olympic lifts. The carryover is: the application of force over a long period of time (called impulse) is important in all applications of force in any event.

8. There is specificity of training, i.e., if training for endurance, the result will be endurance; if training for strength, you will receive strength.

9. Think of strength as an integral part of the whole

performance capacity. Strength is not an end in itself. Strength forms the basis for improvement of speed of movement and application of force.

10. When planning training routines, think of muscle groups. Muscles rarely operate independently of each other in any athletic movement.

11. Sequence of exercise needs careful consideration. This is necessary to insure maximum work of muscle groups with the least amount of fatigue. It is prudent to work a specific muscle group with one exercise, then work the antagonistic muscle group or another muscle group in some other part of the body. For example, after performing presses, do pull downs, or after squats, do leg curls. The routines offered in this chapter are designed to follow this principle.

12. Proper rest and sleeping habits must be firmly entrenched. There is a wide variation between individuals in terms of the number of hours of sleep they need. Eight to ten hours is a reasonable amount for growing athletes in vigorous training.

13. Diet is of great importance in rigorous training. Adequate amounts of protein, vitamins, and minerals must be included in the diet. If weight gaining is the objective, milk provides an inexpensive way to supplement the diet with protein, (as much as a gallon a day). Additional benefits can be obtained if powdered milk is mixed with whole milk. Other protein supplements can be used if the athletes have the money. Caloric intake will control the body weight increase.

14. If training for strength and increase in muscle mass, do not run the athletes great distances or compel them to participate in long sessions of calisthenics. Calisthenics are for warmup and stretching, not for conditioning.

15. Constantly strive to lift as much weight as possible without straining. A good coaching phrase is "Train, don't strain".

16. Starting weights ultimately have to be selected by trial and error because of individual differences. These differences are too great to be able to give an absolute starting weight for everyone. A good rule to follow is select a weight and perform as many reps as possible in one set. If the repetitions are as high as twenty or more, the training load should be 10 or 20 pounds heavier.

17. Sets and Repetitions: During the conditioning period many repetitions and moderate weight should be the aim (3 x 10). During the training period few repetitions and heavy weight should be executed.

18. Weight increases: After the first week, the weight should be increased to five to ten pounds for the upper body exercises, and ten to twenty pounds for the lower body exercises. With the increase in training weight, the repetitions may drop. If so, work with the increased weight until the prescribed number can be performed. When this occurs, go two more workout periods, then increase the weight again. Improvement is not forthcoming unless there is overloading.

19. Insist on proper form and technique in performing the exercises. Cheating, in general, is not a good practice.

20. It is not judicial practice to make up exercises for specific sports skills. Determine the muscles involved in the desired movement; then use the standard exercises for their development. Attention might be focused on the angle of force application when choosing the exercises for each specific event.

21. Motivation of the athletes is important in strength training. First, convince the athlete that he/she will benefit from weight training; secondly, provide experiences whereby he/she can see progress. By nature, weight training is self-motivational. The athlete can see changes in muscle mass and body proportions and experience the increase in strength. This will throw gasoline on the fire.
    A good motivational and training technique is to attempt maximum lifts about every seventh or eighth workout session in the training period.

22. Breathing is extremely important, especially while handling heavy weights. In general lifting, the rule is: exhale during the working phase of the movement and inhale on the non-working phase. This rule needs slight modification in heavy lifting. One should inhale on the non-work phase of the movement and hold the breath until the weight has passed the sticking point.

23. The athlete can get out of training what he/she put into it. If only putting a little time and energy into training, the athlete will not get the same results as one who trains hard. If the athlete wants maximum development, he/she must put some dedication into training. Sell the athletes this philosophy.

24. Coaches cannot expect their athletes to discipline themselves in their strength training program. They must supervise and encourage the athletes to seek higher strength levels.

25. Plateau Breaking. Frequently athletes get stuck at a certain weight. Improvement seems impossible. An effective technique used to break this barrier is to reduce the weight and increase the repetitions (for example, 3 x 12). Carry out this procedure for three to six workout periods. Then return to heavy lifting. This should shock the system and stimulate improvement. If results are not forthcoming, look for other causes for the plateau, e.g., diet or sleep.

26. It is advisable to test strength at the beginning of the training period and periodically thereafter. The athlete should also keep a record of his/her training weights and repetitions. Both provide a basis for proper evaluation.

Plyometric Training

by
Vern Gambetta
University of California

Background

Plyometric training is still a relatively new method of training in the U.S. For the past ten years, the Europeans have used it extensively with outstanding success. Only in the past five years has its value in training track and field athletes been recognized in this country. As a training method, plyometric training bridges the gap between pure strength training and power training (power = speed x strength). This produces the explosive-reactive movements inherent in jumping, throwing, and sprinting.

Plyometric training has been used in various forms all over the world for many years. The fundamental research as to why it is beneficial and the quantification of it in terms of training was done by the Russians in the mid and late 1960's. Many of the jumping drills that are now called plyometric jumping drills have been practiced by triple jumpers and long jumpers for many years. It is just that recent research has defined it so that we can apply it more effectively to our specific training programs.

Definition and Physiological Basis

A strict definition of plyometric training is difficult. Fred Wilt interprets plyometric as those exercises that produce "an overload of isometric type muscle action which invokes the stretch reflex in muscles."

In isotonic (involving movement) muscle action, there are two types of muscle contractions: 1) concentric contraction—the action of the muscle shortening and 2) eccentric—the action of the muscle lengthening. An eccentric contraction occurs when a muscle is loaded sufficiently to lengthen it, even though at the same time it is trying to shorten. The faster the muscle is forced to lengthen, the greater tension it exerts. The rate of stretch is more important than the magnitude of the stretch. In order to achieve high level results from the eccentric contraction (pre-stretching), the concentric contraction which follows must take place immediately. To sum up the basis of plometric training—a concentric contraction (shortening action) is much stronger if it **im-**

*Plyometric boxes drills are vital for jumpers. They should be done both single and double legged.

mediately follows an eccentric contraction (lengthening) of that same muscle.

Plyometric exercises train the eccentric aspect of muscle contraction in order to improve the relationship between maximum strength and explosive power. Many athletes have tremendous strength but they cannot apply this to the specifics of jumping or throwing. They lack the ability to convert this strength to the explosive-reactive action. The key is not increasing strength or power but in relating the two.

As stated previously, a concentric contraction that immediately follows an eccentric contraction is much stronger than if there had been no pre-stretching. "A body movement, requiring an extremely high end velocity (jumping, throwing), can best be achieved by starting it with a movement to the opposite direction. The braking of the opposite movement, provided the change takes place smoothly, creates positive acceleration power for the original movement." Examples of this action would be the backswing in golf or baseball. This braking of the opposite movement activates what is known as the stretch or myotic reflex: The muscle will resist overstretching. The stretch-receptors in the muscle cause a powerful contraction in order to prevent overstretching.

An example in an inanimate body would be dropping a rubber ball from a height. The ball when it hits the ground is deformed to store the energy acquired in the drops. As the ball returns to its original shape the stored energy will be released to bring the ball back to the height from which it was dropped.

The flop stype of high jump is successful because the faster takeoff action results in the stretch reflex action in the muscles of the takeoff leg. It is interesting to note that Dwight Stones' training program includes hopping and bounding in order to train this stretch reflex. Pat Matzdorf did a great amount of plyometric training the two years pervious to his record jump. Plyometric training in the form of hopping and bounding was an integral part of Valery Borzov's training.

Applying Plyometrics

In applying plyometrics to a training program, use imagination. Develop new exercises. Do not be afraid to experiment. In setting up a plyometric training program, keep in mind the following: 1) Maximum tension is produced when the muscle is stretched rapidly; 2) The faster the muscle is lengthened, the greater the tension; 3) The rate is more important than the magnitude of the stretch; 4) Use the overload principle—strength can only be increased if the muscle works at a greater intensity than normal; 5) Do not change the basic pattern of the movement which you are trying to imitate.

East German research has determined that plyometric exercises should be performed in sets of eight to ten repetitions with six to ten sets of various exercises performed in a training session. The research also recommends that 10 to 15 minutes rest be taken between exercises. Remember: Each exercise should be performed at

maximum effort in order to stimulate the neuromuscular system.

A word of caution: Be patient and start out with a few exercises and gradually increase the load. Pay close attention to proper technique in performing the drills because injury potential is high, especially for the young athlete.

Build a good strength base before embarking on an extensive plyometric program. The Russians recommend that unless leg strength is more than double body weight, the athlete should concentrate on pure strength before doing any plyometrics. This is too extreme, but a good strength base is very important.

Plyometric drills should be practiced every other day in order to give the muscles and the nervous system time to recover.

Plyometric Throwing Exercises

Exercise #1—Begin the action of shot putting or discus throwing off an elevated platform 30-40cm high. The athlete lands on the ground in the putting position and immediately performs the remainder of the putting or throwing action. This exercise develops the supporting and driving leg in the throw.

Exercise #2—A 10-20Kg weight is suspended from above. Push the weight out by the left hand and catch and push it with the right in a normal putting action.

Exercise #3—Same as exercise #2, but using a 8-15Kg weight while imitating a discus throwing action.

Exercise #4—The same as #2 and #3 but use a 10-20Kg weight in a javelin throwing action.

Note: In order to increase resistance when using pendulum movement, it is advisable to increase the pendulum swing rather than increase the weight of resistance.

Exercise #5—Using a normal weight javelin, the athlete stands with right leg forward (for right handed throwers), the javelin held in a bent right arm. Next the athlete moves both his right leg and throwing arm back to delivery position with pre-stretched chest and shoulder muscles and immediatley performs a throw.

Exercise #6—For discus throwing—Place a barbell of 50-60 lbs on the shoulders. Twist shoulders to the right and then to the left. Start the motion to the left before the motion to the right is completed and vice versa.

Plyometric Jumping Exercises

Exercise #1--a) A rebound jump off a box 30″ high with a double leg takeoff. The athlete jumps as high as possible after the rebound; b) The same exercise from a higher height; c) The same exercise performed on one leg.

Exercise #2—A hop off a 12-24″ box onto the ground, followed by a triple jump step and jump for distance.

Exercise #3—a) Perform a jump off a 12-24″ box, landing 8″ out from the box and perform a straddle takeoff and b) The same initial action as a) but perform a flop takeoff with a rotation in the air.

> Note: Increase resistance by increasing the height from which you jump. Do not add resistance by adding weight or wearing a weight vest. The young jumper should begin at very low heights, 12″, and progress gradually.

Exercise #4—Repeat hops and bounds for a 30m to 50m distance.

Single leg jumps.

Plyometric Drills for Sprinters

These drills consist entirely of jumping drills. They are designed to improve the speed-strength preparation of the sprinter. The drills are divided into two types of jumps: 1) "Short Jumps" and "Long Jumps."

The "Short Jumps" develop explosive power at the start and the acceleration phase of the sprint. These "Short Jumps" are performed at distances from 30m-100m in various combinations of hopping and bounding. The emphasis when executing these jumps should be on exploding upward off each leg with very little emphasis on forward speed.

The "Long Jumps" help develop an increase in maximum running speed and speed endurance. These jumps are also performed in various combinations of hopping and bounding for distances from 30m-100m. The emphasis in performing these jumps should be on speed of movement while still maintaining powerful takeoffs.

Several factors must be considered in plyometric training for sprinters: 1) The greatest volume of jumps should take place in the Fall or preparatory phase of training. During the season, training should consist primarily of short jumps up to 50m; 2) "Short Jumps" should be performed before sprinting and "Long Jumps" after sprinting.

Bibliography

1. Verkhowshansky, U.V. and G. Chernousov, "Jumps in the Training of a Sprinter," **Track and Field**, Vol. 9, 1974, pp. 16-17, Reprinted in **Yessis Review of Soviet Physical Education and Sports**, Vol. 9, #3, Sept., 1974, p. 62.

2. Verhoshanski, Yuri, "Perspectives in the Improvement of Speed-Strength Preparation of Jumpers," **Yessis Review of Soviet Physical Education and Sports**, Vol. 4, #2, 1969, p. 28.

3. Wilt, Fred, "Why Does Dwight Stones Jump Higher with the Flop than the Straddle Style?" **Athletics Coach**, Vol. #3, Sept., 1976, p. 26.

4. Wilt, Fred, "From the Desk of Fred Wilt: Plyometrics," **Track Technique**, #63, Mar, 1976, p. 1992.

5. Wilt, Fred, "From the Desk of Fred Wilt: Plyometric Exercises," **Track Technique**, #64, June, 1976, p. 2024.

6. "Specific Power in Jumping and Throwing—A Summary of Developments in Plyometric Exercises," **Modern Athlete and Coach**, Vol. 2, #5, Oct/Nov, 1974, p. 7.

5

The Use of Talent Predictive Factors in the Selection of Track and Field Athletes

by
Ken Foreman*, Ph.D.

This is an attempt to bridge the gap between pure chance and that point in time when we can predict with relative accuracy what track and field event an individual is best suited to perform effectively. Recognizing that the state of the art of prediction is still very speculative, the basic assumption is that there is a best event for everyone. It is also assumed that it is the responsibility of the track and field coach to use every tool possible in helping individuals find the event or events for which they have the greatest potential.

The use of prediction factors in the selection of track and field athletes has been a matter of discussion for more than three decades. In 1948 T.K. Cureton found that athletes in different sports and in different events within the same sport manifest specific event related characteristics. Correnti and Zauli reported in 1960 that athletes tended to manifest a wide range of heights and weights, as well as age variability between events, but that they had similar body shapes with the same event. In 1964 Tanner reported a relationship between race and selected track and field events. He also noted that athletes can be separated according to body dimension where specific events are concerned. According to de Garay, body size and type are factors of importance to successful achievement in track and field. So much so he noted in a report given in 1968 that "one ought to look at the grand parents when selecting young athletes".

Wilmore, **et al.**, (1972, 1976) stated that the higher the % of body fat, the poorer the performance in athletic activities. This is particularly true in those events in which one moves his or her body through space. During the same year the writer studied the top 120 female athletes in the world to determine if there were distinguishing characteristics where event specificity was concerned. He noted that the age range among these performers was 16-40, with 79 athletes being older than 25. An additional 26 were older than 30, with 3 being over 35. These data revealed a direct relationship between age and the event in which one participated. The more mature athletes were found in the techinical throwing events and the younger performers in the sprints, hurdles and jumps. It also was noted that the explosive performers, i.e. sprinters, hurdlers and jumpers, were naturally leaner than were those athletes who participated in other events. In like manner, the throwers were significantly taller and heavier than all other track and field performers.

Ryan and Allman noted in the text, **Sports Medicine**, that "size is a factor in all types of sports involving acceleration, i.e., moving ones body over a distance, lifting it, turning it and using it to exert maximum force". It was also noted that taller persons have a greater strength potential in proportion to their size, and a greater respiratory capacity. They are slower to

*Dr. Foreman is the Director of Education and Research for The Sports Medicine Clinic, Seattle Washington.

accelerate than shorter persons and they are at a disadvantage in lifting their own body weight.

Lloyd has stated that the the trend in record breaking in the middle distance events is in the direction of improved oxygen utilization, which is in turn related to greater cardiorespiratory capacity. In delineating those factors which lead to superior performance in track and field, Burke and Tait identified the following: increased size, greater strength, superior skills, better facilities and equipment, more facilities for more athletes, better genetic selection, better nutrition, a more competitive environment and better medical care.

One additional study has some bearing on the selection of track and field athletes. This is the long term Medford Boy's Growth study undertaken by Harrison Clark of the University of Oregon. In this study it was shown that the standing long jump and the jump and reach were excellent predictive measures for future success in the sprints, the long jump and high jump events.

With the advent of the Sports Medicine Laboratory, the identification of the selection criteria has become even more sophisticated. This is to be seen in such activities as the monitoring of lactic acid as a means of evaluating stress, the calculation of oxygen uptake values to determine aerobic capacity and the accurate measurement of muscle power and endurance.

In an attempt to utilize both quantitative and speculative data for the purpose of talent identification, the West German Track and Field Federation has developed selection criteria for all track and field events. These were reported in **Die Lehre Der Leichtathletik** during November and December of 1979. Subsequent to a futile attempt to identify and nurture track and field talent in young children as is practiced in some Eastern Block countries, the DLV trainers worked out a test battery to be administered to teenaged athletes on a twice yearly basis beginning with the year 1976.

These tests are given to young teen agers during March and April with the results used to classify track and field performers according to ability and potential. All of the data accrued are stored in a central computer bank and made available to both local and national coaches upon request. Athletes who manifest outstanding potential are invited to train with the national team.

In addition to the identification of talent, the DVL program seeks to improve the flow of information between local, regional and national trainers, develop criteria for placement of athletes at a specific competitive level, and provide for a common approach to the teaching of technical skills. The selection program is further supported by the use of films and video tapes, medical evaluation and health care and support within the family and community of the athlete. (The following

Throwers are significantly taller and heavier than all other track and field performers.

are) specific, event by event selection criteria established by the DVL Athletics Research Council:

High Jump

1. 30m sprint	4.2 women, not used for men
2. 5 alternate leg bounds for distance	15m with 3 running steps for women 15m from stand for men
3. 5 single leg bounds	15m with 3 running steps for women 18.50m with 6 running steps men
4. Standing long jump	2.20m minimum for women, not used for men
5. Thief vault (5-6 running steps)	Women only, 1.30 meters minimum
6. Scissors jump (5-6 running steps)	1.80m minimum for men
7. Analysis of technique	1.70m for men
8. 800m for time	3:00 for women only

Long Jump

1. 300m sprint from stand	3.8 for men-4.1 for women
2. 5 hops r and 5 hops 1 with five running steps	17.50m for men 15.50m for women
3. 10 alternate leg bounding steps following 5 running steps	28m women
4. Number of bounding strides 30m	no set criteria
5. 1000m for men 800m for women	3:20 for men 2:50 for women
6. Standing long jump	no set criteria

Pole Vault

1. 30m sprint from stand	4.1 for men
2. 60m sprint from stand	7.2 for men
3. 10 jumps from running start	number of jumps counted.. no set criteria
4. 3m rope climb	6.5 seconds
5. 4k shot toss overhead backward	15 meters
6. Rope vault	5 meter rope at 2.5m from cross bar. Measure greatest possible height..no set criteria

Triple Jump

1. 50m sprint from a stand	No set criteria
2. Five jumps following 7 running strides...two feet landing	Evaluate coordination and measure distance
3. 6.25 K shot toss overhead backward	No set criteria
4. Jumping strength endurance test over 50m. The jumper attempts to cover the 50m with the fewest possible strides in the shortest possible time. Mark the last landing before the finish line. Measure the distance to the last landing, and calculate strength endurance. SE = strength endurance, n = number of strides, a = distance from 50m line, t = time $SE = \dfrac{(a \times n + n) \times t}{50 - n}$	

Sprints

1. 30m sprint from stand	3.7 men - 4.0 women
2. Flying 30m sprint	3.0 men - 3.4 women
3. 300m run	36.0 men - 41.0 women
4. 3/30m bounding. Run back between 1, and 2 to repeat. Count bounding strides and total time	No set criteria
5. 3000m run men 2000m run women	12 min 10 min
6. 10 bounds	30m men - 25m women

Hurdles (110 meters - 100 meters)

1. 30m sprint from stand	3.7 men - 4.1 women
2. Jump and reach	No set criteria
3. Single leg bounding r and 1 over 30 meters. Measure distance from last bound to 30m line. n = number of bounds, t = time, a = distance from 30m line, $SE = \dfrac{a \times n + n}{30 - a}$	No set criteria
4. 50m hurdles.....regular spacing	7.8 for women
5. 5 x 5 hurdle shuttle. 30 second recovery between flights. Time from first step down off hurdle five.	35.3 for men
6. 300m run from stand	38.3 men - 44.2 women
7. 3000m run 2000m run	12 min for men 10 min for women

Shot and Discus

1. 30m sprint from stand 50 yds	4.2 for men 6.6 for women
2. Jump and reach	50 cm for men
3. Standing long jump	2.6m for men 86.5" for women
4. Three double leg bounds for distance...from a stand	8.0m for men 22'4" for women
5. Five double leg bounds for distance...from a stand	13.40m for men 36'1" for women
6. Standing put 2.5k shot	25m men
7. 5 k shot toss overhead backward 4 k shot toss overhead backward	15m men 11m for women
8. 800m run	3:20 for women
9. Social cultural evaluation for women only...strong self image. Willing to work with weights. Strong family support.	

The Russian Sports Medicine Council also is working toward the evaluation and selection of talent for various athletic activities. While the precise nature of their program is not readily available, the principle of skill factor evaluation as a criteria for individual selection is noted in the recent article by Komarova and Raschimshanova, (**Lefkaya Atletika**), dealing with ''Ideal Characteristics of Female Discus Throwers.''

These researchers found that world class throwers are exceptionally tall, strong and explosive where movement is concerned. Moreover, they have stated that such characteristics are discernable during the early teens, with speed being developed most effectively between the ages of 11-13, power between the ages of 12-13, and strength between the ages of 13-17.

The potential female discus thrower in Russia must be 5′ 6″ at age 13. Other criteria for selection as potential throwers are fixed standards in the jump reach, the standing long jump, the two hand overhead shot throw, bench press, squat, snatch, clean, the 30m sprint and evaluation of the athletes' reaction time. Specific scores for 12-13 year old girls for several of these measures are:

Standing long jump......6′7″minimum

Vertical jump 15″ minimum

3K shot overhead throw distance....25′3″ minimum

30m sprint from crouch...5.0 sec minimum

The following are this author's observations regarding the characteristics which seem to predispose one to success in the various track and field events. Keep in mind that the force of the human will is the single most important factor in all human achievement. Unfortunately we do not have any simple means of measuring the force of the human will except in the tug of the contest itself.

Factors of Importance in the Performance of Specific Athletic Events

Sprints-Hurdles	Jumps	Throws	Middle Distance Distance
Natural Speed	Power (work-time)	Power (work-time)	
Power (work time)	Strength	Strength	Aerobic capacity
Stride cadence	Morphological factors	Morphological factors	Anaerobic power
Strength			Natural speed
Movement time	Natural speed	Coordination	Low % fat
Naturally high Lean to fat ratio	Coordination Low % fat	Natural speed	Strength

Tests to be used in the evaluation of Specific Performance Factors

Factor	Test
Explosive speed	Flying 50
Power (explosive strength)	Jump, reach, standing long jump, standing triple jump (r-l-r or l-r-l) 5 bounds for distance, the Margaria-Kalamen leg-power test.
Foot speed	Time a runner over 10 yards at the mid point of a flying 50...count the strides and determine strides/sec.
Reaction time	Use a response timer to evaluate reaction (response time to sound, sight and tactal stimuli.
Body morphology	Height, weight, body build....i.e., ectomorphy, etc.
General strength	Push ups, sit ups, chin ups, bench press, lat pulls, full squat to sit, etc. Determination of ratio of strength to body weight.
% Body Fat	Skin calipers, hydrostatic weighing.
Coordination	Soft ball throw for distance, bounding with combinations, performance evaluation using primary sports skill.
Aerobic "Strength"	Maximum stress test with gas analysis, Astrands nomograms using bicycle ergometer, 15 min run, harvard step test, timed 5000.
Anaerobic "Power"	45 sec, 60 sec power run, timed 300, exact distance covered in 2 x 60 sec runs with 3 min recovery between each, calculation of % drop off in time between best 200 and best 400. Best 400 and best 800 etc..
Competitive spirit	Run 800 meters for time.
Self image	Observe athlete in social and competitive situations.

The force of human will is the single most important factor in all human achievement.

The final section of this paper consists of selected data from the U.S. Olympic Training centers. These data were gathered during the summers of 1978 and 1979 and represent a majority of the elite male and female track and field athletes in the United States. The suggested "selection factors for elite track and field athletes" to be found on the final page have been based on the training center data, the material from West Germany and the USSR, and personal experience.

Comparison Between Mean Scores for Elite Male Track and Field Performers on Height, Weight, Age and Measures of Speed, Strength and Percentage of Body Fat

Event	Number	Height	Weight	Age	Jump Reach	Standing Long Jump	%body Fat	50 yard Time
Sprints (100-200)	14	70.34"	157.08#	20.43	26.68"	115.36"	6.61	5.546
400 M	9	70.96"	161.04#	21.65	24.37"	112.92"	6.44	5.767
High Hurdles	11	72.05"	171.06#	19.82	29.08"	116.84"	6.46	5.693
Long Jump	10	74.05"	165.44#	20.80	27.99"	117"	6.98	5.688
Shot Put	12	73.62"	247.55#	24	26.88"	115.36"	14.84	6.180
Discus	15	75.47"	238.65#	23	26.56"	107.66"	13.21	6.174
Javelin	11	73.23"	199.71#	21	25.71"	105.12"	8.48	6.213

Comparison Between Mean Scores for Elite Track and Field Performers on Height, Weight, Age and Measures of Speed, Strength and Percentage of Body Fat - Female

Event	Number	Height	Weight	Age	Jump Reach	Standing Long Jump	%Body fat	50 yard Time
Sprints (100-200)	N = 15	65.51"	126.21#	17.93	20.63	92.86	15.79	6.216
400 M	N = 13	64.43"	123.86#	18.92	19.07	88.69	14.37	6.458
100 M H	N = 8	65.90"	122.12#	19.13	22.69	92.97	13.54	6.266
Long Jump	N = 7	67.21"	133.51#	19.29	21.65	97.96	11.38	6.209
800 M	N = 9	66.31"	115.54#	19.00	17.89	86.88	10.67	6.521
Shot Put	N = 7	69.64"	182.05#	21.29	21.48	86.54	21.21	7.112
Discus	N = 7	72.64"	190#	21.86	20.68	88.0	22.07	6.994
Javelin	N = 5	66.55"	154.99#	20.20	20.23	87.60	18.96	6.965
Pentathletes	N = 9	69.05"	143.88#	21.5	21.1	98.8	11.0	6.31

Comparison Between Weight to Strength Ratios for Elite Male and Female Shot and Discus Performers

Bench press	male 2.03 times body weight	female .95% body weight
Squat	male 2.13 times body weight	female 1.36 times body weight
Power clean	male 1.44 times body weight	female .97% of body weight
Incline press	male 1.33 times body weight	female .70% of body weight
Snatch	male 1.08 times body weight	female .70% of body weight

References

Clarke, H. Harrison, **Physical and Motor Tests in the Medfords Boys' Growth Study**. Englewood Cliffs, N.J.: Prentice-Hall, Inc. 1971

Cureton, T.K., Jr., **Physical Fitness of Champion Athletes**. Urbana, Illinois: University of Illinois Press, 1951

DeGaray, A.L.; Levine, L.; and Carter, J.E.L. eds. **Genetic and Anthropological Studies of Olympic Athletes**. New York: Academic Press, 1974.

Komarova, A. and Raschimshanova, K., "Ideal Characteristics of Female Discus Throwers", **Legkaya Athletika**, No. 5, 1975

Tanner, J.M., **The Physique of the Olympic Athlete**. London: George Allen and Unwin, 1964

Wilmore, J.H., **Athletic Training and Physical Fitness**. Boston, London Sydney: Allyn and Bacon, 1976

6
Planning a Training Program

by
Vern Gambetta
University of California, Berkeley

Principles of Training

Training brings a person to a desired state of fitness and proficiency. The track and field coach aims at developing the highest level of physiological, psychological and technical fitness in his/her athletes. In order to achieve a trained state, there are certain basic principles which must be followed. The following eight principles are essential in building a sound training program:

1) **Specificity**—Stated in the simplest terms, the athlete is what he/she trains to be. This is based on the SAID principle or "Specific Adaptation to Imposed Demands." More directly, it means that following a period of general conditioning, training should be designed to imitate as closely as possible the action of the particular event for which the athlete is preparing.

Evaluate the stresses of the event and apply this to the training program. Do not overload or apply stresses to deviate a great deal from the movement pattern and neuro-muscular coordination demanded by the event.

To insure specificity, the following factors must be taken into consideration: 1) the quantity and type of conditioning demanded by an event; 2) the weaknesses and strong points of the individual athlete; and 3) the most effective technique or type of training to provide the desired result.

2) **Overload**—This principle refers to the amount of work and stress imposed above the normal level to which the athlete is accustomed. The amount of overload necessary to induce a training stimulus varies with each individual. In order for overload to be effective, the amount of work should be increased as the body adapts to the growing demands placed upon the system. An increase in the weights, faster repetition runs on the track, and greater demands on the cardiovascular system in endurance training are all examples of overload. It must be remembered, though, that the amount of training cannot be continually increased. There is a point of diminishing return. At this point, intensity, the next training principle, must be considered.

3) **Intensity**—Intensity refers to energy expended in a unit of time. An example of intensity would be the quarter miler who began running a 550-440-330 workout in October at 75 sec., 60 sec., and 45 sec. At that point in time, after a summer's inactivity, this would be sufficient intensity to overload his system. If he continued to run at the same speed all year, the workout would become progressively easier, the intensity would decrease and there would be little training effect. Instead, each week or two weeks, the athlete should bring the time down by .5 sec. on each repeat so that the intensity is constantly being adjusted to his new threshold of training.

For the distance runner, runs at three times racing distances at 7 min. pace will be sufficient overload at first. Gradually he/she will need either an increase in distance (overload) to four or five times racing distance or faster pace runs (increased intensity). The current thought seems to be to increase the pace (intensity) so that the runner is working at a greater percentage of maximum.

4) **Progression**—Training should be progressive. It should go from the simple to the complex, from easy to hard, from quantity to quality. Also, as stated previously, the overload and intensity should be increased gradually.

5) **Duration**—This refers to the length of training time. This will vary with the event and the objective of the specific workout. A technique workout that is too long in duration can have little beneficial effect.

6) **Regularity**—Training should be set up on a regular basis, daily or twice daily depending on the event. It should be a year-round program.

7) **Recovery**—Every training program should have adequate time for the organism to recover and replenish energy stores. This is the time the body adapts to the stress placed upon it by hard training. Recovery is necessary from day to day as well as from training task to training task. Inadequate recovery time will lead to a decrease in the quality of training and negligible improvement.

A definite rhythmic cycle of work-to-rest should be observed for each athlete. The most common expression of this cycle is the hard-easy pattern. It has been this author's experience that many athletes, especially young high school athletes, require two easy days to recover following a hard day.

It is also important to remember that more rest or recovery is required after high intensity training efforts. It has been found that a 30-90 sec. recovery period is necessary for a low level of effort, and that 3-5 min. is necessary for a higher level of effort.

8) **Overtraining**—This principle was purposely left until last. Overtraining occurs when all the other principles are not followed. It is a state of chronic fatigue. Often times it is as much psychological as it is physical. The cure is either stopping training entirely or drastically changing the training routine to shock the organism. Overtraining is a more dangerous condition than undertraining. It is important to remember Bill Bowerman's classic axiom, "Train, don't strain."

General Training Goals

1) To achieve general conditioning.
2) To achieve event specific conditioning.
3) General strength gains—with special attention given to strengthening those areas of the body directly related to the specific event.
4) Speed—power development.
5) Psychological preparedness.
6) Increase of flexibility—general and specific.
7) Technical improvement in individual events.
8) To allow for individual differences within the context of laws of mechanics.
9) To have each athlete knowledgeable enough in their events to help each other in practice and meet situations.

Factors to be considered in planning training:

I. ● Personality
     ● Ability to concentrate
     ● Ability to relax
     ● Determination.
II. General Athletic Ability
     ● General conditioning
     ● General coordination
III. Speed and Power
     ● The components of speed and power with primary emphasis on jumping, power and ability
IV. Strength
     ● General overall muscular strength, not event specific strength
V. Specific Technical Development
     ● Throwing ability. Specific throwing components: explosiveness, technique
     ● Jumping ability.
       Specific components: explosiveness, technique
     ● Running ability
       Specific components: basic leg speed, running form, endurance.

Intensity is one of the eight essential factors which must be considered when developing a sound training program.

Planning Training

An athlete cannot be in top condition at all times. In setting up his/her training, the peak of conditioning should occur at a specific time. It is important to remember that is is not always the best athlete who wins, but the one who was prepared at that particular moment. This preparation requires thorough and careful planning.

Planning is important because it gives the coach and athlete a control and direction towards the attainment of goals. It reduces the element of surprise in training and competition, and leads to more consistent, reliable performances. The number one goal of planning is to have the athlete reach his or her best performance(s) during the most important competitions. The following plans are aids to this goal:

Daily Training Plan—An outline of the goals and objectives of an individual training session.

Period Plan—A specific plan for that particular training period. There are four periods within the training year, as defined in the section on the yearly plan.

Yearly Plan—An overall plan for the total training year.

Long Term Plan—A plan for several training years. For example, a plan covering the four years from one Olympics to the next.

Career Plan—Often overlooked. A broad overview of what the athlete wants to achieve over his/her entire career.

When planning training also consider the following three factors: 1) WHAT; 2) HOW; and 3) WHEN. The WHAT is the type of condition or training that the athlete hopes to achieve, the HOW is the particular technique or method of achieving this, and the WHEN is the time of the training year in which the athlete should work on this technique or method. For example, a pole vaulter would like to lengthen his approach and raise his hand hold (WHAT). To do this, he should increase his strength through weight training and his speed through sprint work and form drills (HOW). This should be done during the off season in order to allow time to incorporate these changes in technique (WHEN).

Daily Training Plan

In setting up a daily training session, it is important that the workout have a specific goal or objective, and that the athlete is aware of this goal. The session would observe the following sequence of training in order to insure optimum development:

1) Technique—This should immediately follow warmup when the athlete is fresh and receptive to learning.

2) Speed—This should follow technique when it is still early enough in the workout to ensure proper neuromuscular patterning.

3) Endurance—This follows technique and speed/work since it does not require the sharpness in performance that they do.

4) Strength Work—This should consist of either general weight training or plyometrics.

Endurance and strength can be interchanged, depending on the objectives of the workout. This order should be followed within a training week as well.

The Yearly Plan

When setting up this plan, the training year should be divided into four distinct periods: **1) active rest** or **transition; 2) foundation; 3) preparation;** and **4) competition.**

● **Active Rest or Transition Period** (July-August)—This period immediately follows the end of the season. The workload and intensity of training is significantly lower. The emphasis is on rest, recovery and relaxation. This period can be as short as six weeks or as long as eight weeks. It is a time for the athlete to play other games such as soccer, basketball, swimming and cycling. During this period, the distance runner should do some long relaxed running. Field eventers should "play" at their events.

● **Foundation Period** (Sept-Dec)—As the name implies, the foundation for the year is set during this period. It consists of hard physical conditioning. The training load is heaviest at this time. During early foundation (Sept-Oct) little skill work is done. Later on, more technique work is added and workload is created at greater intensity. The development of specific abilities is emphasized.

● **Preparation Period** (Jan-Feb)—During this phase, workload reaches it peak. Intensity is increased. More technique work is done. The emphasis is on direct preparation for the upcoming competitions. Competition is included during this period, but the emphasis is on development of performance. The competitions are a means to an end, not an end in themselves.

● **Competitive Period** (March-June)—Training is altered during this period to increase intensity and to allow for longer recovery periods before competitions and after hard training sessions. More difficult workouts should be done earlier in the week. It is important to note that during the competition period, basic fitness components must not be neglected. For example, if strength training is discontinued, then strength losses can be quite dramatic and result in a significant drop in performance. The whole year points toward this training period.

How can these periods be adapted to the high school track season that begins in February and ends in June? Very few high school programs, either due to state or district rules or interest, are able to have a year-round program. But, this concept can be achieved by compressing the training periods into the normal high school season.

Assuming that training begins February 1 and culminates with the state meet either the first or second week in June, the overall training period will be 17 or 18 weeks in length. This should be divided proportionally:

- Foundation Period—6 weeks
- Preparation Period—6 weeks—8 weeks for the more proficient and conditioned athlete
- Competition Period—6 weeks
- Active Rest—The summer should consist of low key activities maintaining general condition.

The freshmen, sophomores, and the poorly conditioned upper classmen should spend more time on general conditioning and strengthening. Therefore, for them, the foundation period should be longer in length. These athletes will achieve greater improvement in their performances through physical conditioning than through technique training that they are not yet ready to handle. Conditioning yields feet and yards while technique gives inches.

Competition usually begins at the end of the foundation period in late February or early March. Most high schools are commited to a 12-15 meet schedule. It is important to remember that it is physically and psychologically impossible for the athletes to be ''ready'' and ''up'' for each of these competitions. A method to deal with this potential problem is to classify the meets into three categories: 1) development; 2) important; and 3) crucial.

Developmental—Just as the name implies, this meet is used to test a specific ability or technique in the heat of competition. The athlete can try different events, test a different race strategy or make a trial run.

Important—This is a meet against a traditional rival or an invitational in which the athlete should achieve a good mark against good competition.

Crucial—This meet is near and including league finals, state qualifying, and state meet.

Classifying meets in this manner puts each meet in perspective and allows the coach and the athlete to prepare for the ones that really count.

The Olympic Development Committee recommends strongly that the high school athlete compete only once a week. Competing more often does not allow for proper recovery between meets nor does it allow for proper time for training. Experience has shown that more than one competition per week can be counterproductive to the athlete's long term development.

The problem of too many meets generally arises when there is a commitment to a league schedule with round robin dual meets on Thursday and an invitational on Saturday. The solution is to schedule tri- or quadrangular meets early in the season in order to cut down on the number of dual meet competitions.

The Development Committee also discourages doubling the middle distance and distance runners in the 880-Mile or Mile-Two Mile, or some combination thereof, week after week. Research has shown that optimum competition frequency for these athletes is once every 14 days. The explosive event athletes can and in fact should compete more often.

The Training Log

Every athlete in every event should keep a detailed log in order to keep track of progress. It is an important source of feedback for the coach and athlete. The training log provides for evaluation of training and competition, and serves as a valuable tool in planning training for the following year. Daily entries in the log should include the following:

 Warmup
 Goal for the Workout
 The Specific Workout—Number of throws, jumps, repetitions and times
 Drills
 Cooldown
 Weight Training—Exercises, reps, sets and amount of weight lifted, daily body weight, morning resting pulse rate, hours of sleep and any pertinent comments regarding diet that may have affected training. It is very important to note changes: new shoes, new training surface, new living situation. The athlete should also include general comments on how he/she felt before, during, and after the workout.

Preparing for Next Year

Once the athlete has completed a year of competition, it is important to evaluate that year with his/her coach and begin preparing for the next year. The best time to evaluate performance and plan for the following year is during the active rest phase when the past season's positive and negative aspects are still fresh. This evaluation is very important at all levels of development. The analysis should be very objective and as thorough as possible.

References

1) Arbeau, Glen, **Running a la Finland**, Shield Publishing House LTD, Ontario, Canada, 1973.
2) Dick, Frank, ''Periodization: An Approach to the Training Year,'' **Track Technique**, #62, Dec, 1975, p.1968.
3) Falls, H.B., Wallis, E.L., and Logan, G.A., **Foundation of Conditioning**, Academic Press, New York, 1970.
4) Jarver, Jess, **The How and Why of Physical Conditioning for Sport**, Rigby Limited, Adelaide, Australia, 1974.
5) Kruger, Arnd, ''Periodization, or Peaking at the Right Time,'' **Track Technique**, #54, Dec, 1973, p.1720.
6) Popov, V., ''Foundations of Training Planning,'' **Track Technique**, #38, Dec, 1969, p.1217.
7) Rasch, Philip J. and Burke, Roger K., **Kinesiology and Applied Anatomy—The Science of Human Movement**, Lea & Febiger, Philadelphia, 1971.

7
Planning and Administrating a Home Track Meet

by
Bob Covey
Bakersfield College

It is no secret that the modern track and field coach must wear more hats of responsibility than probably any coach in any other sport. Yet, the coach can also gain appreciation from the historical perspective that his/her predecessors very probably wore even more hats, spent more time in classroom responsibilities, coached more sports, and still were faced each Spring with putting the track and field facility back into shape. This comparison is offered because coaches today seem to be putting on a number of meets which are not of the quality they could be. There are many reasons for this. But whatever the reasons, track and field needs more well run meets. The purpose of this chapter is to help coaches set up successful meets by strengthening weak areas in planning and administration.

In planning meets, the time sequence is important. A pre-season organizational letter to all prospective officials is a start. An early meeting, and development of an officials' association is beneficial. The week of the meet requires contact by letter or phone to remind and reconfirm that the officials and support persons are ready. A post season letter of thanks, maybe a hosted barbecue, and some special recognition for service would be greatly appreciated.

The following information brings together guidelines found in most code books relative to official needs at a track and field meet. A track and field meet has the potential to be a memorable, positive experience, but it takes work on the part of the meet manager.

Administrative Needs in Officials and Support Staff

The dual, tri- or quadrangular meet is the very heart of track and field. Yet, it seems to be typically the poorest administered meet. Of course, fewer people are required than in a relay carnival or championship meet, but too often the small meet becomes a "barnyard" due to a careless approach. Below is a list of officials and support staff needed to develop this very important meet.

ANNOUNCER—It is important to develop this person's skills. The announcer will bring stability and enthusiasm for the meet to the competitors and spectators.

STARTER—A coach should work with his/her local, long-time starter to help train younger people. Different starters and recall starters should be used every chance possible.

TIMERS—The number of timers in any given meet should be twice the number of places being picked or scored, plus two. If scoring three places, the coach should use two timers for each place, plus an additional timer for first and one timer for fourth. Of course, if the coach is capable of timing with accuracy all of the competitors, excellent, but most do not have that capability. Sadly, often coaches fall far short of accurate timing in the small meet because they feel it is not important enough to organize it properly.

FINISH JUDGES—Again, the minimum should be implemented, if possible. The minimum should be two on each scoring place plus one each on the next two places. The two-person teams should be instructed on the "torso" concept in track and field and should operate as a team standing on opposite sides of the track.

CLERK OF THE COURSE—For a small meet usually one or two clerks are sufficient to set the runners in their proper lanes on the track. He/she must work well with the starter and announcer to demand that the meet run on schedule and keep the announcer appraised relative to entry changes.

REFEREE—He/she may be the starter, but this is not recommended. The referee must be a well-versed, knowledgeable, and capable decision maker. Often, the starter is expected to be the referee and must stop starting duties to make a judgment. This can be detrimental to the meet.

INSPECTORS—He/she is probably the most understaffed official at a meet. The inspector must be aware of track violations, obviously, and the coach may become more efficient in developing qualified inspectors by recruiting ex-trackmen. It is very important that this position be properly staffed.

MARSHALLS—There may be none needed in a small meet, if coaches can keep spectators off the field.

WIND-GUAGE OPERATORS—Two well trained (takes maybe less than five minutes to train an interested official here) persons are necessary at college meets and are important at increasing numbers of high school meets.

WEIGHTS AND MEASURES—One official trained to work with weights and measures may be needed but is often not necessary in small meets.

SCORERS, RECORDERS—Sufficient scorers and recorders are important to stay with the meet, feeding information to the announcer. Some small meets also have secretaries to type and copy results for release after the meet.

COMMUNICATIONS STAFF—They feed information to the announcer from the field and clerk. This staff also brings results to the scorers and announcers table from the finish line.

SUPPORT STAFF—This large staff consists of block setters, string holders, hurdle crew, hospitality staff (to supply drinks or information to the officials upon request), program staff (some meets supply a free program for the meet, distributed through this staff). In terms of numbers, this is an item that depends on the needs of the meet, the numbers of paid groundsmen also assigned to work with starting blocks and hurdles, etc.

FIELD EVENT OFFICIALS—There should be no less than one trained, adult official to manage each field event. He/she should be supported with at least one additional, trained official in the horizontal jumps and throws, and student support staff persons in the horizontal jumps, pole vault, discus, and javelin for marking and maintenance.

THE MAJOR MEET

Administrative Needs in Officials and Support Staff

The meet manager of a major meet requires more of everything, obviously, but is usually aided by the increased supply of interested help. Nevertheless, he/she has countless items to attend to, and the assignment of officials is always a major headache. The coach should start early in organization, announce a meeting to distribute caps or badges (or both), if used. The following is a guide to administrative needs of a major meet:

ANNOUNCER—He/she needs an assistant handling incoming communications and spotting. This assistant can be called **HEAD OF COMMUNICATIONS**, and in major meets should be working with a phone system or other form of audio communications system to allow instantaneous input to the announcer.

COMMUNICATIONS STAFF—Three to five knowledgeable persons are needed to work on the field and with the clerk to feed information to the announcer through the **HEAD OF COMMUNICATIONS**.

STARTER—Working with the recall starter, these are invaluable persons if they work professionally. In major meets, it is recommended that three persons trade roles to rest the head starter and give the recall starter experience to work as a head starter.

REFEREE—He/she must be a top-notch, knowledgeable official in a meet like this.

Proper planning is one of the keys to a well-run meet.

JURY OF APPEALS—If called for by the rules, this jury of a specified numbers of persons (often by state or regional code) also often acts as the **GAMES COMMITTEE** and **MOST VALUABLE PARTICIPANT COMMITTEE.**

TIMERS—Again the rule is twice the number of places being judged or scoring places, plus two—one as the third timer on first place and one as the sole timer on the first non-scoring (or non-qualifying) place.

PHOTO-TIMER TECHNICIANS—Most major meets today expect or require photo-timing.

PHOTO-TIMER JUDGE—This position requires one trained person reading and recording the results from the photo-timer.

VIDEO-TAPE TECHNICIANS—Many major meets may use video-tape with slow-motion and stop-action capabilities at the finish line with (or instead of) the photo-timer. This system also will need a **VIDEO-TAPE FINISH JUDGE.**

FINISH JUDGE—Following the formula given earlier, the goal is to have two persons judging each place required and additional judges picking one or two places beyond those required, in cases of disqualification. The **HEAD FINISH JUDGE** handles the results, checks with the **PHOTOTIMER JUDGE** and the **HEAD TIMER** before submitting the results.

CLERKS OF THE COURSE—Most major meets work with three to five **CLERKS** to insure that the meet runs smoothly, which means **on schedule.** There are the most important persons to keep the meet running on time.

INSPECTORS—This assignment becomes critical, and trained persons are important. Eight to twelve inspectors are usually necessary to cover all aspects of possible running event violations.

MARSHALLS—These men/women **must** maintain control of the track and field and keep it free of non-competing persons, including coaches and non-competing athletes. This is a thankless job for many, so recruitment of the right person is important. If the field is not kept relatively clear by the marshalls, the entire meet is negatively affected.

WIND GAUGE OPERATORS—Needed here are two experienced or trained persons, one for each gauge. They must report the wind readings for each jump in the horizontal jumps and the 100, 200 and 110 m. high hurdles, to be recorded on the official event sheet.

WEIGHTS AND MEASURES JUDGE—With one assistant, this judge usually can perform his/her task well, if the adequate equipment is available.

FIELD EVENT JUDGES—A major meet requires one **HEAD JUDGE** for each field event, and one **ASSISTANT JUDGE** for each event. Needed in the horizontal jumps, discus, javelin and hammer throw are at least two support persons for marking and maintenance. Two assistants are the minimum needed in the pole vault, and one, minimum, is necessary in the high jump and shot put.

SCORERS, RECORDERS, SECRETARIES—Usually two scorers can keep on top of this task, and the secretaries can become the recorders, usually typing up results and duplicating them at the meet for release upon request to coaches and press.

SUPPORT STAFF—Usually in major meets, the number of block setters equals the number of lanes on the track. This is a chance to bring some interested persons into the meet. Usually students, maybe the cheerleaders, or any group who have taken an active interest in the program can help. The **BLOCK SETTERS** may be dressed alike. The **HOSPITALITY STAFF** may include students who carry the runners' sweat suits to them at the finish line as well as supply food, drinks, and information to the officials. The **HURDLE CREW** numbering eight to fifteen, is essential in moving hurdles in a meet with a normally tight time schedule. The **STRING HOLDERS** should be carefully selected and aware of their responsibility. The **PROGRAM SELLERS**, often a part of the basic meet operation, also require a special type of person.

Now, this list, realizing it is a minimum, and more can always be used, adds up to more than one-hundred persons on the track and field helping with the meet. This is the coach's army, and if well organized and motivated, they will succeed famously for the meet.

Nevertheless, there are often potential problems. The following are comments on a few:

1. The coach must demand that the officials be impartial. They will become emotionally involved with a close meet, but good officials must remain impartial.
2. A time schedule must be planned that is both reasonable and tight. Great meets stay on schedule.
3. In timing races, the coach should instruct the timers to time those races run in lanes all the way by the lane, not the place. This significantly improves accuracy of timing these races.
4. In cases of dispute between the finish judges and the timers, the judge recording the finish results should use the judges' decision over the timers'. In recording the results, then, the timers' time may have to be logically altered in the results.
5. Because the photo-timer often makes the work of the timers seemingly unimportant, instruct the announcer to announce both electric and hand-held marks, and record both sets. This comparison will help the coach discover faulty hand-held watches or less capable timers.
6. More women coaches and officials are needed in track and field. The coach should actively recruit capable women and assign them to good positions.
7. The physical potential that the coach has to work with (i.e., track, pits, standards, ropes with flags,

etc.) is always a problem. A well planned system for repair and purchasing new equipment in time can bring the physical needs nearly up to the level of what the coach desires. Interestingly, physical potential is not as important in providing the quality meet as one might think. Quality track and field meets come from the organization, enthusiasm, and administration of the meet manager, officials, and support staff.

Included is a checklist of officials and equipment to help in setting up an efficient and organized track and field meet.

Track & Field Meet Checklist

Personnel
a. Referee
b. Inspectors (five or six)
c. Scorers (one or two)
d. Marshall and assistants
e. Clerk of the course
f. Surveyor
g. Starter
h. Finish judges (two per scoring table)
i. Timers (four)
j. Head field judge
k. Field judges (two per event)
l. Aids for field judges (two per event)
m. Announcer
n. Physician
o. Official to weigh implements and assistant
p. Awards stewards (as many as there are places)
q. Runners

General equipment
a. Scales
b. Measuring instruments
c. Stickers to be placed on approved implements
d. P.A. system
e. Scorers table and scoreboard
f. Numbers and pins for competitors
g. Large manila envelopes to contain numbers, etc.
h. Press stand or table
i. Official rulebook
j. Local, school, state, national and world records for announcer
k. Awards stand
l. Badges for officials
m. Order of events
n. Instruction sheet mimeographed for each event and clip boards.

Special equipment for Running Events
a. Starting lines
b. Finish lines
c. Relay exchange zones
d. Hurdle marks
e. Lane marks
f. Lime and limer for all above items
g. Hurdles

h. Starter's pistol and cartridges (32 cal)
i. Whistle for starter and referee
j. Score cards for clerk of course
k. Score cards for score keeper
l. Flags for inspectors
m. Pencils for recording places
n. Starting blocks for all events (lanes)
o. Finish post 4 1/2 feet above ground level
p. Platform or steps for finish judges
q. Hammers for each lane attendent
r. Finish yarn (wool)
s. Three or four stop watches checked by competent jeweler.
t. Batons for all relay teams
u. 400 feet of string or cord for laying out track and field
v. Anemometers (two)

Special equipment for field events.
a. **Long jump**
1. Take-off board
2. Jumping pit.
3. Rake
4. Spade or shovel
5. 50 foot measuring tape (steel)

b. **High jump**
1. Jumping pit
2. Standards
3. Crossbars (three or four)
4. Rake and spade
5. Steel tape (10 feet)

c. **Shot put**
1. Three or four shots
2. Shot circle
3. Toe board
4. Distance and foul lines
5. 100 foot steel tape
6. Markers (numbered)

d. **Discus throw**
1. Discus
2. Throwing circle
3. Throwing area must be level
4. Distance lines
5. Markers (numbered)
6. 300 foot tape

e. **Pole vault**
1. Jumping pit
2. Standards
3. Crossbars
4. Forked stickers for replacing crossbar
5. Vaulting poles
6. Planting pit or box
7. Spade and rake or pitch fork
8. Step ladder (20 ft. tape)

f. **Javelin throw**
1. Take-off board
2. Scratch line

Part B
The Running Events

8
Fundamental Mechanics of Running and Hurdling

by
Fred Wilt
Purdue University

Each athlete differs from every other to at least some slight extent in muscle origins and insertions, size and length muscles, bone structure, posture, flexibility, height, weight, personality, and various other features that influence form and technique in running. Because of individual physical makeup, form is strictly an individual proposition, and good form may be described only in general terms. Accordingly, it is a grave error for one runner to blindly copy any aspect of the form of another.

In order to describe running, it is first useful to recognize that race-walking may be superficially described as progression by steps so taken that unbroken contact with the ground is maintained—the heel of the advancing foot contacting the ground before the toe of the rear foot leaves the ground. Walking involves pushing the body forward and out of balance, while it is supported over one leg, and then bringing the swinging, rear leg forward in time to prevent the body from falling. Speed in walking is limited by the step-length—determined by the possible distance between the feet while both are in contact with the ground—and by the time necessary for the rear leg to swing forward to prevent the body from falling with each step.

Human running is a form of locomotion devoid of any theoretical limit on speed on such mechanical grounds as found in walking. Speed is increased in running by causing the body to "float" in the air with both feet on the ground for a short time with each step. Dur-

Because of individual physical makeups, running form is strictly an individual proposition, and good form may be described only in general terms.

ing this time the step is made longer than the span of the legs would otherwise permit. In running, there is never a phase of "double support," when both feet are on the ground simultaneously. The rear leg always starts swinging forward before the front foot contacts the ground. Contrary to walking, there is always a period of "double float" in each running step when both feet are off the ground.

The action of each leg may be arbitrarily divided into three phases, regardless of the running speed:

1. **The supporting phase**. This begins the instant the foot contacts the ground about 12 inches (30 cm.) ahead of a point directly below the body's center of gravity (CG)—Figure 1. It is the shortest of the three phases, and ends when the body's CG has moved ahead of the foot in contact with the ground. The faster the running speed, the closer the foot approaches to grounding directly beneath the body's CG.

2. **Driving phase**. Immediately upon completion of the supporting phase, the driving phase begins and continues until the foot leaves the ground well behind the CG (Figure 2). Throughout this phase the body is propelled forward by extension of levers at the hip, knee, ankle, and toes in that order, acting behind the body's CG in a pushing action. Increased stride length must always result from greater force being exerted by the leg acting behind the body's CG in the driving phase, rather than stretching the leading leg grotesquely forward in the recovery phase, and attempting to ground the foot farther ahead of the body's CG in a futile effort to "claw" the body forward. The runner should have a

feeling of pushing the ground away from behind throughout the driving phase.

3. **The recovery phase**. This starts when the toe of the foot in the driving phase leaves the ground behind the body's CG, and ends when the same foot is again planted slightly ahead of the CG to start another supporting phase.

Body lean in running is a function of acceleration—the greater the acceleration, the greater the body lean. At uniform speed, the body is nearly erect (i.e. no acceleration, no lean). Forward body lean is always greater at the start because it is here that acceleration is greatest. Running into a strong headwind would, of course, require some adjustment in forward body lean, even at uniform speed. The most accurate appraisal of a runner's true body lean may be seen when the knees are closest together while an illusion of forward lean may be observed when viewing the runner from the side at the end of the driving phase when the leg is extended behind the body.

Stride frequency, (cadence) among middle-distance runners is usually around 3½ strides per second. In sprinting, it is around 4½ and occasionally (for brief periods) as much as 5 strides per second.

Stride length at middle-distance speeds varies from 5 to 6 feet (1.5-1.8 m.) while in sprinting it ranges generally between 7 and 8½ feet (2.1-2.6 m.). As a general rule, it may be said that stride length is a function of running speed. The slower the speed, the shorter the stride and the faster the speed, the longer the runner's stride.

Figure 1. The supporting phase

Figure 2. The driving phase.

Both understriding and overstriding are faults. Each runner has his own personal optimum stride length for any given running speed, depending upon leg length, joint flexibility, and numerous other factors.

It requires 43-45 strides to sprint 100 yards, and 47-49 strides to sprint 100 meters. About 1,000 strides are required to run a mile. Top recorded sprinting speed is 36 feet per second (11 m./sec.).

Running speed = candence X stride length. Since maximum cadence among humans seems limited (4½-5 strides per second), the greatest potential for increasing speed is increasing stride length resulting from the exertion of greater force in the driving phase of the stride.

As a runner moves faster and faster, there is less and less time in which to exert force behind the CG during the driving phase of the stride. Thus as running speed increases, the potential for impulse (force X time) is reduced. It is here that we find one great difference between top-class sprinters and those who possess less sprinting speed. The great sprinter can still exert force behind the CG in the driving phase of the stride, even though the time becomes progressively shorter in which to exert such force. Another feature which may differentiate the greater sprinter is his ability to accelerate the leg forward in the recovery phase, which by reaction increases the force exerted by the driving leg.

The height to which the knee is lifted in front of the body during the recovery phase is dependent upon the running speed. The faster the running speed, the higher the knee is lifted in front. The limit of the forward swing of the recovery knee coincides with the completion of the driving phase of the opposite leg.

In all running, including sprinting, at the conclusion of the recovery phase the leading foot sweeps downward, and apparently backward, to initiate the supporting phase of the stride. The outer border of the ball of the foot first contacts the track as the supporting phase of the stride begins. The faster the running, speed the more forward (toward the toes) is the point on the outer border of the foot where contact is first made with the ground. Immediately after this first contact, the heel of the foot comes naturally to the ground. No effort should be made to prevent this. As the heel touches the ground without inhibition, the foot rolls inward, toward the midline of the body. As the body rides forward, over, and beyond the foot which is momentarily flat on the ground, the heel lifts and ground contact is broken with the inside edge of the ball-toe of the foot, to conclude the driving phase of the stride.

It is sometimes argued that running, especially sprinting, is faster if the heels do not touch the ground. This is quite definitely wrong. Work = force X distance. If the distance over which force may be exerted is reduced by failure to permit the heel to touch the ground with each stride, then the range over which work may be accomplished is significantly shortened, and the potential for speed is obviously reduced.

Ideally, the inner border of each foot should touch the ground along a straight line during the supporting and driving phases. The feet should not be placed wide apart laterally, or one in front of the other in a straight line, as both positions cause an inefficient, side-to-side motion when running.

The line of force of the leg through the hip in the driving phase of the stride is offset from the body's CG. Thus, an off-center or "eccentric" thrust of the left leg acting through the left hip, during the driving phase, coupled with the forward lifting of the right leg in the recovery phase of this (right) leg, causes the hips to rotate counterclockwise in a horizontal plane (when viewed from above). The body is lifted simultaneously no more than necessary to counteract the pull of gravity as the runner is projected forward. For every action, there must be an equal and opposite reaction. The reaction to the forward projection of the body is absorbed by the ground. The reaction to the twisting actions caused by the eccentric thrust of the left leg are absorbed by the upper body. In this instance, as the hips move counterclockwise in a horizontal plane, the upper body (arms, trunk, and shoulders) move clockwise in a parallel horizontal plane.

During the running stride the upper body moves either clockwise or counterclockwise in a horizontal plane, in reaction to the hips moving in the opposite direction in a parallel plane. The obvious result is that the right arm and shoulder move forward and backward in coordination with the left leg, while the left arm and shoulder move backward and forward in coordination with the right leg.

Because the cadence is less in middle - and long-distance running, there is sufficient time to allow the trunk and shoulders to absorb much of the reaction to the twisting movements created by the eccentric thrust of the legs. This permits an energy-conserving use of somewhat mild arm action and flowing shoulder-twist as seen in middle - and long-distance running.

In sprinting the cadence is so fast the shoulders cannot twist and untwist quickly enough to absorb the reaction to the frequent and powerful eccentric leg thrusts during the driving phase. For this reason, the sprinter seeks to keep his shoulders steady and absorb the reaction to the eccentric thrust of the legs by forceful and faster (though more tiring) arm action over a wide range. This range of arm motion in sprinting is approximately the same in front and behind the shoulder axis.

The upper arms move relatively straight backward and forward. The lower arms move "around" the trunk in a slight cross-body direction in front, especilly in middle - and long-distance running, but do not cross an imaginary vertical plane bisecting the body into right and left halves. In sprinting the lower arms tend to move more directly backward and forward with less cross-body action than seen in running at slower speeds, and the hands swing as high as eye level in front and no more than about a foot behind the hipline.

During the forward swing of each arm, the elbow tends to remain bent at an angle of approximately 90 degrees, permitting it to move forward more rapidly due to a reduced moment of inertia (mass X radius squared) about its axis at the shoulder. This bend increases somewhat as the hands swing in front of the body.

As the arm moves backward during the driving phase

Every runner has his/her own optimum stride length for any given running speed, depending upon leg length, joint flexibility, and numerous other factors.

of the leg on the opposite side of the body, the angle at the elbow increases (straightens) to the maximum extent at a point when the knees are closest together. As the arm continues backward, passing the hip, it again starts bending at the elbow. As it approaches the end of its path backward, it is again bent to a near 90 degree angle at the elbow, thus increasing its speed of motion to coincide with the final thrust of the leg on the opposite side of the body at the conclusion of the driving phase.

The hands are carried in a relaxed "cupped" position in both sprinting and running at slower speeds, as seen in the accompanying photos.

The arms "follow" the legs and absorb reaction to the eccentric thrust of the legs during the driving phase. Because action and reaction are interchangeable, a fast and powerful arm action may be used in sprinting to speed up the action of the legs.

The head should be aligned naturally with the trunk, and the eyes focused a few yards ahead. It may sometimes move somewhat from side to side in middle-distance running without upsetting body balance, and occupy a role in absorbing the reaction to the action of the eccentric leg-thrust during the driving phase of the stride. It is a mistake to throw back the head at the finish, as this tends to shorten the stride and straighten the trunk.

The essential and involuntary process of breathing should be subjected to the least possible resistance and interference. For this reason, the runner should inhale and exhale through both the mouth and nose.

Athletes who run naturally always find their best and most economical form or style by much training at a variety of speeds over various distances and surfaces. It is therefore unnecessary to "teach" an athlete to run correctly. Difficulty in running form is encountered only when the athlete departs from his natural style and attempts to use some artificially imposed motion, such as overstriding or toe-running.

Sprinting is running at the maximum speed of which an athlete is capable. Anything less than top speed is not sprinting. The form of any one athlete when sprinting will differ in terms of intensity from his form when running at slower speeds. In sprinting the cadence is faster, the stride is longer, the heel of the recovery foot rises higher toward the hip, the knee of the recovery leg rises higher in front, there is less shoulder motion, the arm action is more vigorous, and there is a considerably greater fatiguing effect than when running at lesser speeds.

The start in sprint and hurdles races is accomplished most efficiently with a "medium" starting block spacing. This places the front block 15-18 inches (38-46 cm.)

between the blocks. In the "set" position the front knee is bent at an angle of about 90 degrees, the hips are slightly higher than the shoulders, the rear knee is bent at an angle of slightly greater than 90 degrees, the body's weight is supported equally between the hands and front foot, the head is held in natural alignment with the body, and the eyes are focused somewhere between the starting line and 2-3 feet (60-90 cm.) beyond this line. High hurdlers using an eight-stride approach to the first barrier place the take-off foot on the front block and the lead foot on the rear block. The feet are reversed for the seldom seen seven-stride approach.

Hurdling is sprinting over obstacles. The problem is to clear the barriers in such a way as to interfere least with the athlete's sheer sprinting speed. Thus, hurdling technique is a modification of sprinting form. Because of the exact height and distance between barriers as specified by the rules, and the anatomical limitations imposed upon human locomotion, the possibilities for improving hurdle times are concerned mainly with stride cadence and hurdle clearance, rather than increased stride length.

In the 110 meter hurdles event, the sum of eight strides to the first 42-inch (107 cm.) hurdle, nine times three strides between hurdles (total 27), and five finishing strides is 40. This sum added to the ten strides over the barriers makes a total of 50 strides in the race. For a 13.0 second 120 yards hurdles result, the average cadence is 50 strides divided by 13.0 seconds or 3.84 strides per second. When compared to maximum sprint cadence (4½-5 strides per second), it is obvious that one avenue for improvement in high hurdling is increased stride cadence.

Skilled hurdlers sprint the 110 meter high hurdle event in a time only 2 seconds (or slightly less) slower than their time for sprinting an equal distance without barriers. The average time required to negotiate a hurdle is therefore only 0.2 second or slightly less. Thus hurdle clearance technique should strive to interfere least with normal sprinting action. In achieving such an objective, the hurdler's limbs are displaced in such a way as to avoid contact with the barriers, while landing beyond the hurdle in position to return immediately to normal sprinting action.

Each of the usual eight strides to the first hurdle in high hurdling is longer than the preceding stride, except the final step. Any adjustment in the approach should occur in the fourth, fifth, and sixth strides. The final approach stride is 2-4 inches shorter than the penultimate stride. The purpose of shortening this last step is to rotate the trunk forward so the drive from the take-off foot will project the body with an almost horizontal lean or "body-dip" across the hurdle. This lean must be initiated while the body is still in contact with the ground, as the flight-path of the hurdler's CG while airborne follows a predetermined parabolic path and cannot be altered in the air.

To clear the hurdle, the lead-leg at take off must be lifted fast, with knee well-bent. A high, fast pick-up of this knee encourages continuation of general sprinting

action, increases the force of thrust off the ground by the take-off leg, leaves behind the take-off leg (trail leg) and causes a desirable "splits" position between the legs after take off so the take-off leg may come forward late but last, increases body-dip in reaction to the fast-rising knee-lift, and is much faster than when using a straight lead leg. The speed of lead leg lift determines the speed of hurdle clearance. As a practical matter, the hurdler should try to move the lead knee and foot so fast that the foot cannot be seen, thus producing a wide split between the legs at take off.

As the leading leg is lifted quickly for hurdle clearance at take off, the arm opposite the lead leg is thrust forcefully forward. Some athletes wrap the leading arm (i.e., the arm opposite the lead leg) somewhat across the body, but later straighten and thrust it forward. The arm on the same side as the lead leg remains bent at the elbow in normal sprinting position, in readiness to drive forward in coordination with the trail leg's forward motion for the first "getaway" stride after clearance. *Note*: a "double arm action"—having both arms forward—during the hurdle clearance is not ideal, since this deviates from arm position in normal sprinting.

After full extension of the take-off leg, the heel of this limb rises immediately to the buttock, folding the lower leg to the thigh preparatory to the knee being swung well out to the side, upward and forward to bring the thigh parallel to the ground.

The leading foot reaches its highest point 6-12 inches (15-30 cm.) before the barrier, and the athlete's CG reaches its zenith about 1 foot (30 cm.) in front of the hurdle. From this high point, the hurdler comes down across the obstacle during the clearance.

The near horizontal body-dip initiated at take off permits raising the seat and lowering the trunk in relation to the hurdler's CG. The lower the athlete's flight path over the hurdle, the more quickly he may regain ground contact and continue sprinting.

Before the athlete's seat reaches the barrier, the lead leg begins to straighten, cuts across the hurdle rail, and continues down toward the other side with heel of the foot leading this action.

Ideally, the head and shoulders should face forward at all times, with minimum deviation from their normal positions during sprinting. Dropping the head while over the obstacle may produce a flatter layout during clearance, although this advantage must be weighed against the disadvantage of a possible momentary interference with the athlete's vision.

When most of the body weight is beyond the barrier and the lead leg is well on its way to the ground, the trail leg passes over the hurdle with its foot "cocked" slightly upward to avoid striking the rail with the toes. The crotch reaches the barrier before the knee of the trail leg. As it passes "late but fast" over the hurdle rail, the trail leg is parallel to the ground and makes a right angle with the leading leg.

As it passes about about the hurdle rail, the knee of the trail leg is lifted up high toward and almost to the chest, to insure an optimum "getaway" stride of about 5 fee (152 cm.).

The foot of the lead leg lands 3 feet 9 inches-4 feet 6 inches (114-137 cm.) beyond the hurdle after clearance. The landing point must be beneath and slightly behind the body's CG to insure immediate return to sprinting action. There is nothing to be gained by preventing the heel from touching the ground at this correct landing point. The extreme body dip over the hurdle decreases to the body-angle of normal sprint action (in accordance with acceleration) as the lead foot is grounded.

With the changes in the position of the legs as the hurdler pivots over the hurdle in the just described clearance action, the arms also change position. The leading arm swings back, somewhat bent at the elbow, with the hand carried low. It sweeps backward, outside the knee of the trailing leg, which is now moving forward. If the elbow is bent and the hand carried low, a wide novice "swimming action" of this arm may be avoided.

Hurdlers are sometimes instructed to snap the lead leg down as the hurdle clearance is made in an effort to more quickly regain ground contact. This actually has the effect of prematurely raising the trunk in reaction, although it may not be so obvious as the action of the lead leg because the moment of inertia of this leg about a horizontal axis passing through the body's CG is less than the moment of inertia of the trunk about the same axis. Nevertheless, such a premature raising of the trunk may cause the trail leg to drop, and result in the foot

striking the hurdle rail as it is brought through for the first getaway stride. *Note*: Insufficient body-dip during hurdle clearance is usually the cause of striking the hurdle with the foot or ankle of the trail leg.

Rather than attempting to snap down the lead leg, the hurdler should lift the trail leg through high, bringing the limb through laterally until the knee is near the chest in front, causing the lead leg to move downward in reaction to the upward-forward lifting of the trail leg. The faster the trailing leg is pulled through forward-upward, the faster the lead leg will move toward the ground. This is not to suggest the trail leg should be "hurried" (causing a jump to avoid striking the barrier), nor that it should be delayed. Rather the legs must move continuously throughout hurdle clearance with no "posed" position at any time.

The key to proper stride length between hurdles is often directly related to the length of the first stride after the lead leg is grounded beyond the hurdle. This stride must be a hard-driving effort of about 5 feet (150 cm.). A short first stride is ordinarily caused by lack of trail leg lift.

Clearing the hurdle causes the athlete to rotate simultaneously in several planes while in the air. For the purpose of reference, think of three anatomical planes passing through the body's CG as the frontal (a vertical plane that divides the body into front and rear halves), sagittal (a vertical plane that divides the body into right and left halves), and horizontal (a plane parallel to the ground that divides the body into upper and lower

Hurdling technique is a modification of sprinting form.

halves). As the athlete leaves the ground for hurdle clearance, there is forward rotation in a sagittal plane. As the trail leg is lifted laterally forward-upward, the trunk rotates downward ("sidewise") in reaction toward this upward-moving limb in a frontal plane. As the trail leg continues forward, passing the hurdle rail and sweeps laterally forward-upward toward the front of the body, the trunk rotates toward this forward moving limb in a horizontal plane. As the lead leg sweeps downward toward the ground for landing, the trunk moves upward by reaction in a sagittal plane.

The adverse aspect of these rotations may be minimized by an appropriate body-dip at take off, causing a flat hurdle-clearance, thus resulting in the body presenting a greater amount of inertia in a horizontal plane about a vertical axis passing through the CG. This moment of inertia is increased by the forward extension of the arm opposite the lead leg during the clearance. Such an increased moment of inertia about the vertical axis will permit a less pronounced reaction to the action of the trail leg in a horizontal plane.

The technique of clearing 42-inch hurdles applies generally to clearance of the 30-inch (76 cm.) barriers, with certain modifications. Because the hurdler's CG is well above the low hurdle rail, there is no need for the exaggerated body-dip. Extreme body-dip in clearing the low hurdles would require unnecessarily executing the dip, and then raising the trunk following each clearance. The forward lean at low-hurdle clearance should be merely sufficient to maintain proper sprinting form. There is little rise in head height in clearance. It is not necessary to lift the trail knee to hip level in crossing the barrier. Thus the extreme hip flexibility of high hurdling is not absolutely necessary in clearing these barriers.

The technique of clearing the intermediate (36-inch or 91.4 cm.) hurdles is roughly halfway between that of high - and low-hurdle clearance techniques. The pivot over the hurdle rail is slower than in either of the others. Economy of effort receives more attention here. Less body-dip is required than in high hurdling. Because horizontal speed is slower, the stepping action over the 36-inch barriers is less violent. The trail leg is not lifted so high as in high-hurdling. A first stride of around 5 feet is required after hurdle clearance in this event, as in the case of both the 30-inch and 42-inch barriers.

Hurdling should be considered a sprint race over barriers. The action throughout should present as little interruption as possible to sprinting form. Although for the purpose of description and analysis it may be useful to separate hurdle clearance into various phases, it is in reality a continuous coordinated effort, and not a series of separate parts.

9
Sprints*

Sprinting: Techniques and Fundamentals

by
Brooks Johnson
Stanford University

The objectives of sprinting are the attainment of maximum acceleration, the maintenance of maximum velocity, and the minimization of deceleration in order to cover the required distance in the minimum amount of time. The coach and athlete seek the optimum combination of stride length and stride cadence to the maximum extent possible throughout the race.

Sprint performance can be improved. Areas which may be altered to a certain extent include technical aspects, physiological aspects, and psychological aspects. Technical areas include the start, stride length, stride cadence, and movement patterns of the body. Physiological areas that can be improved through training include anaerobic capacity, muscular strength (primary muscle groups involved in running—arms, legs, feet, upper body—as well as the balance of antagonistic muscles), and flexibility (elasticity of the muscles). Psychological areas include the "sprint personality," inhibiting forces (fear of failure, fear of success, fear of ultimate speed), and race preparation.

The following material deals mainly with the technical aspects of sprinting.

The Sprint Start

The purpose of the sprint start is to accelerate the athlete to maximum speed in a minimum of time. One type of inertia must be overcome and be replaced by another. In the accomplishment of this, certain actions required for maximal effectiveness will conflict with other desirable objectives. For example:

a) the sprinter should assume a position at "set" that permits a minimal reaction time;

b) the sprinter should leave the blocks quickly, maintaining balance while driving forcefully on the blocks with both legs; and

c) a smooth but constant acceleration should be attained.

The problem arises when equating rapid block clearance and immediate early speed with the achievement of maximum velocity in the shortest possible time. The more forceful block exit leads to a smoother, more effective acceleration which permits attainment of this velocity in a minimum amount of time. Great discipline is required in order to restrain and replace seemingly

*This chapter consists of two articles: (1) "Sprinting: Techniques and Fundamentals"; and (2) "400 Meter Training".

The start.

natural actions with those which do not seem as natural, but which may be mechanically more efficient. The ideal start is not easily defined since the actions and techniques vary among successful sprinters.

Block Spacing and Placement

Athletes should use their own body segments to provide proper measurement for the spacing of the blocks, since most athletes prefer not to be burdened with carrying measuring devices to the starting line. A semi-elongated block setting should be used with the pedals separated from 10″ to 18″, depending upon the height and comfort of the runner. The front pedal should be approximately 2 to 2½ foot lengths from the starting line, depending upon the two previously noted factors. The block positions and spacings are best attained when the runner assumes the set position with the following guidelines:

a) an angle of approximately 90° is formed between the thigh of the front leg and the trunk;
b) an angle of approximately 90° is formed by the knee joint of the front leg;
c) an angle of approximately 120° is formed by the knee joint of the rear leg;
d) the front pedal is set at an angle of 55° to 60°;
e) the rear pedal is set at an angle of 80° to 85°; and
f) arms should be at approximately 90° to the running surface and directly under shoulder.

At this point, the block's spacings should be adjusted for the individual. More effective positioning will result through trial and error. The sprinter must feel confident, comfortable, efficient, and powerful in the set position.

Taking Position in the Blocks

At the command, "On your marks", the sprinter who is standing behind the blocks should move forward ahead of the blocks and back into position, placing the feet securely in the blocks one at a time. The feet should be straight and vertical in the blocks, the weight evenly distributed between the hands and feet. The head should be in natural alignment with the trunk and the eyes focused slightly in front of the starting line. The arms should be straight (with the hands supported by a high bridge of the fingers and thumb) and placed about shoulder width apart.

Set Position

On the command "Set", the runner raises the hips and moves the center of gravity forward by raising the knee of the rear leg off the ground and partially straightening the rear leg (to approximately at 120° angle). The shoulders should be moved forward above or slightly ahead of the hands, as the hips rise to a position slightly above the shoulders. The angle at the knee

of the front leg is approximately 90°. There is some difference of opinion as to the head position. Some technicians maintain that a natural alignment of the head with the shoulders and with the eyes focused slightly ahead of the starting line is preferred. Others prefer to elevate the head and focus the eyes down the track. The individual preferences govern these aspects of the set position, and will evolve over a period of time. The attention of the runner should be concentrated on the initial movement actions rather than listening for and reacting to the sound of the gun.

The Starting Action

On the sound of the gun, the reactions begin immediately by picking up the hands, resulting in the raising of the shoulders as the hands move oppositely and vigorously (one forward and up, the other backward), while the legs drive explosively against the blocks. The short but vigorous arm action is coupled with the forceful pull through of the rear leg after its initial drive against the rear block. The front leg exerts maximum force until the knee and ankle joints are fully extended and the foot exits the block pedal. The head remains in natural alignment with the trunk or else the head is already upright, dependent upon the position at "set". There is a pronounced lean, and a straight line can be drawn from the lead foot through the leg, hips, trunk, shoulder, and head at an angle of 30° to 40°. The foot of the rear leg should touch down under or slightly behind the center of gravity. The rate of acceleration depends upon the stride cadence and stride length as a powerful backward thrusting of the legs is achieved during each stride, assisted by a fast and high pick up of the rear knee. As the actions continue, stride length is increased as cadence is maintained. The forward lean will be reduced as the length of time spent applying force against the track is decreased and the supporting leg comes more directly beneath the center of gravity. Maximum acceleration is attained between 40 to 60 meters.

Stride Length

Stride length is defined as the distance between touchdown of the toe of one foot and the touchdown of the toe of the other foot. Stride length may, and usually will, vary from left to right (or right to left) on individuals at the same velocity. This variance may be influenced by dominance, weakness, injuries, and even leg length.

Stride length will vary with the speed of running and during the various phases of a race. Extreme stride length (over-striding) will adversely affect sprint speed as it slows down stride cadence. (If the foot strike is 12-20° in front of the center of gravity, it is considered an overstride).

The coach and the sprinter must determine a stride length which, when combined with a stride cadence, is most productive for the overall race. The stride length will increase as a consequence of increased strength, flexibility, and motor efficiency with maintained stride cadence. Velocity will improve as a consequence.

Stride length may, and usually will, vary from left to right on individuals at the same velocity.

Stride Cadence

Stride cadence is defined as the number of strides per second. Little definitive research has been conducted regarding the ability of runners to appreciably improve this skill. Some researchers have observed that stride rate is determined by the age of 10 to 12 years, and does not appreciably improve in later years. Other technicians note that stride frequency may be increased by shortening the arm swing. However, the balance of stride cadence with stride length could have a detrimental effect on velocity if more is taken away than obtained. This works to the other extreme, too, when arm swing is slowed too greatly as stride length is lengthened.

The stride cadence for sprinters is 4.5 to 5.0 strides per second with little difference found between the sexes. The method for determining stride rate is to divide the number of strides in a race by the elapsed time for that race. For example, in the 1979 World Cup race, Evelyn Ashford, with 47 strides in a time of 11.06, had a stride rate of 4.25 strides per second, while the world record holder Marlies Gohr, who finished second in 11.17 while taking 51 strides, had a stride rate of 4.56 strides per second. This example indicates that the most rapid turnover does not always prove best. Problems of fatigue and relaxation are also involved.

However, the above formula may not be the best means of calculating stride rate as it provides only an

overall rate. Of equal concern are the various phases of the race—start and acceleration, maximun velocity, and deceleration. Again, the little research available seems to indicate that rates for each of these phases does not vary a great deal. However, even a little variation could be significant when three hundredths of a second is equal to approximately one foot in the hundred meter dash at the above speeds. Of real interest is the concern of stride rate in the deceleration phase where good technique might prevent an appreciable loss.

Stride rate is maximized over an entire race by utilizing a full range of motion and attaining the optimum rate early in the race. The key is **optimum rate.** At maximum velocity, the foot is applying force a minimum amount of time; this is one of the reasons that velocity is gradually lost since less impulse is received by each strike of the foot.

Body Position

The term "body lean"—relating to a sprinter—is a matter of considerable controversy due in part to disagreements concerning when body lean occurs and how it should be measured. The controversy arises as to the means of measurement, what body parts are keys to this measurement, and when body lean occurs within the stride phase.

The actual degree of lean is dependent upon: normal posture of athlete, the specific athlete, technique and condition of athlete, wind resistance (greater forward lean is needed to offset a headwind, and almost no lean is needed to benefit from a tailwind), and rate of ac-

The stride rate is maximized over an entire race by utilizing a full range of motion and attaining the optimum rate early in the race.

celeration (forward lean is more exaggerated when acceleration is the greatest, such as at the start of a race, and when acceleration is least noticeable, such as when maximum speed is attained). Only slight lean is required to counter the wind resistance created by the speed of the sprinter. Too much lean may prevent a full stride while an overly vertical trunk position diminishes forward drive—by causing the foot plant to fall too far forward of the center of gravity.

Knee Action

Knee action is an often sought but somewhat misunderstood action. Coaches have noted that great sprinters have "good knee action" and have sought it as a desirable attribute. It is true that higher and faster knee action is more prevalent among great sprinters, reaching close to a 90° thigh position relative to the body trunk. But what is most often observed among great sprinters is the lifting action of the knee during the swing phase of the stride.

Knee lift is the consequence or end result of other actions, and is not self-generated. Proper knee action results from a rapid forward thigh motion which in turn has resulted from a vigorous extension of the pushoff leg from the surface and the passing of the heel close to the buttocks. The "folded" leg thus provides a shorter lever and may be brought forward more quickly, thus attaining a greater height than the more extended leg. Therefore, the high leading knee lift is a product of the thrust of the driving leg in its subsequent flight phase.

However, the degree of lift is an individual matter and is the result of body structure, suppleness, flexibility, and strength. Some great sprinters have been successful with less than artistic heights in their knee actions. On the other hand, some sprinters have employed an excessive amount of lift and slowed their stride cadence to such an extent that best results were not achieved until modifications in technique were made.

As the thigh and knee begin their descent after attaining maximum height, the foot and fore leg continue unfolding and extend forward before commencing their downward and backward movement. The foot strike should be under the center of gravity for most efficiency. Knee lift is most relevant in its relationship to the body position. In order for the foot plant not to have a retarding effect, the foot must move back faster at foot strike and during plant than the center of gravity is moving forward. This can be described as a "pawing motion" as the descending foot srikes the ground. A longer stride is the result of a stronger pushoff.

Foot Strike

Prior to foot strike, the foot descends towards a position beneath, (or nearly so), the center gravity. The common foot strike pattern during sprinting is one that lands on the outside ball of the foot, rolls to the heel,

flattens the arch as weight is absorbed during the full-support phase, rolls back to the ball, and pushes off the insides of the foot at the great toe. It should be kept in mind that the above sequence takes place in a very short period of time.

Arm Action

Varying degrees of opening and closing of the elbow joint are evident in each running cycle. The opening and closing of the elbow joint will vary with the cycle, strength, and stride length of the individual sprinter. The closer the angle remains to 90°, the quicker the arm can be moved through the full range of motion. The opening is greatest just as the arm swings past the vertical on the backswing, and it is least as it reaches the height of the forward swing. The opening varies among individuals and cannot be dictated. The action of the arms serves the following functions: 1) absorbs reaction of leg thrust and allows the shoulders to remain relatively steady; 2) aids in body balance and; 3) aids in maintenance of stride rhythm. The arms and hands are relaxed, with the hands lightly cupped, even when running at maximum velocity.

The ability of a runner to stop an action and immediately initiate another, often directly opposite, action is illustrated by the arm action of top sprinters. As the arm reaches the maximum height of the forward swing, the downward action commences immediately. The suddenness of this action is indicated by the lack of a coasting motion with the arms as the hand will flick upwards, breaking at the wrist, while the arm starts in the reverse direction. Proper relaxation is also demonstrated by the hand flick. Such repeated and vigorous but rhythmical actions require strength of the arm and shoulder girdle muscles.

As the arm swings forward, it travels slightly across the body to compensate for the rotation created by the eccentric thrust of the opposite leg. However, the hand does not cross the midline of the body. The shoulders and trunk are kept steady to avoid any excessive rotation.

Arm and leg actions are interrelated with the arm action complementary to the leg action in direct bilateral opposition. Arm action has been used by some competitors in the latter stages of a race theoretically to spur legs on by increasing or maintaining leg cadence and/or stride length. Such actions, while effective, must be practiced to ensure the maintenance of proper positon and alignment.

Structure of a Sprint Training Program

All successful sprint programs incorporate the following areas of training in varying degrees. The balance and mix between them is dictated by the local circumstances and the coach's individual philosophy. A successful program will emphasize the following:

A. **Drills:** Drills should be a segment skill activity that covers, or is involved in, sprinting itself. Drills should be specific to the sprint activity. Variations in drills include length (duration), speed (intensity), tempo (cadence), surface (grass, sand, track, etc.), and elevation (slight or steep slope). Some of the more popular drills are as follows:

1. **High Knee Drills**—These should be done with a forward lean, as in the sprint action. Example: 2-8 × 10-30m with walk back rest interval.

2. **Bounding**—A series of jumps alternating legs, done with a good sprint posture, emphasizing leg thrust, knee lift, and aggressive arm action. Variations include performing bounding at maximum height, or for maximum length, or at a desired cadence. Example: 2-6 × 20-80m.

3. **Hopping**—A series of jumps on and off the same leg, incorporating the same emphases as bounding. Examples: 2-6 × 20-80m.

4. **Uphill and Downhill Running**—Uphill running improves strength in the specific muscles used in sprinting as well as helping to improve stride frequency. Downhill running is beneficial in improving stride length. Examples: 4-8 × 30-60m downhill (3% decline) running at maximum speed with adequate rest interval. 6 × 150m uphill with 5 min. rest.

5. **Harness Pulling**—Use of a shoulder or waist harness while sprinting against a resistance (person, sled, tire, etc.) over short distances. Example: 4-6 × 30-60m pulling a person offering some resistance.

6. **Towing Drills**—Some research indicates that towing—attaching the athlete to a rope and pulling them along at a speed greater than they would normally run—helps to improve speed development. Obviously, there are inherent dangers in this type of drill and it should be undertaken with the greatest caution. Example: 4-6 × 50-100m at pace .5 of a second faster than normal running speed over the distance, with adequate rest interval.

B. **Strength Training:** It is suggested that strength training involve the following: 1) a year-round approach and plan; 2) total body strength and development; 3) consistency of training (3 × a week); 4) proper technique; and 5) a rational and realistic approach to the amount of weight and repetitions used. (See section on Weight Training.)

C. **Power Training:** This type of training contains the elements of both strength and speed, and is perhaps most directly related to success in sprinting. The power program should contain the same safeguards mentioned under strength training. Drills particularly useful in the development of this component include various forms of bounding, hopping, uphill running, harness pulling, and similar activities involving both overload and speed of movement. (See Drills section.)

D. **Flexibility Work:** (See section on Flexibility Training and Stretching.)

E. **Speed-Endurance Work:** The ability of the sprinter to maintain maximum or near maximum velocity over a major portion of the race is of primary importance. Maximum velocity can be maintained for only 10-20m, hence the ability to continue near maximum pace is crucial in races of 60-400m. The emphasis on speed-endurance should increase from late Fall through the late competitive season. Examples: 6-20 × 30-60m sprinting with a standing or flying start and a short rest inverval of 2-3 minutes; 6-10 × 75-150m sprints with a short rest interval of 8-10 minutes. After several repetitions, a longer rest interval may be taken before commencing a second set.

F. **Endurance Work:** Sprinting is basically an anaerobic activity. It is safe to say, however, that all of the sprint programs recognize the need for some endurance work and cardio-vascular efficiency as well as the development of a high degree of anaerobic efficiency, particularly for the longer sprinters. Philosophies differ as to the amount and intensity of endurance work needed in a successful sprint program. Examples: **Aerobic Endurance**—mostly off-season and on week-ends during season—15-30 minutes Fartlek; 12-20 minutes of steady state running on roads, cross country, etc.; 4-8 × 600-1320m on grass, cross country, etc. **Anaerobic Endurance** (Speed Endurance)—mostly pre-season, early, and mid-season—4-6 × long uphill 200-600m with jog or walk down rest interval; 4-8 × 300m with 2-3 minutes rest interval or heart rate down to 120 b.p.m.; 6-10 × 200m with 1 1/2—2 1/2 minutes rest interval or heartrate down to 120 b.p.m.; 10-20 × 100m with 1-2 minutes rest interval or heartrate down to 120 b.p.m.

G. **Speed Work:** Speed work for sprinters has been characterized by the Russians as being, ". . . running fractional distance at maximal and near-maximal speed." How much and how long this should be is an individual matter. But keep in mind that sprinting is a highly skilled activity and specificity of function is very important. In all of the following examples quality is the goal, and adequate rest intervals should be permitted: 4-8 × 30-60 m flying starts; 4-8 × 20-40 m starts; 4-8 × one-half leg sprint relay handoffs; 4-8 × 30-60 assisted running (towing, downhill, windaided, etc.)

H. **Motor Learning:** An important but often less-stressed factor of sprinting is the development of a clear understanding of the mental and physical activities involved in performing the sprints. The variety of associated movments of the body segments during the start, acceleration, maximum speed, and deceleration phases must take place in proper sequence and at the proper tempo. The training process must include extensive practice of the parts of the whole skill in order to emphasize or correct certain aspects of the total movement. A high level of competence can be attained through such practice as long as there is a proper foundation of strength, flexibility, endurance, and neuromuscular coordination.

The reward factor is very important to the learner. The reward is a far more reliable force in learning than punishment, and the more immediate the better. By maintaining a positive and happy training environment, a higher level of performance can be attained.

Sample Training Schedule

Each workout should begin with a good warmup and flexibility program, and conclude with a cooling down period.

An example of a warm-up is: 800-1600m jog, flexibility exercises, 6-10 × 80-120m acceleration runs of gradually increasing intensity, and more flexibility exercises if needed. The warmup is then followed by the workout which should include drills. The final portion of the workout is the cooldown. This consists of easy running and walking, as well as stretching. Recovery should be nearly complete before the athlete leaves the training area.

Examples of a week's workouts are presented for each training period. It should emphasize that these are examples only and should not be followed blindly, but must be adapted to each individual's situation.

A. **Off-Season**—September, October, November

Monday:	4 × 20m High Knees
	2-6 × long uphills, 300-600m depending upon event and elevation of hill
	Weight Training
Tuesday:	4 × 40m Bounding
	8 × 20m Hopping—R & L
	4 × 8 Hurdles jumping
	10 × 200m on grass at 2/3 speed w/ 2-3 min. R.I.
	1 × 1-2 miles easy run
Wednesday:	4 × 20m High Knees
	4 × 30m Harness runs
	3 (3/4 of event distance at 1/2, 2/3, & 3/4 variable speed; i.e., 100m sprinters run 3 sets of 75m, at half, medium, and fair speed)
	8 × 20m 3-pt. starts
	Weigth Training
Thursday:	4 × 40m Bounding
	Jumping Drills as on Tuesday
	20 minutes Fartlek

Friday:	3 × 30 High Knees
	4-6 × Relay Exchanges, #1 & #3 zone exchanges
	Long Uphills as on Monday **or** 600m, 300m, 300m; **or** 500m, 400m, 300m; **or** 300m, 150m, 150m depending upon event
	Weight Training
Saturday:	Off
Sunday:	Easy Run of 2-4 miles or Fartlek for stretching out and endurance purposes

B. **Pre-Season or Indoor**—December, January, February—Obviously, those teams competing indoors must modify their training schedules to include those requirements specific to sprint competition.

Monday:	4 × 30m High Knees
	4-6 × Sprint Relay Exchanges, #2 zone exchange
	6 × 60m Harness Runs
	500m, 400m, 300m **or** 250m, 200m, 150m
Tuesday:	6 × 20m High Knees
	4 × 60m Fly-ins at 7/8 speed w/ adequate R.I.
	4 × 30m starts at 7/8 speed
	1-2 miles running
	Weight Training
Wednesday:	6 × 60 Bounding
	6 × 30m Giant Hops
	2 (4 × 8 Hurdles Jumps)
	8-10 × 200m or 100m depending upon security) at 3/4 speed w/ 2-3 min. R.I. **or**
	4 laps of 50-100m ins-and-outs
Thursday:	4 × 30m High Knees
	4-8 × uphills, 200-500m in length depending upon event
	1-2 miles running
	Weight Training
Friday:	6 × 20m High Knees
	6 × Sprint Relay Exchanges, #1 and #3 zone exchanges
	6-10 × 20m starts
Saturday:	If not competing—Timed 2 × 110m, or 2 × 220m or 2 × 440m emphasizing various portions of race distance, with adequate R.I.
	Weight Training
Saturday:	Competition
Sunday:	2-4 miles easy run or Fartlek

C. **Competitive Season**—March, April, May

Monday:
4-6 × 20-30m High Knees
6-8 × sprint relay exchanges, 1st & 3rd exchange
500m, 350m, 300m **or** 250m, 175m, 100m (depending on event) at good effort level
Weight Training

Tuesday:
6 × 40m Harness Runs
8-10 × 20-30m Starts alternating 3/4 and 7/8 effort w/ adequate R.I.
2 × 30m Fly-ins at 3/4 speed; 2 × 30m Fly-ins at 7/8 speed all w/ adequate R.I.
2 × 60m Fly-ins at 3/4 speed; 2 × 60m Fly-ins at 7/8 speed, all w/ adequate R.I.
2 (5 × 8 Hurdle Jumps)
1-3 miles easy run

Wednesday:
6 × 20m High Knees
4-6 × 60-80m Bounding
6-8 × sprint relay exchanges, 2nd zone exchange
3-5 × 200m at race pace w/ 3-5 min. R.I. (if 400m)
or
3-5 × 100m at race pace w/ 3-5 min. R.I. (if 200m)
1600m Relay Exchanges
Weight Training

Thursday:
8 × 40m Harness Runs **or**
6-10 × short uphill runs, fast w/ walk back R.I.
3-5 × 80-150m acceleration runs w/ walk back R.I.
2 × 1/2 distance (200 or 200m) at pace minus 1 second

Friday:
Stretch
Light Weights here or after meet on Saturday

Saturday:
Competition
Light Weights (See Friday)

Sunday:
Easy 1-3 mile run

R.I. = Rest Interval

400 Meter Training

by
Clyde Hart
Baylor University

The 400 meter dash is an endurance sprint incorporating the speed of the sprinter and the endurance of the half-miler. It is considered by many to be one of the most demanding and grueling of competitive events. Usually the 400 meter runners will fall into two distinct categories—the sprinter type and the half-miler type. Both of these have had their share of success over the years. Occasionally, one will find an athlete who possesses characteristics of both types.

Physiological Basis of the 400M

The 400 meters is an oxygen-deficient event. The energy used during the 400 meter run is derived mainly from the breakdown of high energy phosphate compounds supplied through the ATP-PC and lactic acid systems. Training emphasis should be on maximizing development of each system.

Proper training will help the athlete learn to deal with the stress that he/she will face toward the end of the 400m. Severe exercise imposes great stress on the body. The athlete must learn to adapt to this stress, or the body will break down. It is known that when the body is gradually put under stress, it will do whatever is necessary for its own well-being to adapt to this stress. When the athlete is conditioned to the stress of his/her event, he/she will be able to perform at a higher level in competition.

Characteristics of the 400M Runner

The following characteristics are helpful in drawing a profile of the prospective 400 meter runner: Most are medium to tall in height and physically strong in build. It is necessary for the runner to have good basic speed. Most world-class runners are capable of maintaining velocity of about 94% of the average velocity of their best 200m time while running the 400m. The stride length as measured from toe to toe will be about 1.3 multiplied by the standing height. It is only slightly less for women 400m runners. Racing stride rate varies from 4½ to 5 strides per second at the world class level. The stride rate decreases as the height and leg length of the athlete increases.

Distribution of Effort

The ability to distribute speed and energy in the most efficient manner over the total racing distance is the primary prerequisite for success in the 400m dash. No one is capable of running the 400m all out from start to finish. Good pace judgment and effort distribution are a must. Remember, the 400m is not a full sprint. Speed at the 100m and 200m can be a tremendous advantage to the 400m runner but only if he/she learns to distribute this energy properly. Generally the outstanding 400m runner will have approximately a one second differential. A good formula for predicting the potential 400m time for a 200m runner is to double the best open 200m time and add 3.5 seconds. It is obvious that the sprinter type has the advantage through the early stages of the 400m; however, if the runner is not trained properly, this advantage can melt away toward the end of the race. The half-miler type will definitely have the advantage from the 300m mark to the finish.

The ideal race pattern should be one of smooth, controlled deceleration with as little tightening up at the finish as possible. The 400m runner should try to cover the first 50m at near top speed. At this point he/she should relax the actions of the upper body while still trying to maintain leg speed. Thoughts should be on trying to settle into the rhythm of the race and getting the next big effort. This will be at the 200m mark. He/she should be trained and conditioned to know that at this point in the race plan there must be a determined effort to increase the actions of the arms and to begin driving and lifting the knees to resume more of a sprinting action. The runner who learns to work this turn from the 200 to the 300m mark will usually find himself/herself in good position to win the race. It is a controlled pickup, one that should allow the 400m runner to come off the final curve even or ahead of the opponents. During the final 100m of the race, the runner must learn to stay relaxed while fighting the effects of fatigue. One of the best ways to do this is by thinking of proper running technique and good form.

Psychological Aspect

The mental makeup of the 400m runner is of great importance in relation to the degree of success he/she may obtain. The event is a controlled sprint which will require a great deal of patience and determination. Quick strategy decisions may be necessary as the race unfolds. It is the thinking person's sprint—not like the shorter sprints, when a bad start or stumble can lose the race for the runner just a few meters into the competition. In the 400m there is more room for error and for experimentation in tactics and strategy.

The strongest personality trait the 400m runner must possess is aggressiveness. It is not a race for the timid. The runner must learn to experience pain and fatigue and be willing to come back for more until he/she has learned to distribute the effort properly.

The strongest personality trait the 400 m runner must possess is aggressiveness.

Training Year

The training year is divided into the following four segments:

I. Off-Season (Summer and Fall—September through December)
II. Early Competitive Season (January-February)
III. Mid-Season (March-April)
IV. Late Season (May-June)

Based on the demands of the 400m event, the training workouts presented are recommended in varying degrees of emphasis during the training year. The time frame during which each workout is used is very important. To derive the most from any training program, proper introduction of a specific workout is a must. Chart I serves as a basic yearly guide for introduction of each type of workout and percentage of emphasis placed on each.

Types of Workouts

1. Speed Endurance. During this workout, the runner incurs a high oxygen debt and subsequent lactic acid buildup. This type of workout is vital to good 400m running. Distances vary from 100m to 600m. Number of repetitions is determined by multiplying the race distance 2½ times—in this case, approximately 1000m. The recovery period is usually around 10 minutes, in order to give the runner almost full recovery to insure quality in the runs. This workout is designed to help develop the lactic acid energy systems.

Examples of Speed Endurance Workouts

a) 10 X 100   5-10 min. rest
b) 6 X 150   5-10 min. rest
c) 5 X 200   10 min. rest
d) 4 X 300   10 min. rest
e) 3 X 350   10 min. rest
f) 2 X 450   10 min. rest

2. Tempo Endurance. These runs are done at a slower pace, to help the runner learn rhythm and tempo. Another vital byproduct of this workout is that it trains the very important phosphate energy sources. The emphasis is on quantity and not on quality. The rest is generally short—usually 2 to 3 minutes.

Examples of Tempo Endurance Workouts

a) 8 X 200   2 min rest.
b) 6 X 300   2 min rest.
c) 50-100-150-200-250-300-350-   Walk same distance for rest.

3. Strength Endurance. This workout involves activities that will last longer than 10 seconds in duration. Such activities will include resistance running, long-hill running, and stadium step runs.

Examples of Strength Endurance Workouts

a) 6 X 150m hill
b) 6 X 60 stadium steps
c) 6 X 15 sec duration harness runs

4. Endurance Running. This is pure aerobic running. It consists of continuous runs of 15 to 45 minutes at a steady state speed. Although the 400m only requires about 5% aerobic running, it is important that the 400m runner get a good base of aerobic running in order to improve oxygen uptake so that his/her recovery time between efforts will be cut to a minimum.

Examples of Endurance Running

a) 15 min at steady state speed
b) 30 min of Fartlek running
c) 6 X 800m on cross country course with 3 minutes recovery time

5. Power Speed. This workout emphasizes speed of muscle contraction. This is usually done with less than 10 reps and no more than 10 seconds per repetition.

Examples of Power Speed

a) Short hill runs of about 60m
b) 10 X 30m harness runs
c) 10 X 10-sec fast rope jumps

6. Event Running. This does exactly what the name implies. The runner will run different distances at a predetermined race pace in order to learn to work on different aspects of running strategy in the 400 meters. This is also referred to as segment running.

Examples of Event Workouts

a) 3 X 300m. First 50m all out. Next 150m, relaxed floating action. All out on last 100m. All timed and recorded.
b) 2 X 450m. The first 200m, 300m, 400m and final 50m are all timed and recorded.
c) 1 X 350m. Quality run, with each segment run as if in the 400 race coming up.

7. Speed. These workouts vary from distances of 30m to 150m. Work done at full speed either on the straightaway or curve. Rest is usually long between runs in order to give full recovery to insure quality. Relay handoff work is included as part of the speed workouts.

Example of Speed Drills

a) 6 X 40m starts
b) 6 X 60m flying starts
c) 6 X sprint relay handoffs, 60m total distance

8. **Strength.** Strength workouts consist of both general and specific strength development. General strength development is done through the traditional weight-lifting programs of both free weights and machines. Specific strength work is achieved through specific plyometric drills.

Examples of Strength Training

a) 30 min. traditional weightlifting workout (1 set, 13 reps)
b) Explosive jumps for the development of starting power and acceleration
c) 3 sets of 10 hops each leg
d) Fast 50m bounding runs with barbell

Training Concepts

Before the coach plans the 400m workouts, there are several concepts that merit strong consideration. The basic one is the concept of going from quantity to quality. All workouts should follow a progressive pattern. Standardize workouts so that the speed over the running distance, the distance itself, and in some cases, the rest interval, will progressively shorten. The principle of overloading is also an important consideration. An example of this would be running 2 X 600's in training, beginning in the fall with 60 seconds for the first 400. The 400m time is gradually lowered (to 50-52 sec.) with the runs reduced to 500m. The distance is once again shortened to 450 meters. The runner is then expected to run these at 50 seconds. Although the runner is getting less distance, effort is becoming more intense—thus more stress is being put on the body.

Another factor to consider in planning 400m workouts is that it takes a hard run of around 40 seconds in order to incur a significant lactic acid buildup. With this in mind, the ideal distance to work lactic acid training is 350m. Most quality 400m runners cover this distance in slightly over 40 seconds. Thus, they are working a few seconds into lactic acid buildup. By running this distance, the runner can accomplish several of these runs in a workout session, whereas it is difficult to have a 400m runner perform more than one quality 400m run in a session. The coach can add approximately 7 seconds in the early session to a runner's 350m time to predict 400m time. In the late session, this conversion factor can be lowered to around 5.5 to 6 seconds.

Finally the coach must become personally involved in the race strategy of the 400m runner and be more than just a trainer. Time the different segments of the workout runs as well as competitive races. Let the runner know beforehand how long he/she should take to come through the 200m or the 300m, in order to get an idea of what kind of pace he/she is running. Oftentimes, the race will dictate what pace the runner will have to carry in order to be competitive, but this is no excuse for not having the runner mentally ready to perform at a certain level. It will give the athlete valuable confidence if he/she has been through different checkpoints at a certain time in practice.

Although weight training and flexibility play major roles in training the 400m runner, space does not allow a detailed discussion of these subjects. Weight training was mentioned briefly earlier in this chapter, but flexibility - which should play a vital part in the daily training program of the 400m runner - will not be discussed except as mentioned in the sample workouts. (Refer to chapters on weight training and flexibility.)

Chart I: Percentage of Emphasis Chart

Types of Workouts	Fall	Early	Mid	Late
Strength	100	100	100	100
Speed Endurance	75	90	100	100
Tempo Endurance	100	100	100	75
Strength Endurance	100	90	80	70
Endurance Running	100	20	10	5
Power Speed	20	60	70	80
Speed	25	80	90	100
Event Runs	25	90	100	100

Emphasis is given in terms of % of use recommended for each workout in relation to each segment of the training year.

These workouts can be applied to all levels of 400m runners, but performance times given in this sample are for a potential 46-second quarter miler; so adjustments should be made accordingly.

Chart II: 400 Meter Running Exercises

Exercise	Brief Description	Benefits	Season
Endless Relay	Baton is kept moving, rest and run are controlled	Endurance, stamina, exchange work	All
Australian Pursuits	Sprints & slow jogging for total of 3 min.	Endurance, speed, kicking drill	All
Long hill	100m or more, slow runs.	Endurance, stamina, knee lift	Fall/Early
600 meters	Pace 400, pick-up last 200.	Endurance, stamina	Fall/Early
500 meters	Pace 400, pick-up last 100m.	Endurance, stamina, knee lift	Early/Mid
350 meters	Quality and training distance, add 5.5 - 7 sec to predict 400m time.	Mental preparation, endurance, stamina	Early/Mid /Late

300 meter event	200m slow pace, last 100m faster.	Mental preparation, endurance, running efficiency	Early/Mid and Late
450 meters	Pace 400 and pick-up relaxed last 50m.	Mental preparation, endurance, stamina, knee lift	Mid/Late
Short Hill	Less than 100m fast runs	Speed, leg drive, stamina	Mid/Late
Flying Bears	Repeat 100's with jogging.	Speed, strength, running efficiency	Mid/Late
320 meters	Quality distance, add 10-12 sec for 400 time.	Mental preparation, speed, running efficiency	Mid/Late
Speedmaker	Short 50m sprints jogging.	Speed, strength, running efficiency,	Mid/Late
150 meter Build-ups	50m 1/2 speed, 50m 3/4 speed, 50m near full speed.	Running efficiency, speed, endurance, mental preparation	Early/Mid /Late

400 Meters
Sample Workouts

I. Fall (September through December)

Monday
1. Warm-up: 1 mile cross country run.
2. Flexibility exercises.
3. 2 x 600 **Speed** 60 sec. 400/ **Rest** 15 min.
4. 3 x 300 **Speed** 50 sec/**Rest** 1 min.
5. 3 x 300 **Speed** 40 sec/**Rest** 5 min.
6. Cool down: 1 mile cross country run.
7. Weights.

Tuesday
1. Warm-up: 1 mile cross country run.
2. Flexibility exercises.
3. 10 x 200 **Speed** 30 sec/**Rest** 3 min.
4. 6 x 150 long hill runs. **Speed** fast/**Rest**; jog back.
5. Cool down: 1 mile cross country run.

Wednesday
1. Warm-up: 1 mile cross country run.
2. Flexibility exercises.
3. 4 x 350 (Event Run) **Speed** 48 secs/**Rest** 10 min. (50 fast—150 relaxed, 200 time 28 sec—100 picked up fast —last 50 steady and keeping good form).
4. 3 x 200 **Speed** 30-29-28 sec/ **Rest** 3 min.
5. Cool down: 1 mile cross country run.
6. Weights.

Thursday
1. Warm-up: 1 mile cross country run.
2. Flexibility exercises.
3. 600-400-200-400-600 **Speed** 30 sec pace/ **Rest** 5 mins.
4. 6 x 100 strides **Speed** medium/ **Rest** 1 min.
5. Cool down: 1 mile cross country run.

Friday
1. Warm-up: 1/2 mile cross country run.
2. Flexibility Exercises.
3. Two mile cross country timed run.
4. Weights.

Saturday
No organized practice; encouraged to do 3 miles running.

Sunday
No organized practice; encouraged to do 20 minute Fartlek.

II. Early Season (January-February)

Monday
1. Warm-up: 1 mile in and outs (100 sprint/100 walk, 3 laps, faster each lap, 4th lap run 200, 26 sec).
2. Flexibility Exercises.
3. 2 x 500 **Speed** 56 sec 400/ **Rest** 15 min.
4. 3 x 200 **Speed** 30-29-28 sec/ **Rest** 3 min.
5. 8 x 10 second rope jumps/ **Rest** 10 sec. repeat.

Tuesday
1. Warm-up: 1 mile in and outs.
2. Flexibility exercises.
3. 8 x 200 **Speed** 28 sec. **Rest** 3 min.
4. 6 x 150 long hills **Speed** fast/ **Rest** jog back.
5. Weights.

Wednesday
1. Warm-up: 1 mile in and outs.
2. Flexibility exercises.
3. 4 x 300 (Event Run) **Speed** 42/ **Rest** 5 min.
4. 3 x 200 **Speed** 30-29-28/ **Rest** 3 min.
5. 6 x 10 sec rope resistance runs **Speed** fast/ **Rest** 10 sec.

Thursday
1. Warm-up: 1 mile in and outs.
2. Flexibility exercises.
3. 1 x 350 **Speed** fast/ **Rest** 15 min.
4. 4 x 200 **Speed** 26 sec/ **Rest** 5 min.
5. Weights.

Friday
1. Warm-up: 1 mile in and outs.
2. Flexibility exercises.
3. 3 x 200 **Speed** 30-29-28/**Rest** 3 min.
4. 1600 Relay hand-off work.

Saturday
Meet.

Sunday
No organized workout, encouraged to do light cross country running, about 20 minutes.

III. Mid Season (March-April)

Monday
1. Warm-up: 1 mile in and outs.
2. Flexibility exercises.
3. 2 x 450 **Speed** 52 sec 400/ **Rest** 15 min.
4. 3 x 200 **Speed** 28-27-26/ **Rest** 3 min.

Tuesday
1. Warm-up: 1 mile in and outs.
2. Flexibility exercises.
3. 6 x 200 **Speed** 26 sec/ **Rest** 3 min.
4. 5 x 20 sec long rope resistance runs. **Speed** slow/ **Rest** 3 min.
5. Weights.

Wednesday 1. Warm-up: 1 mile in and outs.
2. Flexibility exercises.
3. 4 x 300 (Event Run) **Speed** 42 sec/ **Rest** 5 min.
4. 8 x 100 short hill runs **Speed** fast/ **Rest** walk back.

Thursday 1. Warm-up: 1 mile in and outs.
2. Flexibility exercises.
3. 3 x 200 **Speed** 26-25-24 sec/ **Rest** walk 200.
4. 3 x 150 (Build-ups) **Speed** slow-med-fast/ **Rest,** walk back.
5. Weights.

Friday 1. Warm-up: 1 mile in and outs.
2. Flexibility exercises.
3. 3 x 200 **Speed** 26 sec/ **Rest,** walk 200.
4. 1600 relay hand-offs.

Saturday Meet

Sunday No organized practice; encouraged to do some cross country running, about 20 minutes.

IV. Late-Season (May-June)

Monday 1. Warm-up: 1 mile in and outs.
2. Flexibility exercises.
3. 1 x 450 **Speed** 50 sec 400/ **Rest** 15 min.
4. 3 x 200 **Speed** 26-25-24 sec/ **Rest,** walk 200.

Tuesday 1. Warm-up: 1 mile in and outs.
2. Flexibility exercises.
3. 4 x 300 **Speed** 42/ **Rest** 5 min.
4. 4 x 200 **Speed** 28-27-26-25/ **Rest** 3 min.
5. Weights.

Wednesday 1. Warm-up: 1 mile in and outs.
2. Flexibility exercises.
3. 1 x 320 (Quality run) **Speed** fast/ **Rest** 15 min.
4. 3 x 200 **Speed** 26-25-24 sec/ **Rest,** walk 200
5. 8 x 80m short hill **Speed** fast/ **Rest,** walk back.

Thursday 1. Warm-up: 1 mile in and outs.
2. Flexibility exercises.
3. 3 sets speed makers **Speed** fast/ **Rest** jog (50m all-out sprints—50m swing down —50m slow jog—repeat until 4 all-out sprints are done.) 3 min rest between sets.
4. Weights.

Friday 1. Warm-up: 1 mile in and outs.
2. Flexibility exercises.
3. 2 x 200 **Speed** 26 sec/ **Rest,** walk 200.
4. 1600 relay hand-offs.

Saturday Meet

Sunday No organized practice; encouraged to do a little cross country running, about 20 minutes.

The ability to distribute speed and energy in the most efficient manner over the total racing distance is the primary prerequisite for success in the 400m dash.

10
Hurdling*

Hurdling

by
Vern Gambetta—UC Berkeley
Dick Hill—San Diego State University

Introduction

Hurdling is a sprinting, rhythmic event. To a beginning hurdler, this may seem an impossibility. The beginner will view the hurdle as a barrier and consider jumping over it. But hurdling is not a jumping event. The first lesson in hurdling is that all one needs to clear a hurdle is an elongated running stride, with as little deviation from correct sprint form as possible.

Since hurdling is a sprinting event, a hurdler's most important physical characteristic obviously is **speed.** To substantiate this, examine the time for world records in the hurdles: 13.00 for the men's 110m hurdles, 12.36 for women's 100m hurdles, 47.13 for men's 400m hurdles, and 54.28 for women's 400m hurdles. Those are good flat sprint times even before adding the 1-2 seconds or more spent ''in the air,'' clearing 10 barriers. The key to good hurdling, then, is adapting one's speed to the distance between hurdles. In order to achieve this, the hurdler must have a highly developed sense of **rhythm.**

The next vital physical attribute of a hurdler is **flexibility.** A good hurdler must have trememdous ''range of motion'' in the joints, particularly in the hips, knees and ankles. Also very important and often overlooked is the necessity of flexibility in the lower back and shoulder points. When the average person looks at a

*This chapter consists of two articles: (1) ''Hurdling''; and (2) ''400 Meter Hurdles''.

72

proficient hurdler, the first impression is one of suppleness or looseness.

Size is also valuable to hurdlers. Few outstanding male hurdlers have been under 5' 8". The average height and weight among male high hurdlers in the 1976 Olympic Games was 6' 1", 175 pounds. The female finalists in these Games averaged 5' 6 1/2" tall and 138 pounds.

Coordination and **balance** are additional key attributes for the hurdler. When sprinting a 42-inch barrier at full speed, a great amount of both is required. These can be improved tremendously through practice of proper **technique**.

Hurdling Technique

Start*

Since hurdling is basically a sprinting event, the mechanics of the start do not vary much from that of the sprint start. In order to get eight strides to the first hurdle, the take-off foot should be placed in the front block. If the hurdler wants seven strides to the first hurdle, the take-off foot should be placed in the rear block. Most hurdlers seem to prefer eight strides unless the individual is very tall and needs to chop his/her steps to get eight. Eight strides seem to put the hurdler in a better position into and off of the first hurdle. (A run-up of nine or 10 strides leads to a pitter-patter cadence.)

Place the front block 16-18 inches from the starting line and the rear block 16-20 inches behind the front one. Some modification of the position of the block either forward or backward may be necessary, depending on the approach to the first hurdle. If the hurdler is having to jump and feel crowded by the first hurdle, move the blocks back. If too far away, move them up. Experiment and find the most efficient, comfortable position.

First Strides*

The first three strides out of the blocks are the same as in a sprinter's start. On the fourth stride, the hurdler begins to concentrate on the first hurdle. This forces him/her to get up into a sprint angle sooner than normal.

In perfecting the approach to the first hurdle, make any adjustments on the fourth, fifth or sixth strides. The first three and last two should be kept constant. The last stride is slightly shorter to permit the hurdler to get his/her center of gravity slightly ahead of the take-off foot. This puts him/her in a better position to attack the hurdle.

* **The start and strides to the first hurdle are basically the same for men and women. The other technical areas in this section refer mainly to the men's 110m hurdles. The variations in technique of the women's 100m hurdles are discussed in the next section.**

The key to good hurdling is adapting one's speed to the distance between the hurdles.

This approach sets the pattern for the entire race. It should be as fast as possible so there will be maximum horizontal drive. This drive results in a faster, more efficient hurdle clearance. In competitive situations, a hurdler can put great pressure on opponents by leading at the first hurdle.

Take-off

The take-off distance from the hurdle depends on four factors: (1) the height of the athlete; (2) speed of the approach; (3) length of the lead leg, and (4) speed of the lead-leg action. On the average, the take-off distance is 6' 6" to 7' 6" from the hurdle in the men's hurdles.

Effective take-off action is necessary to insure sufficient body lean and clearing the hurdle with the least amount of upward movement. The lean or "dip" into the hurdle makes it possible to raise the seat and lower the trunk in relation to the center of gravity.

The action of the take-off foot as it leaves the ground is exactly the same as in sprinting. Take-off should be up on the ball of the foot. Toeing out the take-off foot, a common fault, results in a loss of drive over the hurdle. It often causes the trail-leg ankle to smash the top of the hurdle.

Good take-off action, high on the toes, lifts the center of gravity high enough for efficient hurdle action. Another common fault is to take off flat-footed. This results in lift, which causes the hurdler to clear the hurdle with a jumping action.

As mentioned, the body's center of gravity is slightly ahead of the take-off foot. The hip and shoulders should be square to the hurdle. A tendency among beginners is to lean forward with the lead-arm shoulder, which causes imbalance into and off the hurdle.

The lead-knee action is an exaggerated sprint stride. The hurdler should imagine that he is going to drive the knee through the hurdle. Fast lead-leg action causes increased drive off the take-off leg. The action of the two legs is directly related. The legs, working in opposite directions, have the effect of leaving the take-off leg behind, causing a split position over the hurdle.

A fault among novices is swinging up a straight lead leg in a goose-step action, similar to punting a football. This requires a greater take-off distance which, in turn, causes the action to slow down significantly.

According to hurdling expert K. O. Bosen, "Since the speed of the lead-leg action determines the overall speed of hurdle clearance, it is a point to be stressed in training." This is often neglected in the hurdler's technique work. A majority of time is spent developing the trail leg, while little work is done on the lead leg. Sound advice for the young hurdler would be to spend more time on drills for the lead leg.

Many hurdlers have the tendency to swing the lead leg slightly out or in and also toe in or out. This is inefficient. The leg should be directly in front of the hip with the toes pointed straight up.

Action in Air

The take-off (trail) leg folds up as a natural reaction to the drive off the ground. The action is essentially the same as when a sprinter's rear leg folds up, the only difference being that the hurdler's trail leg is brought around to the side. As the leg crosses the hurdle, it is bent at the knee with the foreleg against the thigh. The toes of the trail leg are turned out. The action of this leg is continuous, on the move the whole time to prevent a floating or "posed" position in the air.

When viewed from the side, the trail-leg knee crosses the hurdle at the same time as the hip. If the trail leg precedes the hip, the hurdler can correct this by using a more pronounced lift and drive at take-off. It is wrong to attempt to delay the trail leg in midair.

After clearing the hurdle, the knee is brought through so that just before the lead leg hits, the trail knee is under the armpit. This insures a good getaway (first) stride off the hurdle, which puts the hurdler in good sprinting position for the next hurdle. In the men's hurdles, in this first stride, the lead foot comes down 3' 9" to 4' 6" beyond the hurdle.

The arms work in an exaggerated spring action. It is important to emphasize the lead arm action, as this balances the lead leg. The hurdler raises the lead arm to about shoulder height and bent at the elbow. He drives it straight ahead, not across the body. The swing of the trailing arm is very controlled. It swings to the side to counteract the mass of the trail leg. This arm action helps dip the body weight forward and down.

The hurdler leans from the hips with as flat a back as possible. Rounding the shoulders or hunching the back is undesirable. A double-arm action (both arms thrown forward) is not mechanically sound as it deviates too much from normal sprint action. It will get the hurdler lower over the hurdle, with a pronounced dip, but is not effective coming off the hurdle because it can cause severe balance problems. The single arm forward, or what is more commonly termed an "arm-and-a-half" action, is more desirable.

Hurdling techniques: (a) take-off—photos #1-4; (b) action in air—photos #5-10; and (c) landing—photos #11-12.

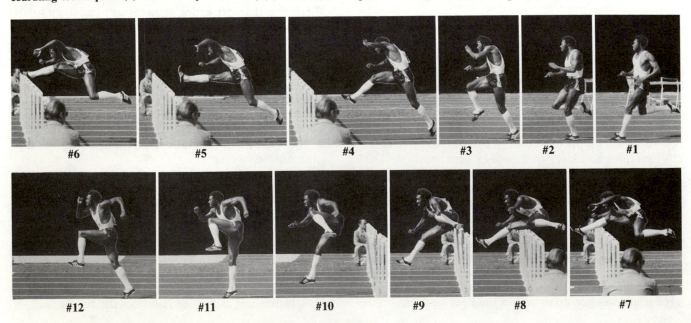

#6   #5   #4   #3   #2   #1

#12   #11   #10   #9   #8   #7

On clearing the hurdle and between hurdles, the runner focuses on the rail of the upcoming hurdle. He should avoid snapping the lead leg down, which causes the trunk to rise prematurely. This leg comes down as a result of the pull-through of the trail leg and the torso rising. The faster the trail leg, the faster the lead leg gets back to the ground.

Landing

At the landing, the athlete's body weight is directly over or just in front of the lead foot. The landing is on the ball of the foot, not flat-footed. This places him in position for a good getaway stride. It also allows for an immediate pickup in sprint rhythm. The arms come into play as soon and as vigorously as possible off the hurdle.

The getaway stride is the result of the high knee action of the trail leg. It is a full, driving sprint stride. A chopped first stride reduces momentum. At times, it is off-center from the other strides. This balance problem causes the hurdler to run an extra distance between each hurdle. Ideally, the lead leg and trail leg land in line with the take-off point.

The hurdler takes three sprint strides between hurdles. The last stride is slightly shorter than the other two. This raises the center of gravity and places it slightly ahead of the take-off foot. The hurdler does not stride or bound between hurdles, but drives and maintains a slight lean, staying up on the balls of the feet.

Run-in

Hurdle races often are won or lost in the 15-yard run-in after the last hurdle. By this time, most competitors are fatigued. The hurdler who gets back into sprint action soonest has the best chance of winning the race, provided, of course, he is in a position to do that.

Technique in the Women's 100 Meter Hurdles

There are some fundamental differences in technique between men's 110-meter and women's 100-meter hurdles. In the first place, the lower height of the women's hurdles (33 inches) does not pose the same problems with raising the center of gravity as does the higher men's hurdles. The hurdle action does not have to be quite as pronounced.

Due to this lower height, the action of the lead leg is very important and differs somewhat from the men's hurdles: the female hurdler leads with a bent knee into the hurdle and then, at the last instance, flicks the lower leg out in a karate kick fashion. This results in the lead leg momentarily locking on top of the hurdle. The locking action activates a stretch reflex which results in a very active snap down of the lead leg off the hurdle. The lead leg comes down quickly and the returns to sprinting action is as fast as possible.

The action of the trail leg is also different from that in the men's hurdles. Due to the low height of the hurdle, the thigh is brought through at a downward angle. The trail leg is not brought around as in the men's high hurdles. Because of the low height, the leg is essentially kept under the body with the trail leg toe everted to avoid hitting the hurdle. The action of both legs is much closer to normal sprinting action.

Forward lean is not as pronounced because it is not as necessary. Exaggerated body lean would only cause balance problems. This again varies with the size of the hurdler. The short woman hurdler is going to have to use a more accentuated forward lean than the tall hurdler.

As previously mentioned, the total clearance stride for women's hurdles is shorter than for men's hurdles. The distance from take-off to landing is 9' 4" to 9' 6". The distance from take-off to the hurdle is 6' 0" to 6' 6" and from the hurdle to the landing, 3' 0" to 3' 4".

Hurdle Training

A good method to insure the hurdler is working at top speed is to use split timing as a guide to training. Start the watch on the flash of the gun and stop it when the lead foot hits the ground off a particular hurdle. If the time taken at the third hurdle for example was 4.9, it would indicate that the hurdler would run from 14.5 or 15.0 seconds at that pace for the full 10 hurdles. (See accompanying charts.)

Split timing can be taken during a race as well as in practice to pinpoint a weakness in various parts of the race. For example, in the 110m high hurdles, if the athlete's time over the third hurdle was 4.7 and his split was 9.5 at the seventh hurdle, he needs more endurance work.

Another way to predict hurdle time is to take the time at the halfway point and project a final mark. For men, double the 60-yard time and subtract one second. For women, take the time at 55 yards, double it and subtract 0.7. For the less experienced hurdler, less time should be subtracted. Experimentation will reveal accurate figures for each individual.

Hurdling Drills

Many hurdlers do not spend enough time to thoroughly master the techniques of the hurdles. Hurdle drills should be part of each day's workout. It is important to train daily on a specific aspect of hurdle technique, even if only during the warmup period. The drills are performed as follows:

1. **Lead-leg drill.** Complete the lead-leg action over the side of the hurdle. Concentrate on leading with the knee and keeping the toe up. Also, do not swing the lead leg to either side. Work over five hurdles five times.

2. **Trail-leg drill.** Execute a trail-leg action over the side of the hurdle. Concentrate on pulling the trail leg through quickly and emphasize proper arm action. Work over three or five hurdles. A good drill for working on drive into the hurdle.

3. **One-step hurdle drill.** Begin over low hurdles and progress to intermediates. Place 10 hurdles 8-10 feet apart. The object is to go over the hurdle with good technique. The lead foot comes down, one stride is taken, and the hurdler takes off again over the next hurdle. A good drill for working on quickness of the overall hurdle action. This drill can also be done over the side of the hurdle, using either the lead or trail leg. Repeat about 5-8 times in workout.

4. **Five-stride drill.** Place the hurdles 12 or 13 yards apart, depending on the speed of the hurdler. Use five sprinting strides between hurdles. This enables the hurdler to work on hurdle technique at near maximum speed with a little less effort than is required to three-step. A good drill for endurance when done over 10 or 12 hurdles. This drill should be confined to fall and early pre-season, since it does tend to change rhythm slightly.

5. **Place hurdles reduced distance apart** so the hurdler can easily take three strides between hurdles. A good drill to work on the proper rhythm between hurdles especially for anyone who has trouble getting three strides between hurdles.

6. **Five up and back.** Place five hurdles at normal spacing in one direction and five hurdles adjacent in the opposite direction. Using five steps between hurdles, go down and back, making one trip. Begin with 3-5 and try to build up to 10-12 trips. A good drill for hurdle endurance. This drill could be modified for speed-endurance by moving the hurdles 12 yards apart and taking five strides between them. Another variation would be to place the hurdles nine yards apart and take three steps.

7. **Sprint hurdling.** The hurdler must face the problem of adapting stride length to the distance between hurdles and then increase speed between hurdles without changing the stride length.

In order to increase speed between hurdles, increase the distance between hurdles to seven strides. This allows two strides to correct a bad landing and five for sprinting. The drill is set up using hurdles one, three and five. Two and four are removed. Hurdle three is four feet nearer to hurdle one and hurdle five is eight feet closer to hurdle one than normal. For women, the hurdles are moved in six and three feet, respectively.

Other suggested drills: Run the first five hurdles at 42 inches high, the next five to 39 inches. Run the first five high hurdles and next five intermediates (36 inches). Run four hurdles, skip the next two, and run the final four.

The primary concern of the hurdler should be fast *hurdling* in training, not simply sprint training. Too much sprint training on the flat can interfere with the consistency of the stride pattern needed for hurdling and lead to a different rhythm.

Speed-endurance is an important factor in hurdle training, as form usually begins to deteriorate after the seventh hurdle. This is where races can be won. Many hurdlers make the mistake of training only over three and five hurdles, and lose form and speed in the last part of the race. He/she should train over three, five, six, eight and occasionally 10 hurdles.

Hurdlers should also practice sprint work between two points in a definite number of strides. Occasionally, the hurdler should take starts with an extra stride to the first hurdle in an attempt to increase speed. Gun starts over three and five hurdles should be an integral part of hurdle training.

Training should emphasize the following areas: (1) technique, (2) rhythm, (3) speed, (3) endurance, (4) strength and (5) flexibility. The emphasis on each of the areas changes with the time of the year. In the Fall and pre-season, the emphasis is on speed-endurance, rhythm, strength and flexibility, with some attention to speed and technique. During the season, the emphasis in primarily on speed and technique while maintaining some strength work and flexibility training. The training should be kept as specific to hurdling as possible at all times.

Hurdle Faults and Their Correction

Fault #1—Excessive Body Lean—Jacknife Position over Hurdle
  Cause: Poor sprint mechanics—excessive forward lean between hurdles
  Correction: More work on correct sprint mechanics. Upright body carriage.

Fault #2—Hurrying the Trail Leg.
  Cause: The hurdler is afraid he/she will not clear the trail leg.
  Correction: Work on the side of the hurdle both walking and running. Lower the hurdle.

Fault #3—Locking the Leg.
  Cause: Leading with the foot rather than knee.
  Correction: Lead leg drills emphasizing knee drive into the hurdle.

Fault #4—Jumping Action over the Hurdle
  Cause: Take-off too close to the hurdle, forcing an upward trajectory rather than forward.
  Correction: Lower the hurdles. Mark the take-off point. Increase speed by running lower hurdles.

Fault #5—Snake Action between Hurdles.
  Cause: Imbalance off the hurdle due to a poor hurdle stride. Lack of flexibility.
  Correction: Emphasize good take-off with hips and shoulders square to the hurdle and the lead knee driven straight into the hurdle. Flexibility exercises.

Fault #6—Jarring on Landing off the Hurdle.
    Cause: Not enough lean in landing due to premature straightening of the body over the hurdle.
    Correction: Emphasize maintaining body lean during the hurdle stride.
Fault #7—Premature Turning of the Take-off Foot.
    Cause: Desire to start trail leg action early.
    Correction: Emphasize full extension of trail leg off the ground before everting the toe.
Fault #8—Shoulder and/or Hips Not Square to Hurdle.
    Cause: 1) Poor arm action in sprinting. 2) Reaching across with the lead arm. 3) Driving lead knee across the body.
    Correction: Work on lead knee and lead arm action against a wall. Good sprint mechanics.
Fault #9—Inability to Get Three Steps between Hurdles
    Cause: Lack of speed or poor hurdle technique.
    Correction: Work on lower hurdles with a reduced spacing.

Hurdling for Beginners

One can learn to hurdle at any age, but it is suggested that the earliest be age 10. This is when a young person can begin to grasp the concepts of hurdling and attend to the lengthy teaching progressions.

During the learning stages, the height of the hurdle and the distance between the hurdles should be adjusted to the individual's stride pattern and height. This will give the beginner confidence and, most important, will allow a rhythmic sprint stride rather than an artificially adjusted stride to clear the hurdle. Hurdles placed at regulation invervals can cause many problems for the beginner such as overstretching the strides, alternating lead leg and jumping. At times, there is little resemblance to sprinting in their action.

Age-group hurdle competition should be set up at shortened intervals—for example, 11 or 12 yards to the first hurdle and 7-9 yards between hurdles—so the race is better adapted to the young runner's stride pattern. If hurdle placement is adjusted to their stride pattern at first and then moved up gradually to regulation spacing, beginning hurdling will be a more positive experience.

Learning Progression for the Hurdles

Possibly the best way to teach hurdling is with the "sticks-and-bricks" method developed by Geoff Dyson of Britain, world renowned authority on the mechanics of track and field. The advantages of stick-and-bricks are: (1) it emphasizes hurdling as a rhythmic sprinting event; (2) it can be used with one person or with a group as large as 50; (3) it can be taught in a very short time; and (4) very little equipment is needed—some bricks, shoe boxes or blocks and sticks.

If working with a group, divide the runners into three lines according to the height of the individuals—one line for the shortest people, another for those of medium stature and the third for the tallest. People of different heights of course have different stride lengths, and adjustments in "hurdle" spacing are made accordingly.

Now, progress through these steps:

1. Have each individual sprint 20-25 yards as fast as possible. Emphasize the need to maintain a constant rhythm and consistent stride pattern.

2. Teach each individual proper foot positioning at the start. If the athlete does not find it too uncomfortable, teach the start with the left leg back and right leg forward. This will result in a left lead leg when hurdling, which is desirable when running intermediate or low hurdles on the turn. Emphasize the same foot positioning at the start each time or the stride pattern will change. Using this positioning, have each individual sprint the entire distance once again.

3. Teach the beginners to run eight steps to the first hurdle. Have each one sprint all-out, counting aloud through 13 steps. The eighth step should be on the right foot. Each individual should do this twice in order to develop a consistent stride pattern. The third time, place a stick midway between the eighth and ninth strides.

4. Have everyone run through again and place a stick on the ground between the 12th and 13th strides. Emphasize a rhythm as smooth and unbroken as possible. Have them run through again; place another stick between the 16th and 17th strides. (If running more than three hurdles is desired, continue this pattern of putting a stick midway between every fourth stride.) The hurdler should not be conscious of the sticks. Constantly emphasize good sprint form: high knee lift, good rear leg push-off and vigorous, relaxed arm action.

5. Put two bricks flat on the ground for each stick and put the stick on the bricks. Have each person sprint over these twice. Next, turn the bricks on edge, raising the stick a little higher. Run through twice more. Then raise the bricks up on end and run through them twice. Add the width of another brick to raise the height again, and run through two or three more times. There should be no mention of the trail leg, lead leg or, for that matter, hurdling until the stick reaches 24 inches in height.

6. Point out that normal running action will result in the knee hitting the stick. Demonstrate trail-leg action: (a) as the lead leg starts downward, the trail leg should start back up; this will give a split position. (b) As the trail leg comes up, turn the knee and trail leg toes outward. (c) Continue through in a normal running action; emphasize the need for a good "first stride" off the hurdle. (d) Emphasize how the arm opposite the lead leg goes forward; it is very important that the arms be vigorously used on landing.

7. The athlete should practice the following lead-leg action a few times without a hurdle: (a) Stand on the take-off leg. (b) Swing the leading knee up, flip the leg out and "chop" down. (c) Drive the opposite arm forward at the same time; this lead-arm action is necessary for balance. (d) Cut the trail leg to the side, toes out; the lead hand comes back, outside the trail leg.

8. The athlete combines the lead leg and trail leg action. Walk through the combined action two or three times away from the hurdle.

9. When the stick has reached a height of 24 inches, teach the action of everting (turning out) the toes of the trail leg. Introduce exaggerated arm action over the hurdle for balance. This is best done by having everyone imitate the hurdle action on the ground.

10. The athlete should now be ready to run over an actual 30-inch hurdle. Place the hurdle just where the sticks were, adjusted to the step pattern. Have each hurdler run through three hurdles about three times. Then place pole vault or high jump standards beside each hurdle and set the crossbar about 18 inches above head height. As the athlete gains confidence over the hurdles, lower the crossbar. This will add in achieving better "lay-out" position over the hurdle. With increased speed, size and maturity, the athlete can gradually move the hurdles to regulation spacing and still maintain good sprinting action.

11. Raise the hurdles about three inches at a time. (This step will take substantially longer than previous ones.) The athlete should avoid training too long over low obstacles. As the athlete gains confidence, raise the hurdles. Pad the hurdles with foam rubber the first few times the hurdles are at a new height. This will prevent painful bruises and scrapes and will allow the hurdler to be more aggressive.

Remember, this should be a positive experience. Patience is very important here. The beginner should not move to the next step until he/she feels confident. Constantly stress sprinting and as slight a deviation from sprinting form as possible. Refrain from timing hurdlers too soon. It is more important that the beginner get a feel for what he/she is doing before being timed, although an occasional race with someone of comparable ability could be beneficial.

There are some fundamental differences between men's and women's hurdling.

100m-110m Hurdles Sample Training Programs

A. **Off-Season** (Summer-Fall): Weight lifting 3 days per week.

Preface: During the early summer months (June/July—Mid-August), we recommend involvement with related activities such as: basketball, volleyball, swimming, tennis etc.

Mon.—Distance run (2-3mi.), hurdle drills (15 Hurdle (H) volume, 1-mile turns and 1-mile straights with jog in-between (alternate respiratory patterns between breath-holding, expiration, breathing).
Tues.—500-600-700-800m with 70 sec. at 400m staircase (up & down).
Wed.—280m back-off (build-ups) by 60m, i.e., over last 50% at 3/4 spd.
Thurs.—15 hurdle back-off volume (spaced 3m short)—strength and endurance.
Fri.—Same as Tuesday
Sat.—Same as Monday
Sun.—Rest

B. **Early Competitive Season:** Weight lifting 3 days per week.
Mon.—15 hurdle back-off 4 × 200m (1/2-3/4 spd.).
Tues.—Sprint Schedule
Wed.—Attacking 2nd 5 hurdle vol. (6H-10H), 3 @ 6-10H—9m, 3 @ 6-10H—8m, 3 @ 6-10H—7m.
Thurs.—Grass fartlek run for 3 mi., and 5 × 180's.
Fri.—Blocks over 3H, then jog and stretch.
Sat.—Competition
Sun.—Rest

C. **Mid-Season:** Weight lifting 3 days per week.
Mon.—15H back-off vol.
Tues.—3-5H tech. work and/or 2nd 5H backoff, plus 1/2 sprint sched.
Wed.—Sprint schedule.
Thurs.—Starts with 2H, 3 . 1-3-5H, 3.160m at 1/2-3/4 to full build-ups.
Fri.—Rest (flexibility exercises)
Sat.—Competition
Sun.—Easy, continuous 25-30 min. run.

D. **Late Season:** Weight lifting 3 days per week
Mon.—Sprint work-out
Tues.—Blocks over 2H, 5. attacking 2nd 5H, 3.200m.
Wed.—Sprint schedule
Thurs.—Blocks over 2H, acceleration declines 10-20° grade) over last 20m at dist. of 160-110— 80-60-40m (1/2-3/4 then, 3/4-full speed), 3.160m.
Fri.—Rest
Sat.—Competition
Sun.—Rest

400 Meter Hurdles

by
Ken Gibson—Old Dominion University
Vern Gambetta—UC Berkeley

The intermediate hurdles in one of the most physically demanding events in track and field. It requires the speed of a quarter-miler, the stamina of a half-miler, and the suppleness and technique of the high hurdler. From a technical point of view, the greatest problem facing an intermediate hurdler is deciding the number of strides to take between hurdles and then to master that chosen stride pattern.

Another complication in the intermediates is the fact that the race is run around two curves. To lessen this problem, it is recommended that the hurdler lead with the left leg. This permits him/her to run on the inside of the lane, making the curves easier to negotiate.

The beginner who does not have a preferred lead leg should learn to lead with the left. It is also advisable that he/she learn to hurdle off the "wrong" foot. This will prepare the athlete for all eventualities. Should the step be off, he/she will be able to clear the hurdle without losing form. In addition, alternating legs can be used effectively to make a transition in stride pattern.

Technique

Approach to the First Hurdle

The athlete should choose a number of strides to the first hurdle which feels comfortable and which results in a good transition to striding between hurdles. Twenty-two strides is recommended because it closely resembles the stride rhythm that the hurdler takes between hurdles. In the case of 22 steps, the lead leg should be placed in the rear block. For 23, the lead leg should be placed in the front block. Twenty-one, 23 or 24 strides may be acceptable, depending on the individual.

The speed to the first hurdle is slightly less and is more controlled than in the flat 400m. The last four to five strides before take-off should be as close as possible to the same stride rhythm used between hurdles. The beginning hurdler could benefit by counting the number of strides to the first hurdle to help insure proper step pattern: Count each time the take-off foot hits the ground. For 22 steps, the take-off foot will hit 11 times. For 23 steps, the take-off foot will hit 12 times.

To develop confidence in this run-up, the hurdler should practice running to an imaginary first hurdle or a stick placed on the ground where the hurdle would be. He/she should run through enough times to develop consistency and confidence, then put the hurdle up in the lane.

Hurdle Form

Form in the intermediates is a compromise between high and low hurdle technique. Many coaches and athletes feel that hurdle form is not as important in the intermediates. This is a serious misconception. Good form allows the hurdler to flow over the hurdle with only a slight deviation from normal running form.

The action is similar to that of the high hurdler except there is less of a "dive" into the hurdle, and less flexibility in the hip is required because of the lower hurdle height. The running action over the hurdles is not as pronounced. This allows for an economy of effort and as little deviation in the stride pattern as possible. The action with the lead arm is similar to that of the high hurdler but not nearly as pronounced. In the intermediates, the hurdler should carry the arms lower to the sides. The lead-arm action should be parallel to the leading leg.

Continuity of action is even more important here than in the high hurdles due to the added factor of fatigue. By correcting faults and perfecting technique, the hurdler can complete a race with much less effort. It should be remembered that fatigue will magnify faults in technique. Many hurdlers twist their upper bodies over the hurdle, which causes them to land off balance. It then takes them a stride or two to get back to normal running action. The athlete should keep the shoulders and hips square to the hurdles at all times.

In order to master action over the hurdle around a curve, the athlete should practice hurdling in all lanes, not only the one that is most comfortable. Training on the bend is even more vital to the right-lead-leg hurdler who has a greater tendency to trail a foot around the hurdle and thus risk disqualification.

The length of the flight over the hurdle is approximately 7' 0" to 7' 6" in front and 4' 0" to 4' 6" beyond that hurdle. To avoid disturbing the stride pattern, the athlete should not attempt to chop down the lead leg.

Strides between Hurdles

In order to excel in the intermediates, it is necessary to develop a stride pattern that fits perfectly into the space between hurdles. This will vary with individuals but should not include any chopping or overstriding. For most male athletes, the best stride pattern between hurdles is 15 steps. For the female beginner, 17 may be necessary at first. But, this is not practical for too long because it will lead to chopping the strides. A good rule of thumb to remember is to use as few strides as possible without overstriding.

It would be best to maintain the same stride pattern for the whole race. Many athletes have used 15 or even 13 all the way, although the former can lead to chopping and the latter to overstriding. A possible solution to the problem of strides between hurdles is to take 14, 16 or 18, but these would necessitate the added skill of alternating lead legs. Due to fatigue, most athletes have to change their stride pattern to a greater number of strides during the race. Usually this changeover takes place after the fifth, sixth, or seventh hurdle. It involves a great deal of practice to change without a serious loss in momentum or hurdle form. This is also complicated by the fact that this change often occurs on the turn.

The number of strides a hurdler should take between hurdles lies in his/her natural stride length. The following are common stride patterns and the required length of stride for each: 17 strides—6' 1"; 16 strides—6' 6"; 15 strides—7' 0"; 13 strides—8' 0".

To reach 13 steps requires an eight-foot stride which can quickly fatigue the normal athlete. This can cause

serious trouble if carried too far into the race. The more experienced hurdlers usually go 13 for five or six hurdles and then change to 15. The changeover shifts in rhythm from a longer stride to a quicker cadence. This does not mean chopping. To facilitate the change, some hurdlers find it beneficial to run on the outside of the lane. This has the effect of adding a little distance and thus, extra steps. But this can pose a problem of trailing the foot around the hurdle. Fatigue can also aid the changeover, as it will force the hurdler to change to an increased number of strides.

Hurdling on different track surfaces can change the stride pattern drastically. In the warmup, the hurdler should survey the condition of the track and choose the stride pattern accordingly. Tartan and similar surfaces will facilitate a fewer number of strides. The hurdler should also take into account the wind and other weather conditions.

Relaxation and concentration can be very important in the continuity of action and stride pattern. The hurdler must stay as relaxed as possible in order to maintain form. Concentration on one's own race plan is essential. If an opponent inside or outside goes out faster than expected, the hurdler should not panic but have confidence in his/her own race plan.

The greatest problem facing an intermediate hurdler is deciding the number of strides to take between hurdles and then to master that chosen stride pattern.

Run-in

The athlete must anticipate the run-in by clearing the last hurdle as relaxed and with as good as form as possible. After clearing the last hurdle, he/she should think the same as a quarter-miler finishing the race, concentrating on correct action with the arms and quickening the leg speed. This is the point where the speed endurance of the athlete is most evident.

Training and Drills

Split timings as a guide for training can be used effectively in the intermediates as in the highs. They can determine proper pace at any hurdle and the point in the hurdle race where problems begin to occur. To determine splits, take the time at the landing of the lead foot off the hurdle. Check this time with the following charts to derive the final time:

SPLIT TIME CHART—400M/400Y HURDLES—MEN*

Time at landing after	48.0	49-50	50-51	52.0	53.0	54.0
1st hurdle	5.7	5.9	6.0	6.1	6.3	6.4
2nd hurdle	9.7	10.0	10.2	10.4	10.7	10.9
3rd hurdle	13.7	14.1	14.4	14.7	15.1	15.4
4th hurdle	17.7	18.2	18.6	19.0	19.5	19.9
5th hurdle	21.7	22.3	22.8	23.3	23.9	24.4
6th hurdle	25.8	26.5	27.1	27.7	28.4	29.0
7th hurdle	29.9	30.8	31.5	32.2	32.9	33.7
8th hurdle	34.2	35.2	35.9	36.8	37.6	38.5
9th hurdle	38.5	39.7	40.4	41.6	42.5	43.4
10th hurdle	43.0	44.3	45.1	46.5	47.5	48.4
Total time	48.0	49.6	50.5	52.0	53.0	54.0

From: ''The Hurdle Races'' by K. O. Bosen, in International Track and Field Coaching Encyclopedia by Fred Wilt and Tom Ecker, Parker Publishing Company, West Nyack, N.Y., 1970.

WOMEN'S 400M TOUCHDOWN TIME CHART

Target Time	H1	H2	H3	H4	H5	200	H6	H7	H8	H9	H10	Run In
52	6.1	10.3	14.5	18.8	23.1	25.0	27.5	32.0	36.7	41.4	46.3	5.7
54	6.3	10.7	15.1	19.6	24.1	26.5	28.7	33.4	38.2	43.2	48.2	5.8
56	6.5	11.1	15.7	20.3	25.0	27.0	29.8	34.7	39.7	44.9	50.1	5.9
58	6.7	11.5	16.3	21.1	25.9	28.0	30.8	35.9	41.1	46.2	51.8	6.2
60	6.9	11.9	16.9	21.9	26.9	29.5	52.0	57.2	42.5	47.9	53.4	6.6
62	7.1	12.3	17.5	22.6	27.8	30.0	33.1	38.4	43.9	49.5	55.2	6.8
64	7.3	12.6	17.9	23.3	28.7	31.0	54.2	39.8	45.4	51.1	57.0	7.0

Pace judgment in the intermediates is of prime importance. Normally, the first half of the race is run two seconds faster than the second half of the race. To determine this pace, take the split time at the fifth hurdle and add 1.8 to two seconds. This will give the 200m time, as the fifth hurdle is short of a 200.

Basically, the conditioning for the intermediate hurdler is the same as the training for the quarter-mile. Each hurdler should be capable of running a fast 600. This race is similar in terms of energy cost to the athlete. Fall and early season training should be directed towards running a good 600.

In training, at least half of the intermediate hurdler's repeats should be run over hurdles to work on pace judgment and economy of effort. In the Fall, when running repeat 500's, 400's, 300's, or 200's, it is beneficial to put two or three hurdles arbitrarily somewhere in the distance. During this time, the hurdler should not be concerned with stride pattern but with adjusting to an upcoming hurdle, clearing it with good form and coming off the hurdle with good sprint action.

The intermediate hurdler should run his/her drills over hurdles out of the blocks. Typical workouts are run over three, five and seven hurdles.

In order to work on "transition" (changing the number of strides between hurdles), the hurdler should begin at the third hurdle and run the prescribed number of strides (13 or 15) between the fourth and fifth hurdles. Then he/she should change to 15 or 17 steps and run over the sixth and seventh hurdles to complete the transition to the new rhythm. This should be repeated five or six times in a workout.

Another good intermediate drill is to run the first 200 on the flat and the last 200 over hurdles. This serves as a good indicator of potential time.

A valuable workout in the Fall or early season is the up-and-back drill on grass. On opposite sides of a football field, two hurdles are placed facing one way and two hurdles facing the other way, each set being the proper distance apart. The athlete should attempt to run them in 15 or 17 strides, jog across the field and repeat the same going back. Up and back counts as one trip. The hurdler should begin with six trips and progress up to 10. This can also be done on the track. It is a good drill for step pattern and endurance.

The following drill simulates the conditions the hurdler will face the last three or four hurdles of a race: At the end of a 400, 500 or 600m run, the hurdler should go over one or two additional hurdles. This teaches him/her to adjust steps quickly, and to hurdle when fatigued.

Another drill, the 12-hurdle exercise, is basically a strength workout. The 11th hurdle is placed five meters from the finish line and the 12th, 30 meters (33 yds) beyond the line. This drill should not be used too often, especially within a week of a race.

An excellent drill to teach correct rhythm for the various stride patterns is to reduce the distance between hurdles. The hurdles should be set so that the same stride length that is required to run 15 or 17 strides is run in seven or nine strides. This is done by multiplying the stride length in meters times the number of strides to be run and adding 3.00 meters for the hurdle stride. For example:

Length of stride for 16 steps	# of steps to be run in workout	Hurdle stride		
2.00	X 7	+ 3	= 17 meters

The hurdles should be placed 17.00 meters apart which will give the hurdler the same stride length and rhythm as in the normal spacing. This allows the hurdler to do more work on hurdles at the correct rhythm without fatigue becoming a big factor. It also allows him/her to work hurdles on the turn, thus perfecting all important turn technique.

11
Relays

by
Mel Rosen—Auburn University
Jim Bush—UCLA

Relay races are a popular and exciting feature of track and field. They are a team event in an individual oriented sport. Therefore, they give the opportunity for teamwork and cooperation not available in the other events. The 400m sprint relay is the first running event of a track meet. A win in this relay can be a boost to other members of the team. The 4 X 400m—1600m relay is the last running event of the meet and oftentimes can be the deciding factor, giving the meet an added air of excitement. It is important to note that in team scoring competition, the relays are scored five points to the winner, zero points for second place. This helps lend to the excitement of relays, making them an all or nothing proposition.

The key to good relay racing is the baton pass. The shorter the relay, the more important the baton pass becomes. Many meters can be gained through smooth, efficient relay exchanges. In fact, with proper and well-timed passing, it is possible to defeat a team of better runners whose exchanges are inferior.

4 X 100m Relay

The Pass

The main objective in the pass is to keep the baton moving at top speed throughout the relay. This is insured through proper timing of the outgoing and incoming runner so that both are at maximum speed when the exchange is made.

The key to good relay racing is the baton pass.

The recommended technique of passing is the alternate downsweep method. In this, the #1 runner carries the baton in his/her right hand, passing to the #2 runner's left hand who in turn passes to #3's right hand. The third leg passes to the anchor leg's left hand.

The second, third and fourth runners are allowed a 100m acceleration zone and a 20m exchange zone in which the baton pass must be executed. The 10m acceleration distance is used by the outgoing runner to build up speed so that the baton is exchanged with both runners at near top speed.

For a smooth, efficient baton exchange, the outgoing runner should use two checkmarks. He/she should measure the first checkmark, the "go" point, in foot lengths (using the foot). This mark will vary from 15-25 foot lengths back from the acceleration zone depending on the speed of the incoming runner. The second should mark the beginning of the actual exchange. It is usually placed halfway through the exchange zone.

The pass should take place as follows: When the incoming runner hits the "go" mark, the outgoing runner leaves his/her position, accelerating to top speed as soon as possible. When the outgoing runner reaches the second point, he/she should put the hand back, palm up, presenting a steady target for the incoming runner. A good rule of thumb is that both runners should execute the pass with both arms fully extended. The exchange should be completed in the last third of the passing zone.

If the incoming runner overruns the outgoing runner, then the outgoing runner must move the "go" point checkmark further out. If the opposite happens, then the mark must be moved in closer to the zone. It is important to note that the primary responsibility for the pass rests with the incoming runner.

The outgoing runner may start either in a standing or a crouch position. It is a matter of personal preference, as long as it gives the runner a clear view of the "go" checkmark. The key is that the outgoing runner be adept at going on a visual cue—the incoming runner hitting the "go" mark. If the receiver is going to receive the baton in the left hand, then he/she should stand on the outside of the lane with the incoming runner on the inside.

Selection of Personnel

The following should be considered in selecting the best athletes to run the four segments of the 400m relay:

1) The distance each person is to run with the baton. Not every runner runs the same distance on each leg. Assuming that the pass is executed just beyond the middle of the passing zone, each athlete runs approximately the following distance:

In the 1600m relay, the runners use a visual pass.

	Total Distance Run	Distance Run with Baton*
#1 runner	101.5m	101.5m
#2 runner	121.5m	99.0m
#3 runner	121.5m	99.0m
#4 runner	120.0m	97.5m

*This totals 397. The extra three meters is gained by the free distance gained in each exchange.

3) The second and third runners must be very reliable in both receiving and passing the baton since they must execute both. The 200m-400m runner is effective here. The third leg also requires good turn running. The anchor runner should be the most reliable runner under pressure. Many times a hurdler who is used to maintaining concentration is a good person to anchor. The anchor runner must be a pressure performer.

Keeping in mind that the whole is greater than the sum of its parts, it is important to remember that the team with the four fastest runners does not guarantee the fastest relay team. A good indicator to evaluate how close a team is to running its potential is an efficiency rating. This is determined by totaling the open 100m times of the four individual runners and subtracting that from the actual relay time. The ideal difference should be about 2.5 seconds.

1600m(4 X 400m) Relay

The Pass

In this relay the runners use a visual pass. The incoming runner carriers the baton in the right hand and passes to the outgoing runner's left hand. The primary responsibility for the pass rests on the outgoing runner

due to fatigue on the part of the passer. The receiver should time the take-off based on how strong the incoming runner is finishing the last 200m. Once the receiver determines this, he/she should take five fast accelerating steps, turn the head back to the left, reach back with the left hand, and take the baton in such a manner as to present a good target. As soon as the outgoing runner is clear of the traffic of the exchange zone, the baton should be switched over to the right hand. He/she must sprint hard through the first turn to establish position.

Selection of Personnel

Recommended considerations are as follows:

1) Assess the strengths and weakness of each athlete -both physical and psychological—to maximize the potential of the relay.

2) The first three legs are run flat out, very similar to the open 400m. The last leg becomes more of a tactical race, depending on whether the team is ahead or behind.

3) The runner on the second leg must be aggressive and prepared to run a very strong, fast 200m. This person also must break for the pole either at the exchange or after the 100m mark.

4) The team order can be adjusted to keep the team in the race. It is possible to hide a weak leg if the oppenents' strengths and weaknesses are known.

5) A good order is to run the second strongest runner first and the strongest last, with the two weakest in the middle.

Summary

The relays offer a unique blending of individual talent into a cohesive team. It is particularly challenging for the coach to determine the best athletes for each position in the relay and maintain team unity without sacrificing individual pride.

Part of the "art" of coaching is recognizing that there are many ways to reach a particular goal and then convincing your athletes that your way is best.

12
General Principles for Middle, Steeplechase and Long Distance Runners

by
Roy Griak*
University of Minnesota

Coaching is both a science and an art. Almost everyone knows the science of coaching...the miles, reps, recoveries and the like. The art of coaching, wherein we "listen to the athlete", senses how the individual is responding to the work loads prescribed. A part of the art also is recognizing that there are many ways to reach a particular goal and then convincing your athletes that your way is best.

MIDDLE AND LONG DISTANCE RUNNING

I. **TECHNIQUES**
  a. Stride length: A basic rule to remember is the the slower the race, the shorter the stride; the faster the race, the longer the stride. Stride length must be adjusted accordingly when economy of effort is a prime consideration. Concentrate on lifting the knees just enough for the feet to clear the ground during the recovery phase. Knee lift any higher will result in wasted energy.
  b. Arm action: The faster the arm swing, the faster the leg movement. Action of arms should be relaxed and natural. Hold the palms of hands inward, fingers cupped, with thumb resting on top of second joint of index finger. This action will help to keep the arms to the side of the body. Arms swing freely from shoulder sockets. Hands move in a straight line from the middle of the body back to the side of the hip.
  c. Foot placement: Foot placement should be under the knee during the driving phase. The foot should strike the ground slightly in front of the center of gravity. Land low on the ball of the foot. During the supporting phase, the foot should be flat on the ground. Do not land heel first during supporting phase. During the recovery phase the driving leg leaves the ground behind the body. As the foot leaves the ground, the lower leg folds up toward the thigh and the heel rises towards the hip. Minimize a high knee lift. During the driving phase the stride begins when the center of gravity has passed ahead of the foot in contact with the ground.

*Coach Griak edited this chapter. He was assisted by Al Baeta, Terry Crawford, Larry Ellis, Dr. Ken Foreman, Harry Groves, Don Hessel, John McKenzie, Jim Meilke, Jerry Quiller, Bill Squires, Gary Wieneke, and Herm Wilson

d. Body lean: Run tall, with hips forward. Head will be in line with torso and erect. Focus eyes straight ahead, approximately ten yards.

e. Run with rhythm.

f. Breathing: Breathe steady and with an even rhythm. Inhale and exhale through a partially open mouth and the nose.

II. **TRAINING OBJECTIVES**-Keep in mind that the main goal of training is to develop aerobic endurance and maintain speed for the full distance of the race, stamina first, then speed.

a. Proper warmup and cooldown (emphasis on stretching and flexibility).

b. Speed work—top speed efforts of 10-15 sec.

c. Stamina—hard endurance runs of four to eight miles.

d. Strength training—weight training.

e. Sprint technique training.

f. Gradual adaptation to stress—patience, long range program.

g. Maintain rhythm and patterns.
   1. Training (the entire year).
   2. Daily routine.
   3. Diet.

h. Endurance runs—relaxed efforts slower than race pace.

i. Flexibility—type, frequency, before and after training.

j. Tactical considerations.
   1. Reacting to tempo changes during competition.
   2. Pace work.

k. Proper running technique.

l. Types of training needs and frequency.

III. **STRUCTURING A TRAINING PROGRAM— GUIDELINES TO CONSIDER BEFORE FINALIZATION OF A TRAINING PROGRAM.**

a. Hill training.
   1. Uphill running at various grades and distances means developing speed and strength. Bounding triple jump style is an excellent strength builder and conditioner.
   2. Down hill running at a very slight grade (3%) is a method of developing leg speed.

b. Moderate training sessions after hard training day, or hard, easy easy, hard day pattern.

c. Long easy runs for recovery.

d. Train twice a day. Morning runs are usually a slow tempo. Some athletes are now having three training sessions per day, two of which are slow tempo work. When training more than one workout per day, consideration should be given to the individual's maturity and development stage.

e. Allow time during workouts for flexibility training, preferably before and after the training sessions. With the increase of volume running, the need for flexibility work is of utmost importance.

f. Weight training consisting of high repeats with light weights is recommended. However, a recent trend is a balance of heavier weights with fewer repeats for additional strength training. Individual activities such as dips, pull-ups, and sit-ups, should be included on a daily basis. Strength training two or three days per week is recommended.

g. A year-round training program with the following phases:
   1. Active rest—following the competitive season of four to six weeks. Have volume running the time for other physical activity.
   2. Marathon phase—heavy volume running.
   3. Competitive phase (pre-competitive phase, competitive, and championship phase).

h. Tempo running—lactic acid build up is minimal. This type of training stimulates the athlete both physically and mentally. Include distances of 8 to 15 miles at pace to suit the individual.

i. Peak of competitive season, decrease volume of distance runs and increase maximum effort runs. Repeat runs of three to ten minutes. This type of training should be considered three to four weeks before the desired peak performance.

j. Every consideration should be given to the mental and social aspects when planning training.

k. Use training methods two or three times per week where the athlete trains in an aerobic state (running without oxygen) for middle distance events (800-1500). i.e., training at a tempo faster than race pace.

l. Consider a longer interval of time between competitions. A nine to fifteen day cycle is more realistic than a seven day cycle. This would allow an athlete proper recovery, followed by hard training necessary for proper development.

m. It is very important to train at moderate stress and not strain. The type of training is more important than mileage alone.

n. Patience is a virtue in training and racing.

o. A major consideration in selecting training routines is to remember that the body adapts to what it is given.

p. There is little or no value in doing two speed sessions one after the other.

q. A runner must build the ability to convert from a rapid stride to a finishing kick or sprint.

r. Training must include some work at the exact rhythm and pace of the planned competitive effort.

s. Train to race—the body should delight in the battle, the thirst of competition.

t. All workouts and competitions should include a warm-up and cool-down.
   1. **Warm-up** A proper warmup should include at least 3/4 miles of easy running, 10-20 min of flexibility work, and 6-8 good acceleration runs (70-110 yds).

2. **Cool-down** A proper cool-down should include a recovery run of 1 to 6 miles and 10-15 min. of flexibility work.

u. More must be gained from training than physical strength. A great deal of psychological strength must also be gained. Mental toughness and inurement to fatigue are planned aspects in a total training program.

v. There are many off season training considerations but the most important for the middle distance and distance runners is the building and maintenance of an aerobic base.

w. Strength training: Set up a general weight training program three times per week during the off season and one to two times per week during the competitive season. Use a strength training program that is available to the coach and athlete.

1. Free weights: Includes dumbells (short bars), barbells (long bars), and rowing. Alternate bent-arm swings with dumbells (3-8 lbs. with each arm), 2 sets of high repetitions (20-50 reps each arm).

2. Universal gym: Appartus of weights and pulleys, with stations for leg, chest, shoulder presses, pulls, curls, chinning, bent over rowing, dipping, and hip flexions.

3. Nautilus machines: Each station works a single muscle group. Each machine has a cam that varies the strength of resistance according to the strength of the muscle as it goes through the motion. A Nautilus machine gives a muscle a total workout throughout its full range of motion.

4. Strength training should be a slow controlled movement with complete flexion and extension of muscles involved. Begin with two sets of 8-12 repetitions for arms, shoulders, neck and upper back. Begin with 12-20 repetitions for lower back and legs. Pre-competitive programs may include the following: inclined press, half squats, toe raises, leg curls, sit-ups (twisting), bench press, curls, neck raises, and bent over rowing. The following are recommended during the competitive season: bench press, jump squats, curls and box drills, and stadium steps.

5. Circuit training: This is a very effective method for general strength training. There are as many individual exercises and/or circuits as the creative coach can devise to meet his/her athlete's needs. A sample circuit would be:
   (1) Step-ups.
   (2) 4 or 6 count burpees (4 count includes one push-up/6 count includes two push-ups.
   (3) Bent knee sit-ups.
   (4) Pull-ups.
   An athlete would spend 30 seconds at each station with a 30 second recovery between exercises. The period of work and rest would vary as the athlete's condition improves. Two circuits are recommended. Circuit training may be included into the program 3-4 days per week.

x. Types of training: All types of training play an important part in a balanced training program. Training must be used in correct amounts at the proper time. A gradual adaptation to stress must be a prime consideration. A coach must realize the effects that various training exercises have on the body.

A Nautilus machine gives a muscle a total workout throughout its full range of motion.

The best way to condition the middle and long distance athletes is on a program that requires the following weekly mileage: 800m-runner—30-50 min., 1500m runner—40-60 min., and the 3000m, 50-70 min., It is strongly recommended that athletes do not train more than 70 min./week for any event.

Consider the following types of training in setting up a program:

1. **Slow continuous running** 10 to 20 miles, usually on Sunday as recovery run, heart rate approximately 150 per min. Eight minutes per mile may be the tempo desired for a high school athlete. Aerobic training (with oxygen).

2. **Fast continuous running** - Tempo is faster, heart rate in the range of 150 beats per min-180 beats per min. Aerobic training (with oxygen); however, anaerobic training (without oxygen) may take place to a small degree.

3. **Interval running** - Formal training of slow-fast variety. Variables are distance of fast run, inter-

val of rest, number of repetitions, time of fast run, and any type of recovery period. Recovery period could be jogging or walking. Example: 4x440 (70 sec with 220 jog recovery).

4. **Hill running** - Uphill running should be timed on set course. Downhill running a very slight grade from 200 to 300 m. for leg speed developement.

5. **Fartlek** (speedplay) - Informal slow-fast running. Run on golf courses or parks with emphasis on fast running. Fast runs on golf course from hole to hole with varying jog recovery would be a form of Fartlek activity. Include hill running at fast tempo.

6. **Surges** (interval sprinting) - Running alternate sprints for a specific distance (100m) and jogging (200m) for a distance of 5000m. Develops aerobic endurance.

7. **Accelerated sprints** - An accelerated sprint from jogging to sprinting.

8. **Hollow sprinting** - Sprint, jog recovery, sprint, and walk recovery before next repetition. Example: sprint 100m, jog 100m, sprint 100m, walk 100m.

9. **Repetition running** - Involves a longer interval of run than in interval training with complete recovery usually by walking. Example: run 3x800m in 2:00 with a walk recovery—pulse rate below 120 beats.

10. **Race pace tempo running** - Race can be broken down into whatever increments desired. Inform the athlete of his pace for every 50-100m during interval of run.

11. **Speed running** - Top relaxed effort at 150m or less.

12. **Speed endurance running** - Top relaxed effort at 200m through 600m.

13. **Stress endurance running** - Top relaxed efforts of 700m through 1200m.

IV: SAMPLE TRAINING PROGRAMS

As the training of the middle and distance runners must be perceived wholistically, the athlete must be perceived wholistically. The athlete needs to improve aerobically, anaerobically, in terms of strength, flexibility and endurance, as well as technique and mental aspects. How one accomplishes all of this cannot be clearly delineated in the mere printing of a schedule. The art of applying knowledge is the genius of coaching. What is known is that the stress loads necessary to "get there" must be 80 percent or more of the athlete's current level of development in a specific biophysical factor...although a 60 percent stress load is sufficient to maintain that which has already been built up.

The Wholistic Approach - The wholistic program covers twevle months. (When working with high school athletes it is recommended that a general format be developed for a period of three years). The table below suggests how one could emphasize the development of the fuel systems during a one, two and three year training cycle.

Long Term Development of the Energy Systems Essential for Competitive Racing At 800-1500-3000 Meters

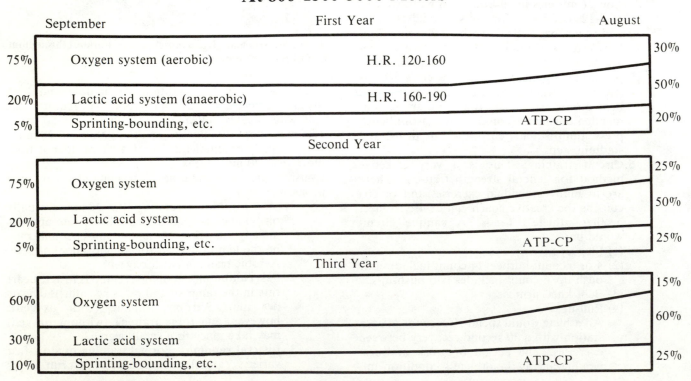

A Comprehensive Training Program for Middle Distance Runners

Month	Sept	Jan.	May	August
Total Miles	300	280	280	200
Elements				
Strength training weight work	3 time/wk ••••••••••••••••••••••••••••••••••••••			2 time/wk
bounding	1 time/wk ••••••••••••••••••		2 time/mo	
depth jumping		1 time/wk		
Flexibility work	Daily •••			
Long distance-slow (Oxygen system)	4 time/wk ••••••••	3 time/wk ••••••••	2 time/wk ••••••••	1 time/wk
Long distance-fast (Oxygen system)	1 time every other wk ••••••••••••••••••••••••••••••••			
Fartlek (Oxygen-lactic acid)	1 time/wk ••••••••	2 time/mo ••••••••••••••••••••••••••		
Power runs (Lactic acid)		1 time/mo ••••••••	3 time/mo	
Interval running (Oxygen-lactic acid)		1 time/wk		
Interval training (Lactic acid)			2 time/wk ••••••••••	1 time/wk
Hill work (Oxygen-lactic acid)	1 time/wk ••••••••	2 time/mo ••••••••	Occasional use for peaking	
Sprint work (Lactic acid)			1 time/wk ••••••••••	2 time/wk
Pace work (Steady state)		2 time/mo ••••••••	1 time/wk	

TYPICAL TRAINING FORMAT

Fall - September

Monday	Anaerobic run (8-12 miles).	1st session
	Weight training...upper body.	2nd session
Tuesday	Morning run-low aerobic (5-6 miles).	3rd session
	Fartlek (45 minutes with some short, high intensity bursts).	4th session
Wednesday	Hill work...continuous, aerobic-anaerobic.	5th session
	Weight training.	6th session
Thursday	Morning run-low aerobic (5-6 miles.)	7th session
	Afternoon aerobic-anaerobic-aerobic:	
	4 easy miles...1 hard mile...4 easy miles.	8th session
Friday	Active rest...i.e., hiking, swimming, cycling, etc.	9th session
Saturday	Aerobic run (10-14 miles)-morning.	10th session
	Weight training - afternoon.	11th session
Sunday	High aerobic run (8-10 miles).	12th session
Monday	Morning run-low aerobic (5-6 miles).	13th session
	Fartlek (30 min with some high intensity running). Finish workout with several 220's at adjusted pace.	14th session
Tuesday	Morning run-low aerobic (6-7 miles).	15th session
	Weight training . . . preceded by several form strides on the grass.	16th session
Wednesday	Active rest . . . i.e., hiking, swimming, cycling, etc.	17th session
Thursday	Hill work . . . repeats, aerobic-anaerobic-aerobic (400 m flat, 300 m 10-15% grade, 400 m flat run out).	18th session
Friday	Morning run-low aerobic (3-4 miles).	19th session
	Afternoon run-low aerobic (3-4 miles).	20th session
Saturday	Competition in cross country followed by weight training-light.	21st session / 22nd session
Sunday	Recovery run (8-12 miles).	23rd session
Monday	Rest.	

Total miles—approximately 150, 11.5 training sessions/week. Two days of active rest. A mix of both aerobic and anaerobic training, though the major commitment is to aerobic or base running. During the second 14-day training cycle, the number of training sessions/week increases to 12.5. It is assumed that each session will be preceded by 15 minutes of stretching.

TYPICAL TRAINING FORMAT
(Continued)

Winter — January

Monday	Fartlek (60 min including warm-up. Run with a friend and share the joy together.)	1st session
	Weight training.	2nd session
Tuesday	Morning run-low aerobic (5-6 miles).	3rd session
	Internal work . . . repeat 200's, 400's or 600's at adjusted pace time. To be run within time limitations, i.e. repeat 6 with 3 min for both running and recovery.	4th session
Wednesday	Aerobic run (8-12 miles).	5th session
	Weight training . . . light with 10-12 reps/lift.	6th session
Thursday	Hill work . . . repeats, aerobic-anaerobic-aerobic (400 m flat, 400 m 10-15% grade, 400 m flat).	7th session
Friday	Morning run-low aerobic (3-4 miles).	8th session
	Off the track pace work . . . preferably on grass and in open terrain: 400's, 600's, 800's.	9th session
Saturday	High aerobic run (8-10 miles) 3-4 easy . . . 2-3 hard . . . finish easy.	10th session
Sunday	Weight training.	11th session
Monday	Morning run-low aerobic (5-6 miles).	12th session
	60 second power run for distance. Finish workout with several easy miles.	13th session
Tuesday	Morning run-low aerobic (5-6 miles).	14th session
	Pace intervals at adjusted times . . . 200's, 400's with short recovery. (work on strong side with higher intensity-fewer reps for anaerobically oriented runners).	15th session
Wednesday	Morning run-aerobic (6-8 miles).	16th session
	Hill bounding in the afternoon (30 min). Finish with fast striding on grass . . . 10x150.	17th session
Thursday	Morning-weight training.	18th session
	Aerobic run (8-12 miles).	19th session
Friday	Morning run-low aerobic (5-6 miles).	20th session
	Fartlek funnel (5-4-3-2-1 min of running at adjusted pace for time. Running time and recovery time is the same). Finish workout with 3-4 easy miles.	21st session
Saturday	Active rest . . . i.e., hiking, swimming, etc.	22nd session
Sunday	Morning run-aerobic (3-5 miles).	23rd session
	Time trial at 3/4 race distance.	24th session
	Weight training.	25th session

Total miles approximately 140, 12.5 training session/week. One full day of rest and one day of active rest. A mix of both aerobic and anaerobic training with an emphasis on the strong side for each individual. Each session should be preceded by 15 min. of stretching.

Spring - April

Sunday	Complete rest...or an easy recovery run depending on the athlete's sense of fatigue.	1st session
Monday	Morning run-low aerobic (5-6 miles).	2nd session
	Interval training 4x400 pace, 4x200 faster than pace 4x150 finish kicks...short recovery.	3rd session
Tuesday	Morning run-low aerobic (5-6 miles).	4th session
	Aerobic run (6-8 miles).	5th session
	Weight training.	6th session
Wednesday	Interval training 2x400 pace, 2x550 or 660 slightly off pace, 3x300 faster than pace with short recovery.	7th session
Thursday	Morning run-low aerobic (5-6 miles).	8th session
	Aerobic run (6-10 miles).	9th session
	Weight training.	10th session
Friday	Funnel 550 or 400, 300, 200, 150 with recovery a heart rate of 120 beats/min.	11th session
Saturday	Competition.	12th session
Sunday	Weight training.	13th session
	Recovery run or rest, depending on the athlete's sense of fatigue.	14th session
Monday	Morning run-low aerobic (5-7 miles).	15th session
	Sprint workout...repeat 150's, 200's. Finish with 2-3 easy miles.	16th session
Tuesday	Hill work aerobic-anaerobic-aerobic 400 pace, 200-300 at 10-15% grade at 70% of pace, 400 run out to recovery. Heart rates 120-190-120.	17th session
Wednesday	Fartlek run (45 minutes with joyous abandon).	18th session
	Weight training.	19th session
Thursday	Morning run-low aerobic (4-5 miles).	20th session
	Interval work 3x200, 1x500 or 700, 3x150.	21st session
Friday	Race simulators 4x200 or 300 at anticipated pace for first, second, third and fourth quarters of the athlete's race. Recover to 120 H.R. between each.	22nd session
Saturday	Competition.	23rd session
	Light weight workout to follow.	24th session
Sunday	Complete rest.	

TRAINING PROGRAM 5,000 - STEEPLECHASE

Mid-Season

Sunday	12-15 miles.
Monday	am: 3-5 miles; pm: 40 min Fartlek
Tuesday	am: 3-5 miles; pm: 4x440(75), 4x440(73), 4x440(71), 220 Jog Recovery, 440JR between sets, 3 miles run - 1st and 3rd mile on track at 6:00 pace.
Wednesday	am: 3-5 miles; pm: 3 miles Fartlek.
Thursday	am: 3-5 miles; pm: 3x880 at goal pace at this phase of runners development - 3/4 JR - 4x110 cut-downs (16-15-14-13).
Friday	am: 3-5 miles; pm: 5 miles at slow continuous pace, 7:00-7:30 pace. If competition on Saturday is pm 3-5 miles.
Saturday	Competition.

Off Season

		Daily Mileage
Sunday	12 to 15 miles @ 7 to 9 minute pace.	= 15
Monday	am: 3-5 miles; pm: 8 miles @ 7 pace.	= 11
Tuesday	am: 3-5 miles; pm: 10 miles @ 7-9 min pace.	= 13
Wednesday	am: 3-5 miles; pm: 7 miles, hills.	= 10
Thursday	am: 3-5 miles; pm: 10 miles @ 7-9 min pace.	= 11
Friday	am: 3-5 miles; pm: 6 miles @ 6 min pace.	= 9
Saturday	am: 10 miles at 8 min pace.	= 10
	weekly mileage total	= 79

Late-Season

Sunday	8 to 10 miles.
Monday	am: 30 min run; pm: 2x3/4 in 3:30, 440JR, 6x330 cut-downs: 3 at 52, 3 at 50 with 110 JR.
Tuesday	am: 3 mile run; pm: 30 min Fartlek.
Wednesday	am: 3 mile run; pm: 2 miles easy - 6x165 accelerations - 1x 880 (2:08), 3x200, JR, 3x100 flat out.
Thursday	am: 2-4 miles; pm: 20 min run.
Friday	pm: easy run - strides.
Saturday	competition.

Pre-Competitive

Sunday	3/4 to 1 hour run at 8:00 min pace.	= 8
Monday	am: 3-5 miles; pm: 7 miles of hill running.	= 10
Tuesday	am: 3-5 miles; pm: 10 miles at 7:00 to 8:00 pace.	= 13
Wednesday	am: 3-5 miles; pm: 8 miles Fartlek.	= 11
Thursday	am: 3-5 miles; pm: 12 miles at 8:00 pace.	= 15
Friday	am: 3-5 miles; pm: 7 miles hill running.	= 10
Saturday	12 miles at 7:00-9:00 min pace, recovery run.	= 12
	weekly mileage total	= 79

THE STEEPLECHASE

The steeplechase became an Olympic event in the 1920's. It was standardized by the International Amateur Federation in 1954. World records became acceptable at this time. However, the steeplechase has never been fully accepted with great interest in the United States by the track and field world.

Lack of success in this event rests entirely with high school and college coaches. The steeplechase should be a standard event in high school competition. On this level, the event should be reduced in distance from 3000 meters to 1500 meters. It should be held in every high school invitational meet where there is a steeplechase facility. State championship meets should include the steeplechase if the facility is available.

Since few quality steeplechasers practice the water jumps with regularity, it is not necessary for high schools to have a water jump facility. The coach and athlete merely need to take an interest in the event, practice proper hurdling technique, and develop appropriate training habits.

On the college level, coaches must stop treating the event as an afterthought. The standard practice by college coaches is to put those athletes who lack talent for the 1500 meters, 3000 or 5000 meters in the steeplechase event. In other words, if the athlete cannot excel at any other event, the steeplechase becomes an alternative.

This attitude regarding the steeplechase in the U.S. must change. The event is exciting and challenging. It is a middle distance event which requires agility, endurance and strength, concentration under fatigue, and courage to continually attack solid obstacles.

Strategy

Fluid momentum as one clears each barrier, expending energy effectively throughout the race, is a major goal to be established. One can use an even pace, attack the pace early and hang on, or attempt to finish with a strong burst of speed. However, using various strategies in the steeplechase is more difficult due to the barriers. The barriers and water jumps are equalizers. One may be very good at running between the barriers but may not be able to hurdle well. Such a runner will lose his advantage to one who has more strength and whose hurdle technique is perfect.

It is best to establish a good position during the race, to run the most economical pace possible, and to finish the last 200 to 400 meters as strongly as possible. Few runners have successfully taken the pace out quickly and survived the race as a high place winner. The fatigue factors in the steeplechase are just too great for this type of approach.

Mastering the barriers means mastering the race. Training for the steeplechase does not vary greatly from standard training for other middle distance and distance events. The poorest part of the race for American steeplechasers is clearing the barriers. Poor hurdling technique breaks up the momentum of the race and consumes a large amount of strength. This poor technique is a direct result of coaches and athletes not putting emphasis on proper hurdling. An estimated ten seconds or more could be trimmed off of most steeplechasers' times by merly clearing the barriers more efficiently.

Olympic development films show steeplechasers blocking in front of the barriers on their heels, as a straddle high jumper might do, landing with their center of gravity far behind the lead leg and coming to a near halt on the far side of the hurdle. The leg is in poor hurdling position, the arms out of control, and the clearance too high over the barriers. A general explanation is that the steeplechaser in the U.S. lacks technique and confidence regarding barrier clearance which restricts them from applying solid racing strategy.

On the water jumps, the most common errors are blocking in front of the barrier, standing up on the barrier and jumping off, landing with the center of gravity behind the landing leg, poor arm control, and dropping the head and chest upon landing in the pit. Again, a lack of emphasis and practice time accounts for these problems.

With momentum a key to performance, perfect barrier technique is a must. All good steeplechasers hurdle the barriers or use a combination of hurdling and stepping up on the barrier in the later stages of the race. The ideal situation would be to hurdle the barriers throughout the race with the ability to alternate lead legs. Alternating will prevent any chopping.

The second best method to maintain momentum is to hurdle all the way, leading with the same leg. Since there is no way to accurately measure a step pattern between barriers, it is suggested that an athlete put a mark on the track four to six strides back from each barrier. Upon hitting that mark, a runner attacks the barrier with four to six even strides. This can be sufficiently practiced so that such marks are not needed in a meet.

Stepping on the barrier is easily taught and a very natural thing to do. After hurdling throughout most of the race, stepping on the barrier can prevent chopping and gives a runner a sense of security and a safety margin. By stepping on the hurdle near the end of the race, the runner does not have to worry much about step patterns, effort of clearance, and stumbling upon landing.

Training Factors

Solving the problem of barrier clearance is merely a matter of practice. However, since a steeplechaser puts emphasis on strength and endurance training, hurdle technique suffers. There seems to be a deep seeded problem in the steeplechaser's willingness to practice the hurdles, and that factor is a fear of injury. A lack of confidence in their athletic ability and lack of flexibility promote this attitude.

Hurdling work should be properly supervised by a coach. The water jump has an injury risk and should not be extensively practiced. However, enough practice must be attained to become proficient at the task. In clearing the water jump, one should attack the barrier, jump upward and forward, placing the lead leg foot on the barrier and letting forward momentum move the body across the barrier. As the weight moves to the far side of the barrier, push off the barrier with the right foot. In landing, the left foot comes through and lands in water about one foot deep, while the right foot comes off the barrier and lands outside of the water in running stride. Do not try to jump completely across the water. Keep the head and chest up with a slight forward lean upon landing. Dropping the head and chest upon landing causes one to stumble or even fall upon leaving the water pit. The arms need special control in order to facilitate a forward and level flight across the barrier. Keep the arms in close in good running style while taking the barrier. As one pushes off the barrier, one should keep the arms low and push them forward. Upon landing, get back into running style as quickly as possible.

There is no need to develop an endurance and speed training program that is specially designed for this event, since there are multiple training programs for middle distance and distance runners. However, a combination of long distance runs, intense distance runs, interval, speed, and hurdling should be used. It must be remembered that the steeplechase is a technique event and vast improvement comes to those athletes who strive for perfection.

The steeplechase is a middle distance event which requires agility, endurance and strength, concentration under fatigue, and courage to continually attack solid obstacles.

Training Program
Steeplechase

Mid-Season

Sunday	1 to 1 1/2 hour continuous run.
Monday	am: 3-5 miles; pm: 5 miles Fartlek.
Tuesday	am: 3-5 miles; pm: 15 min hurdle and water jump, 12x440(70) without hurdles, 440JR.
Wednesday	am: 3-5 miles; pm: 1 to 1 1/2 hour Fartlek.
Thursday	am: 3-5 miles; pm: 10x220(35) 220JR, 5x330(52) 220JR.
Friday	30 min easy run.
Saturday	Steeplechase interval running 8-10x430(75) 440JR - with hurdles and water jump **or** 3x 860 (2:20), 3 min JR, 8x430 (75), 3 min JR with hurdles and water jump.

Second week 2x1,000 (race tempo) 30 min easy jog recovery, next 1,000, run 1st 880 slower than race pace, last 220 accelerated.

Late-Season

Sunday	45 to 1 hour Fartlek.
Monday	Same as mid-season.
Tuesday	am: 3-5 miles; pm: 1x440(68), 330 JR.
Wednesday	am: 3-5 miles; pm: 1x860 (2:20), 440JR, 6x150 at 3/4 effort, 220 JR, 1x3/4 (3:20), 880JR, 3x150.
Thursday	30 min easy Fartlek.
Friday	3-5 easy.
Saturday	Competition.

Water Jump

Keep landing leg bent and body c.g. low. Push forward as c.g. passes barrier—do not stand on the barrier.

Trailing leg lands in water after coming off barrier. Land with head upright and a slight forward lean to chest.

Leading leg lands just outside pit with body in balance ready to begin normal stride.

OTHER TRAINING PERSPECTIVES FOR MIDDLE LONG DISTANCE RUNNING

Tactics and Strategies

The objective of tactics and strategies is two fold. One is to improve an athlete's time for a race, and/or the other is to finish in a higher place in the race.

Strategy is defined as the overall plan or plan(s) for a race, such as sitting and kicking the last 110 or running even pace quarters, etc. Tactics is defined as the specific acts that either initiate an action or is a specific act to counteract a competitor's action. The strategy or strategies for a race are carried out by a series of tactics. In addition, unplanned tactics may be used depending on the actions of the competitors.

It should be noted that strategies for placing higher only really have a chance of working provided the competitors are relatively equal in ability. For example, if a miler's best is 5:00, and the other miler's best is 4:30, any strategy is probably worthless, regardless how well they might be executed. Often coaches and athletes set up good strategies that appear not to work and are a source of frustration. The fault may not be with the strategy as much as with the varying developed talents of the competitors.

Factors to be considered when determining strategies are as follows:
1. strength(s) of the athlete
2. weakness(es) of the athlete
3. strength(s) of opponents
4. weakness(es) of opponents
5. What constants can the athlete be relatively sure of (for example, athlete A always starts off at 30 seconds for the first 200.)
6. weather conditions
7. uniqueness of track and stadium
8. predictability of race effort
9. lane assignment
10. qualifying procedures if having prelims
11. start and finish line

Tactics a competitor might use are as follows:
1. even pacing
2. surging
3. kicking (short, medium, or long)
4. slowing the pace
5. setting up boxes
6. avoiding boxes
7. running into the wind
8. running with the wind
9. running into the curve
10. running around the curve
11. running out of the curve
12. running large field
13. starting in lanes
14. starting from a waterfall
15. starting in boxes
16. protecting ones self from contact
17. counter tactics
18. leading
19. following or sitting
20. fade from the front
21. predictability of race effect

Determining an athlete's strengths and weakness must be done relative to his or her opposition. For example, an athlete may have a great kick but his or her opponent might have a greater one, therefore the strategy of sit and kick would be running for second place.

The following are areas to evaluate strength and weakness for each athlete and their opponents:
1. pace judgment. For example, in a mile race 1st lap, 2nd lap, & 3rd lap
2. ability to surge
3. ability to lead
4. ability to follow
5. ability to kick off fast pace
6. ability to kick after leading
7. ability to kick after following
8. ability to run a fast mile
9. ability to run in traffic
10. ability to keep "contact" during middle part of race
11. ability to react
12. ability to be aggressive or initiate action
13. ability to run into the wind
14. ability to run on windy days
15. ability to run on cold days
16. ability to run on hot days
17. ability to handle pressure
18. ability to take a risk or gamble
19. ability to handle the unexpected

Strategies for placing higher only really have a chance of working provided the competitors are relatively equal in ability.

Four basic strategies are:

1) Sit and kick - Unfortunately, this strategy is over used by the beginner through the world class runners. Determining the place to kick depends on a large number of factors. The two main ones are the strength of the athlete and the pace of the race. A real sprint kick is difficult to maintain for longer than 100 yards. Coming off the final turn, accelerating to top speed, and receiving the sling shot effect as the athlete enters the straightaway should be done regardless of strategy.

2) Even pace - Even pace is the most efficient and economical way to run a middle distance or distance race. For example, all of Dave Wottle's 200m splits at Munich were in the 26 sec range for this 800m gold medal race. However, the ability to run in traffic and get out of boxes was required for that race. Frequently even paced runners will find themselves in last place at the 220 and 440 marks of the mile run. If the athlete can overcome this position psychologically, this is often an excellent strategy, especially when the pace is way beyond the capabilities of the competitors.

3) Another strategy is to push the 3rd lap of the mile or the 3rd 220 of an 880 or the last mile of a 3 mile. This strategy forces the kickers into staying up on the pace. Most kickers have a reluctance to do this. Internationally, many of the mile or 1500 races

follow this strategy. These races seldom came down to a big kick over the last 220 but a gradual picking up of the pace where the 2nd lap and the 4th lap about the same pace as the 3rd. As a result of this strategy, the field gradually spreads out over the last 50 yards.

4) Predictability of race effort may be used as a strategy or as a tactic. Divide the race up into its parts based on the difficulty and energy needed to pass an opponent. For example in an 880 yard race, assuming that all athletes' best time is about 2:00.0, most athletes run the first 220 below pace (26-28 seconds). Therefore the difficulty to pass is around 80-90 percent, because a lot of energy will be needed if it is the athlete's strategy to take the lead by the end of the first 220. Then the 2nd 220 is usually run around 30 seconds so the percent of passing difficulty drops to 60-70 percent—a much better time to pass, all other factors being equal. The 3rd 220 is usually run around 32-34 seconds and the passing difficulty factor changes to 40-60 percent. The 4th 220 is usually run around 30 seconds and the passing difficulty factor due to fatigue is 90-100 percent because everyone is trying to go as fast as they can at that point of the race. Therefore, the conclusion based on this concept of predictability of effort would be that the best time to pass is during the 2nd and 3rd 220's of an 880.

Predictability of race effort may be used as a strategy or as a tactic.

Evaluation of Training Concepts

Type of Training	Purpose and Desired Result
Hill runs of 6-12 miles done steady and easy.	**Recovery** run usually on Sunday a.m. Some minor leg strength and anaerobic development takes place to a small degree. Hill runs are usually mentally stimulating.
10 miles easy to 7:00-9:00 per mile.	Promote recovery and mentally relaxing.
6-10 miles fast at 6:00-7:00 or better pace.	**Endurance, stamina and strong stride** development. Mental toughness.
10 to 20 x 400m (with 200m jog) Progression on this workout as time comes down over the months of jog interval is shortened. If the recovery jog drops from 3:00 in September to around 60 seconds in June. In cross country, run 15 to 20 x 400 is always run **all out.**	Anaerobic development, pace and tempo development faster than pace. The final 400 is for kick buildup.
4 - 6 x 800m (with 3:00-5:00 minute rest in cross country and 400m jog on track).	Anaerobic development, pace and tempo development faster than pace.
Hill repeats on up hill from 100 to 400m long, 6-10 repeats with jog downhill. This workout should be done on a set course and timed. This will give an idea of quality of the workout. Also athletes should be put in groups.	Anaerobic, muscle strength, hill running technique.
Downhill repeats from 200 to 300m, 6 to 8 repeats. The downhill should be less than 3 percent. Steeper incline can cause injury. This workout is usually part of another workout that finishes with it.	This is to develop leg turn over speed, quickness, and strength.
1 mile x 4 up hill or over cross country course in the fall. Take 3 to 5 min jog for recovery between each run. When condition is at peak toward the end of the season, the recovery jog will be 3 min.	This is done the last four weeks of the season. Same purposes as for 1.6 mile. Mentally stimulating.
5-7 miles at easy pace over cross country course with 6 x 600 at race tempo.	The purpose of the training is to change up pace off a fairly good tempo. The 300's down a very slight hill assists with leg turn over tempo. Builds strength in legs and hips without fear in injury. Mentally refreshing workout.
Fartlek - each type of Fartlek should be conducted on a designated route with controls on each run, or jog. Set up a course where runs are 200 to 400m with one longer run of 800m in each 2 miles. Grass areas are better than road or hard top areas.	**"Speed play"** as it was originally designed by the Swedes. Anaerobic development.
European Fartlek are runs 20 to 30 min in length on grass areas. Run surges of 440 yds, 4 to 6	This makes a change of pace pickup.
times during run. This workout can be done on the track on occasion with 15:00 minute or 5000m runs.	
Hole to tee runs at golf course with a jog from tee to hole. Runs should be pace of race or faster. Distances vary and recovery jogs vary.	
Circuits over a 1 1/2 to 2 mile course with bounding, striding, hopping, and sprinting with calesthenics.	Overall conditioning, general physical hardness, strength, endurance.
6-10 mile runs with 3/4, 1, 2, 3 mile pickups in the middle of the run off 7:00-8:00 pace. These are moderate or semi-hard runs.	Change of pace.
Measure mile (usually on a track) at 3/4 to 7/8 effort or race pace. Continue on off track at 8:00 min mile pace to 2 1/2 mile mark on routine. Run a 3/4 mile (measured) at 3/4 to 7/8 of race pace. The run continues at 8:00 min mile pace back to the track or original area, run another 3/4 mile at same pace as or faster than the first mile.	Change of pace on hard runs. Confidence run. Mental toughness builder.
Race or time trial - these may be used and are, in fact, for training and development.	This is to measure the **total** runner - physical, mental, social, etc.
Repeat 1, 1 1/2, 2, up to 5 miles on cross country course. These have been done 3/4, 1/2, and 1/4 effort in descending order with 5 minutes recovery jog between. This is a late season workout in cross country.	Teaches pace, builds **physical** and **mental toughness.**
4-6 x 600 (880) on track.	This workout enables the runner to change from the "400" concept by extending the run to 600. Pace and tempo development. The final 600 is run at maximum effort.
6-10 x 200m with slow walk recovery.	This is speed and mechanics training.
Repeat 150's off turn.	This work is designed to develop sprint mechanics and is essential to all runners. It appears the "body" forgets sprint action unless it is practiced.
3-4 miles on cross country course at 7/8 to 3/4 effort followed by a mile jog repeated by a 2 mile at 1/2 effort.	This late season workout, is highly aerobic, competitive, and affords an opportunity to get the steady driving pace needed for meet competition over racing terrains.
Long runs of 6 to 10 miles on roads and trails. These runs are usually done on Sunday a.m. and are used more frequently in the winter and spring than hill areas.	Aerobic training - recovery.

Part C
The Throws

13
Fundamental Mechanics of Throwing

by
Tom Ecker
Cedar Rapids, Iowa Public Schools

The throwing events can be divided into two general categories—the nonaerodynamic events (the shot put and hammer throw) and the aerodynamic events (the discus throw and javelin throw).

In the nonaerodynamic events, there are only three factors that determine how far the implement will go—the speed of the implement at the moment of release, the angle of release, and the height of release. In the aerodynamic events, however, besides the speed, angle and height of release, there is one other important factor—the effect air resistance has on the implement as it travels through the air.

In each of the four throwing events, the athlete begins by imparting horizontal force to the throwing implement—toward the direction of throw in the shot and javelin, around the body's vertical axis (which allows for some simultaneous vertical force during the turning) in the discus and hammer (Figure 1). Then, just before releasing, a nearly vertical force is added. It is a great lifting force in the shot and hammer, but less in the discus and javelin, where release angles are not so high (Figure 2). The summed effect of all the horizontal and vertical forces exerted on each implement determines its angle of release and its exact speed of release.

The force exerted is dependent to a large extent upon the thrower's mass and the length of his levers. Since the reaction at the moment of release will cause less relative backward movement in his upper body, a heavier athlete can exert more effective force over a greater distance than can a lighter athlete. It is obvious, then, that in the throwing events the heavier the thrower, the more advantage he has, if all other factors are equal.

It is essential that the various body forces contributing to the throw be exerted in the proper order—timed to build on previous forces—in order to provide the greatest possible speed at release. As the implement increases in speed before its release, the parts of the body in a position to contribute must be able to move faster than the implement is already moving, if there is to be continued acceleration. This requires the larger, slower muscle groups of the athlete's body to be brought into play first, followed by the smaller, faster groups as the implement approaches maximum speed prior to release.

Speed of Release

In all throwing events, speed of release is the most important factor. In fact, a small percentage increase in release speed will always bring about a greater percentage increase in distance, if all of the other factors remain constant. For example, a 10 percent increase in speed of release in shot putting and discus throwing produces an increase of as much as 21 percent in distance.

While the athlete must continually attempt to increase the implement's speed at release (in order to obtain an increase in the distance thrown), he must avoid increas-

Figure 1.

Figure 2.

ing one velocity component (horizontal or vertical) without also increasing the other. Otherwise, the angle of release is likely to be too high or too low and the distance of the throw will be reduced, even though the release velocity has been increased.

Ground Reactions

The forces that can be applied to the implement—both vertical and horizontal—require resistance from firm ground; as the athlete thrusts against the implement, he receives a counter-thrust from the ground beneath him. This is called ground reaction and is an important part of Newton's third law of motion. "To every action there is an equal and opposite reaction; or the mutual actions of two bodies in contact are always equal and opposite in direction." Without the resistance from the ground, the powerful actions of the thrower would bring about equal and opposite reactions within his body and the implement would not travel very far.

A 160-pound (73 kg.) person sitting on the ground exerts 160 pounds of force against the ground and the ground pushes back with 160 pounds of force. However, if the 160-pound person decided to jump to his feet, he would have to push against the ground with a force greater than his body weight and the ground would "react" with an equal force, allowing him to lift his body into an erect position.

If the 160-pounder in a standing position suddenly pushed against the ground with a force of 260 pounds (118 kg.), the ground would push back with an equal force of 260 pounds and the person would have 100 pounds (45 kg.) of lift—either to lift himself off the ground (as in the jumping events) or to help him lift something away from the ground (as in the throwing events).

From this, two important points become apparent: (1) The forces that contribute to the acceleration of a throwing implement can be initiated much more effectively while the thrower is in contact with the ground, but not nearly so effectively while he is in the air. (2) The greater the forces applied against the ground, the greater the results in forces against the implement.

Angle of Release

No matter which of the throwing events is being considered, there is a particular optimum throwing angle for every attempt, no matter what ability the individual thrower happens to possess. However, it is not necessarily the same angle for each thrower in an event, or even the same angle for an individual athlete's different attempts in the same competition.

The optimum angle for the projection of a missile is 45 degrees—if the point of landing is at the same level as the height of release. However, since all of the throwing implements are released above ground level, the optimum angle of release must necessarily be less than 45 degrees. How much less depends upon the height of release, the speed of release and, in discus and javelin throwing, on the aerodynamic properties of the implement.

In the shot put, the optimum release angle is between 40 and 42 degrees for good throwers. The angle can be plotted by bisecting the angle formed by a line drawn from the shot at release to the eventual landing point, and a vertical line drawn through the shot at release (Figure 3). Obviously, the greater the velocity of the shot at release, the higher the release angle must be.

In the shot put, the optimum release angle is between 40 and 42 degrees.

Distance of Put in Feet	Optimum Release Angle
25	37° 10'
30	38° 25'
35	39° 20'
40	40° 00'
45	40° 35'
50	41° 00'
55	41° 25'
60	41° 40'
65	41° 55'
70	42° 10'
75	42° 20'

Figure 3. Optimum release angles.

Because of the effects of air resistance, the opposite is true in discus and javelin throwing. The greater the speed of release, the lower the optimum angle of release. Optimum angles range from 35 to 40 degrees in the discus throw and javelin throw.

In the hammer throw, because the hammer nearly touches the ground on its way to being released, the optimum release angle is only slightly below 45 degrees, no matter what the hammer thrower's ability.

A thrower who wants to raise his angle of release must do so by increasing the vertical velocity of the implement before releasing it. (He could also do it by decreasing the horizontal velocity, but the implement would not go as far.) A shot putter who wants to raise his angle of release during the arm strike, for example, is unable to make an appreciable change; his speed across the circle coupled with his speed of ''lifting'' the shot has already effectively determined the angle of release before his arm has a chance to make a contribution.

Flight Curves

Shots and hammers describe nearly perfect parabolic curves as they travel through the air; disci and javelins describe aerodynamic curves that would be parabolic were it not for the lift and drag effects of air resistance.

Parabolic curves. The moment a shot or hammer is released and is free in the air, the entire flight path of its center of gravity is determined. The speed and angle of the release and the force of gravity after the release cause the implement to follow a perfectly regular curve called a parabola, or parabolic curve.

As was mentioned earlier, release angles are determined by the combination of horizontal and vertical velocities. Once the implement is air-borne, the horizontal component is unaffected by outside forces (except some air resistance), but gravity gradually slows the vertical component to zero and then reverses the process, causing the implement to travel progressively faster and faster as it falls. The result is a parabolic curve. The length of the curve (the distance over the ground from release to landing) is determined by the horizontal component; the height of the curve is determined by the vertical component.

Aerodynamic curves. Because of the design of disci and javelins, air resistance causes them to follow flight curves that are not parabolic. As a discus or javelin sails through the air, the air flowing over the implement moves faster than the air flowing underneath, air pressure is diminished above the implement, and a lifting force is created which helps the implement to sail a greater distance than would have been possible without the aerodynamic design.

For the first portion of discus flight, the angle formed between the plane of the implement and the direction of the relative wind (the angle of attack) is a negative angle and there is no lift. This changes as gravity begins to slow the discus. The last half of the discus flight is marked by a positive angle of attack, and the discus experiences a pronounced lifting.

The javelin's angle of attack is positive throughout most of its flight. Even while descending point first, the javelin is inclined at an angle to the relative wind and is continuing to gain distance as it glides toward earth.

The Implements

Not only is it important for an athlete to attempt to learn the most advantageous throwing technique and to follow the most beneficial training program, it is also important for him to select the throwing implement that will provide the greatest possible distance.

Shots. Not much can be said about shots, or about the advantage one shot might have over another. The rules determine the weight and shape; only the size may vary.

There is a slight advantage in selecting a shot that is smaller in size. The international rules allow the 16-pound (7.3 kg.) shot to be as small as 4 3/8 inches (11.1 cm.) in diameter, 3/4 inch (0.2 cm.) smaller than the maximum allowed. NCAA rules allow it to be even smaller—4-7/64 inches (10.4 cm.) U.S. high school rules allow the 12-pound (5.4 kg.) shot to be as small as 3 7/8 inches (9.8 cm.) in diameter, also 3/4 inch smaller than the maximum size allowed.

Because it encounters less air resistance in flight, the smaller shot will travel slightly farther than the larger shot with the same effort. Recent research shows that a 62-foot (18.9 m.) effort with a 16-pound shot that is 4 3/8 inches in diameter will travel 2 3/8 inches (6.0 cm.) farther than one that is 5 1/8 inches (13.0 cm.) in diameter. This is not a great difference, of course, but keep in mind that the difference between the gold and silver medals in the 1972 Olympic Games was less than 1/2 inch (1 cm.)!

Surprisingly, there is also a slight aerodynamic advantage in selecting a shot with a rough surface. As the shot travels through the air, a low-pressure pocket forms behind the shot, creating drag and reducing velocity somewhat. Because of the effect the type of surface has on the air passing nearest the shot, the size of the low-pressure pocket behind the shot is reduced when a "rough" shot is used. Thus, drag is reduced and the shot travels farther. The difference is approximately 4

When a discus is thrown, the thrower applies both translational and rotational kinetic energy to the discus—translational energy the distance and rotational energy for the stabilizing spin.

3/4 inches (12.1 cm.) in a 62-foot effort.

Disci. The exact size, shape and weight of a discus is determined by the rule books, but the distribution of weight within the discus is not. Because of differences in the distribution of weight (which cannot be detected by calipers or scales), some disci can be thrown farther than others, even though released in exactly the same way.

Every discus has a certain amount of inertia, which is determined by the distribution of mass within the discus. If a great amount of mass is concentrated in the center of the discus, it has a low moment of inertia; if most of the mass is distributed around its outer edge, it has a high moment of inertia.

When a discus is thrown, the thrower applies both translational and rotational kinetic energy to the discus—translational energy for the distance and rotational energy for the stabilizing spin. Because a hollow discus with the weight distributed to the outside has a higher moment of inertia than a "solid" discus, its spin continues for a longer time while in the air, allowing it to stay level, gyroscopically. Since the hollow discus continues to spin in the air and does not "peel off" so soon, it sails farther before landing.

While there are obvious advantages in selecting a hollow discus for competition, there are equal disadvantages in selecting a molded rubber or plastic discus. Rubber or plastic disci may be less expensive, and they may be easier to grip than the metal-rimmed, wooden ones, but they will not travel nearly as far. The lead pellets that are molded into rubber and plastic disci settle to the center, which can provide nothing but disadvantage for competition. Molded disci have low moments of inertia, they cannot spin as well in the air, they peel off very rapidly, and they do not go as far.

Javelins. Javelins are aerodynamic implements designed to sail maximum distances according to the abilities of the particular throwers. As a thrower's ability increases, he must begin selecting javelins designed to stay in the air longer.

The aerodynamic principles governing javelin flight are very complicated and are not completely understood. However, it is easy to understand one of the aerodynamic factors contributing to the forward rotation of the javelin in the air—the relationship of the javelin's surface area to its center of gravity.

Since javelin's are released in a point-up position but most rotate into a point-down position before landing, the tail section (everything behind the javelin's center of gravity) must have a greater total surface area than the front section. The tail section "catches" the air and the javelin slowly tilts forward. Because it is traveling through the air point-first, wind resistance is minimal as the javelin leaves the thrower's hand. But as the javelin begins to slow and more air catches its tail section, the javelin rotates forward around its center of gravity.

The greater the distance thrown, the slower the forward rotation in the air must be. Obviously, the javelin that is going to be thrown 250 feet (76.2 m.) must be designed so that it turns over in the air more slowly than the javelin that will be thrown only 150 feet (45.7 m.). Thus, the amount of surface area on the tail of the javelin (the part that catches the air) must be proportionately less if the javelin thrower's ability is greater in order to get the longest possible throw.

This is where javelin design and javelin selection become important. The thrower must select the javelin that will turn over just enough during the time it is in the air so that it lands almost flat, but with the point hitting first.

Hammers. The maximum and minimum dimensions for hammers, as designated in the rule books, allow for two different ways to gain valuable distance.

The formula for determining release velocity in hammer throwing is $v = wr$ (Release Velocity = Turning Speed x Effective Radius of Turning). Thus, even if the thrower does not increase his turning speed, his release velocity will be increased if he is able to increase the effective radius of turning. At a turning speed of 2 revolutions per second, an increase of 1½ inches (3.8 cm.) in effective radius is worth approximately 7 feet (2.13 m.) of increased distance in the throw. At 2.3 revolutions per second, the increase is close to 10 feet (3.0 m.).

International rules allow the hammer's maximum overall distance from the bottom surface of the head to the uppermost surface of the grip to be 3 feet 11¾ inches (121.5 cm.)—1½ inches (3.8 cm.) longer than the minimum length allowed. NCAA rules allow the distance to be even longer—4 feet 1/64 inches (122.0 cm.) or 1 19/32 inches (4.0 cm.) longer than the minimum.

The size of the head may be as small as 4 inches (10.2 cm.) in diameter by international rules, ¾ inches smaller than the maximum allowed. Also, the rules allow the head's center of gravity to be ¼ inch off-center, away from the handle. Therefore, the distance from the handle to the head's center of gravity may be as much as 3 feet 10 inches (117.9 cm.) (with maximum length, minimum head size, and the head's center of gravity off-center by ¼ inch), or as little as 3 feet 7 7/8 inches (111.4 cm.)

To insure maximum performance by providing the longest possible effective radius of turning, it is obvious that the thrower should select the hammer with the greatest possible distance between the handle and the head's center of gravity.

14
The Shot Put

by
Phil Delavan—University of Texas
Tom Pagani—Stanford University
Tom Tellez—University of Houston

Introduction

The shot put is the simplest of all the throws. It is basically a linear action confined to a small area. There are no aerodynamic factors involved.

The modern technique of throwing is relatively new, being invented by Perry O'Brien in the early 1950's. Technical aspects of the throw have been constantly refined and perfected.

The primary prerequisites for success in shot putting are speed, agility, coordination, explosive strength, and size. Too often the emphasis is placed on size in the selection of talent, to the exclusion of the other factors. Physical size is only one factor and should be evaluated as such. The following chapter discusses the basic technique of the throw and the fundamentals of a training program, encompassing both weight training and technique training.

Technique

The Grip

The shot should be held high on the fingers (while still maintaining control). The higher it is held, the better and quicker the release the athlete will have. The shot may be held in the palm of the hand and rolled up onto the fingers before or at release. This is a very precarious grip, but is used successfully by many athletes.

The number of fingers that are put behind the shot put is a matter of personal preference. There may be three or four. If it is three, the little finger is usually curled down and used as a guide to stablilize the shot. In any case, the thumb will determine how high the shot is held on the fingers by how it is placed below the shot. The thumb plays very little part in the grip if the shot is rolled upon the fingers. In either case, let the athlete determine the most comfortable and effective grip for him/her.

Position of the Shot on the Neck

To get the correct positioning of the shot put on the neck, look at the release of the shot as it is delivered. The shot is delivered with the thumb down. Too many times, the shot put is placed against the neck with the palm in towards the neck and elbow dropped near the torso. The athlete has to apply pressure against the neck to hold the shot in.

Position at the Rear of the Ring

The position at the back of the ring is the most important part of the throw because if anything is out of alignment at this point, it will have an adverse effect on the distance of the throw. The center of mass must be located over the ball of the supporting foot, the shoulders hunched and the back rounded. The torso should be parallel to the ground. The knees are bent at approximately 120° angles. At no time should the free leg ever be brought forward so that the knee swings in front of the knee of the supporting leg. The angles of both knees should be approximately the same—120°.

The Glide

The glide is initiated by a slight settling or unseating of the hips toward the front of the circle. At this point, the right leg and the left leg should be driven simultaneously. The supporting leg should drive in an upward fashion while the free leg should drive toward the toe board. The angles of both legs should increase simultaneously.

By driving the supporting leg up and the free leg forward, the athlete will initiate the angle of the throw. This will be approximately 39 to 42°. If one were to trace the path of the shot at it goes through the putting motion, it would create a slight S and would be delivered at this angle of 39 to 42°. (Fig. 1) The hips will rise faster than the shot. They will also flatten at the center of the ring and almost appear to settle slightly as the athlete reaches the power position. It is very important that the supporting foot, when it drives up, also rotates so that when landing in the center of the circle, the foot placement is at 90° to the toeboard. Force can only be applied in the shot put when the athlete is on the ground. The rotational force of the supporting foot must be made while the foot is in contact with the ground. The free leg should be driven as close to the surface of the ring as possible. If the free leg has a tendency to get too high, there is a delay in its plant at the front of the ring. The supporting foot should not drag across the ring, but be in the air and planted at a 90° angle. If the supporting foot does drag, this indicates that there has not been enough force in its upward movement and there has been a premature unseating of the hips.

Position in the Center of the Ring

The supporting foot should be at 90° and the free leg placed slightly in the bucket (a toe-heel relationship). The right (supporting) foot should contact at least the center of the ring for most athletes and should continue to rotate forward. The knee of the supporting leg will rotate forward as the foot continues to rotate. The right hip rotates forward so the belt buckle points in the direction of the put.

In the power position at the center, the right leg should be at 120°, the left leg still extended and only slightly bent. As the rotational force of the right foot and hip take place, the center of mass is moved forward towards the left leg—at the front of the toe board. As

this center of mass is moved forward, the free left leg will move to an angle of approximately 120°.

At this point it is important to consider the action of the free arm. At the rear of the circle, the free arm should hang loose and relaxed in a vertical position. As the glide is made to the center of the ring, the free arm and shoulder open slightly as a natural reaction. The shoulder and arm holding the shot, however, must stay back, such that if the shot put were dropped, it would hit outside of the supporting foot at the center of the circle.

The Put

The action initiated by the forward rotation of the supporting foot creates an upwards explosion. As this is all taking place, the free arm, which is hanging relaxed and loose, opens and straightens in a manner so that it becomes parallel to the shoulders.

At this time, the weight moves more onto the front foot. As the front leg straightens, the elbow of the free arm is bent, shortening the radius of the free arm. As the front leg is extended in an upward motion, the rotation of the free arm is stopped. This causes a blocking of the left hip and a transfer of power to the right side of the body. There is actually a change of the rotational force of the body from around the center of mass as the shot putter begins to put at the center of the ring to the left hip and shoulder as he/she posts the left side in the putting action.

As the radius of the free arm is shortened, it has a tendency to lock the chest out. The shot will actually pull away from the neck to the point of the putting shoulder. As the transfer of power takes place, the shot is accelerated very quickly. The supporting arm merely tries to keep up with the shot and at this time accelerates in a slapping or putting action to give the burst of speed to the shot as it leaves the hand. The shot leaves the hand with the thumb in a down position. There is a tremendous amount of finger and wrist snap at the end giving the shot the final acceleration.

The Follow Through

The follow through is nothing more than a natural following of the supporting arm across the body after the shot is released. Because of the rotational force of the body, the feet have a tendency to switch positions, the supporting foot going to the front of the ring, the free foot back towards the center. When the athlete lands on the front foot, if there is a tendency to foul, the putting arm should continue to be driven under and the back leg thrown towards the left sector line.

Timing is of the utmost importance. The coach of a shot-putter must particularly watch the athlete at the starting position. The slightest unseating will result in an imbalance, causing the athlete to have a poor put.

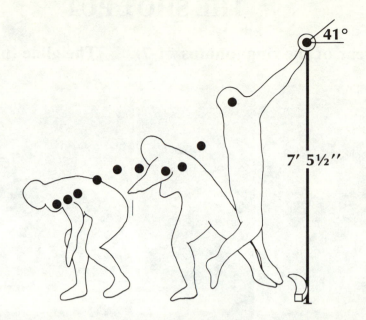

DIAGRAM 1. PATH OF SHOT: SIDE VIEW

Figure 1. Path of shot—(above) side view; (below) top view.

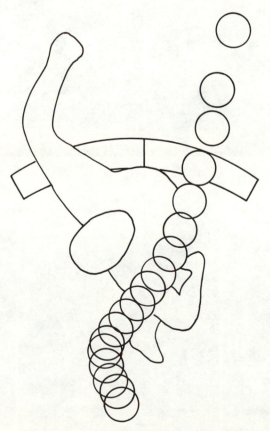

DIAGRAM 2. PATH OF SHOT: TOP VIEW

THE SHOT PUT

Position at the rear of the ring (photos #1-7).   The glide (photos #8-13).

#1   #2   #3   #4   #5

#6   #7   #8   #9   #10

#11   #12   #13

The position in the center of the ring; the put; and the follow through (photos #14-22).

#14   #15   #16   #17

#18   #19   #20   #21   #22

Training Objectives

The coach should concentrate on the athletes' weaknesses. If the athlete is overweight, more running should be included in the program. If the athlete needs quickness, then short, quick sprints and accelerations should be used. Every shot putter should be encouraged to do short quick bursts of speed such as 40 meter sprints, 60 and 80 meter build-ups and starts from the blocks.

Training emphasis should be on developing proper technique. This can be done through drills, controlled throwing, films, film loops, still pictures, and video. This does not mean that the coach should copy a particular technique, but strive to develop the basic fundamentals talked about previously in this chapter.

Structure of a Training Program

A. Drills

1. Conditioning	Purpose
• Throwing heavy shot (4 lbs over competition weight over a 10′ bar from the power position.	To aid the athlete in learning upward leg explosion
• Foot-twists-back and forth perpendicular to a line.	To aid in the ability to turn foot parallel to centerline in the power position
• Heel-toe-inside-outside foot walking	To aid in the development of lower leg muscles
• Back hops on one leg.	To aid in the development of the muscles involved in pulling the supporting leg under the body
• Back hops with a crossbar across shoulders.	To aid in learning control of shoulder position during the glide
• Start glide on a low box and throw.	To aid in the development of "stretch reflex of the supporting leg."
• Overhead throws over the back.	To aid in the conditioning of the back and legs.

	Also used to develop the idea of the summation of forces: the back and legs are used before the arm.
Backward standing long jump	To aid in the development of "explosiveness" in the muscles used to start the throw
Throwing without using the arm holding shot, executed from the power position	To aid in learning to throw with legs first and then the upper body

2. Crossing the Circle	Purpose
• Towel drill-for right foot. Towel placed 3″ behind the foot at the rear of the circle.	To aid in the ability to get the right foot "under"
• Towel drill-for left foot. Towel placed just outside where foot should land at the toeboard.	To aid in correcting the thrower who steps "in the bucket"
• Rope-for left arm. Thrower holds rope in left hand with partner holding other end of the rope.	To aid in learning to keep the shoulders closed
• Glide-down a slot. Small pieces of wood are placed beside the supporting foot to guide the foot straight across the circle.	To aid in learning foot alignment in the glide
• Signal drill. Athlete glides from the back to the power position in the center of the circle, stops, notes correction, then throws on verbal command from the coach.	To aid in correcting position in center of the circle
• Letter "A" drill. Thrower drops from the back of the circle, extending both legs.	To aid in learning extension of both legs during the glide

- High jump cross-bar-glide. Cross-bar placed over the circle one foot over shoulder height. Athlete must glide under the bar.

  To aid in learning to keep the back low during the glide

- Walk in turn throw. Thrower steps into the ring from the rear, turns and throws.

  To aid in learning the turn as a possible new technique

3. Throw

- High jump cross-bar throw. With full glide, normal weight shot is

  Purpose
  To aid learning to lead with the hip and throw off the back foot

thrown over a high jump bar.

- Illustrate "long drive". Teaching Progression

  a) Athlete places feet against toe-board with upper body torqued.
  b) Right foot is dropped back.
  c) Athlete pushes from that position.

  To aid in demonstrating the need to push over as long a distance as possible

The proper positioning of the shot against the neck requires that the athlete applies pressure against neck to hold the shot in.

B. Strength Training

The lifts that are essential for shot putting are as follows:

1. Push or Power press from military position
2. Incline press from 45°
3. Bench press
4. Squat (in power rack and bottom pinned for safety)
5. Power clean

Alternate exercises should include all of the Olympic lifts. The following is a yearly strength program using these lifts:

July

1. Two to three week rest after last meet.
2. Last week or two of July should be broad base work.
3. Lift 3 days a week.
4. 6 to 10 reps working on 60 to 65% of max in each lift.
5. Work correct technique.
6. Do a lot of pulling movements.

August

1. A continuation of the broad base work.
2. Lift 3 days a week.
3. Continuation of technique work in each lift.
4. Lifts should still be high reps at about 70 to 75% max.

September-October

1. Lift 4 days a week.
2. Continue technique work, resting from heavy lifts.
3. No max lifting.

November

1. Test max early
2. Lift 4 days a week.
3. Work heavier base work.
4. 4 to 6 repetitions.

December

1. Drop repetitions severely
2. Length of workout decreases.
3. Intensity and quality of lifts up.
4. First day of work week is base work.
5. Lift 3 days a week.
6. Pyramid workouts. Examples:
   a. 1 set of 5 at 70%
      increase 10 lbs and do 4 reps
      increase 10 lbs and do 3 reps
      increase 10 lbs and do 2 reps
      increase 10 lbs and do 2 reps
      until the athlete cannot hit a double
   b. 5 sets of 5 at 75%
      5 sets of 3 at 85%
      5 sets of 2 at 90 to 95%

January

1. First week same as December.
2. Sample workouts 2 weeks before first meet:
   a. Monday—5 sets of 5 first day
   b. Wednesday—set work
      1 set of 5   75%
      1 set of 3   85%
      2 sets of 1   90 to 95%
   c. Week of competition—
      1. Monday—5 sets of 5 at 75%
      2. Wednesday—5 sets of 3
                    5 sets of 2
                    5 sets of 2
      3. Friday—warmup sets in reps of 8-6-4, work few reps, heavy load in sets of 4-3-2, doubles or 3, 2, 1 + 1

February or through the Indoor Season

1. Keep up base work on Mondays.
2. Other two days, fewer repetitions and more quality lifts.
3. There should be no max lifting in this period of time.
4. Test after the indoor season for maximum lifts.

March

1. Back to base work and technique.
2. Lift lighter weights—75% of new max.
3. One day a week do heavy triples and doubles.

April through Regular Outdoor Season

1. Same as January.
2. Lifts will be heavier because of new max.
3. Any large meets (2 days heavy lifting). Examples:
   a. Day base
   b. One day of quality work

From the Conference Meet through June and Nationals

1. Spend time on finer points of technique in the competitive event.
2. Split routine:
   a. Monday—pulls
   b. Wednesday—presses and squats
3. The athlete should lift as he/she feels, keeping the level of intensity up and cutting back to two days a week.

Keep in mind there is nothing marginal about any weight program. The athlete has to be conscientious, dedicated and have the proper diet to make it work.

C. Technique Training

1. **Off Season:** To correspond this with the weight training program, the athlete should take July

and August and do a minimal amount of throwing, relax, and enjoy other activities. A conditioning maintenance program is important here and should include some running. September, October, and November should be a time that is spent working on technique and any major technical changes. At least 2 to 3 days a week should be spent on drills and easy ring work.

2. **Early Competitive Season:** December, January, and February should be spent on intensified technique work. Workouts should be held 4 to 5 days a week. The number of throws a day will depend upon the athlete. It does little good to continue putting in a practice session when the form begins to fall apart.

3. **Mid Season:** March and April should be spent with fewer throws a day in practice, but the intensity of the throws should be higher. Work on the finer points of technique.

4. **Late Season:** This is a time when the number of throws are reduced. Throwing in practice should be reduced to 2 or 3 days a week and the volume of throws reduced considerably. Work should be on the finer points of the technique.

The lighter work load should result in a sharp feeling. This is not the time in the season to make any changes in technique.

D. Flexibility

If an athlete is extremely tight, a flexibility program should be used to enable the athlete to perform the basic putting technique. A general stretching program should be used as a part of the regular warmup to prevent injuries.

E. Endurance Work

The only place running endurance should concern a coach is if the athlete is overweight. If this is the problem, overdistance running should be a part of a reducing program.

Endurance from the standpoint of putting is to insure that the best put comes within the official six throws. The practice program should also be strenuous enough to insure enough endurance to take an athlete through a qualification round, preliminary round the finals.

Endurance from the standpoint of putting is to insure that the best put comes within the first six throws.

To be a good performer, a discus thrower must aspire to throw between 5 and 10,000 throws over an eleven month time period.

15
The Discus

by
Dr. Paul Ward

I.   INTRODUCTION

This discussion of discus throwing has as its objective the promotion of understanding the application of discus technique and throwing on a superficial level. Therefore, the coach and the beginning discus aspirant will benefit from its step-by-step progression. Male or female coaches or throwers will benefit equally from this information. The training and technical applications are exactly the same for both sexes. The advanced coaches and throwers will benefit from many of these ideas also.

The critical variable from a technical viewpoint is the number of throws performed. To be a good performer, one must aspire to throw between 5 and 10 thousand throws over an eleven month time period. The increase in strength and size through scientific functional weight training programs dominates the objectives for physiological training.

When talking about discus technique, think of the circle as being a giant clock. The back of the circle is at 12 o'clock and the front at 6 o'clock (See Figure 1).

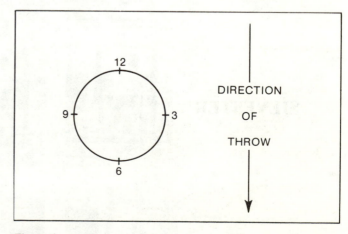

Figure 1.

	#1 Starting Position	#2 Transition	#3 Turn	#4 Drive Foot Landing	#5 Power Position
WILKINS					
SILVESTER					
POWELL					

	#6 Start of Leg Hip Drive	#7 Free Side Block	#8 Release	#9 Reverse
WILKINS				
SILVESTER				
POWELL				

II. GENERAL DESCRIPTION OF DISCUS TECHNIQUE

The sequence photos shown on the opposite page contain 9 basic positions in discus throwing.

They are:

(1) Starting Position
(2) Transition
(3) Turn
(4) Drive Foot Landing
(5) Power Position
(6) Leg and Hip Drive
(7) Free Side Block
(8) Release
(9) Reverse

The discus thrower must not segment his/her thinking into positions although for discussion and understanding, it is helpful to isolate key positions. It is important that the thrower pass through these positions with conformity to good mechanics. Three ex-world record holders from the United States are shown; Wilkins, Silvester and Powell.

The maximum distance a discus will travel is dependent upon the release speed (velocity), and the optimal release conditions, the latter being influenced mainly by aerodynamic factors. The discus turn and delivery is a combination of rotational and linear forces properly integrated, the most important being the rotational.

The discus thrower rotates through 1¾ turns (approximately 630°) and while rotating the total system moves linearly only 8′ 2½″ at the most. If the complete throw takes 1.34 seconds, then the linear velocity of the total system is 6.13 feet per second (8.21 ft. ÷ 1.34 sec. = 6.13 fps). The release velocity of good discus throwers is somewhere between 80 fps and 85 fps. Thus, the linear velocity accounts for only 7% to 8% of the release velocity. This translates into 15.5 to 17.7 feet in a 221.4 foot throw. The predominate forces then are those which relate to the turning and delivery action of the discus which are primarily rotational in nature. (These figures have been taken from a research report presented by Juris Tarrauds at the Annual Detroit News Clinic, NCAA Indoor Track & Field Championships, Cobo Hall, March 10, 1977. "Computerized Biomechanical Cinematography Analysis of Discus Throwing At the Montreal Olympics".)

The following is a general description of the technique of discus throwing.

A. **THE INITIAL STANCE AND PRELIMINARY SWING** (Sequence Picture: Frame #1)

From the rear of the circle the thrower executes not more than two preliminary swings using the entire body-not the arm alone. These movements set the rhythm for the throw and prepares the body for movement across the circle. A longer backswing is generally preferred for beginners. Most of the weight starts on what will be the free swing leg.

B. **THE TRANSITION** (Sequence Picture: Frame #2)

To start the turn, the thrower unseats slightly to the rear oblique while transferring and lowering considerable weight to the pivoting foot. The pivoting foot turns between 90° and 120° (pointed at 8 or 9 o'clock) in the direction of the throw. The driving foot should not linger on the ground, but its movement must be properly timed and activated as the weight is shifted to the pivoting foot. A delay in its activation precipitates a falling out of the back of the circle which usually puts the thrower in the bucket in a poor power (throwing) position. It is extremely important to transfer most of the body weight on the pivot foot with the body rotating in an erect position.

C. **THE TURN** (Sequence Picture: Frame #2, #3, #4, and #5)

The turn is initiated by using the free arm and pivot leg, unseating slightly and lowering the center of gravity. Additional rotational forces are then produced by the swing (free) leg. The movement of the swinging drive leg serves to produce most of the rotational force by its wide high sweep and subsequent movement to the middle and down toward the center of the circle, while the discus is held far back. This is where most of the torque is developed in the throw. The action of the pivot leg is a jump-turn, and the pivot foot is almost pulled forcefully off the rear of the circle by the highly active and properly directed swing leg drive.

The swing leg races ahead of the erect upper body producing a torqued position. The drive foot lands somewhere between 12 and 3 o'clock. The weight remains on the toe of the drive foot while the entire lower extremities of the driving side rotate in the direction of the throw. The discus is held far back while the free arm is extended at the elbow and is beginning its horizontal swing backward initiating the delivery of the discus. The free (front) foot must land as soon after the swing (driving) foot as possible with the body weight well over the rear leg. If the front foot is allowed to float the torque is rapidly dissipated.

The free foot must be positioned no more than six inches from the center line while the drive foot should be positioned approximately in the center of the circle. The center of gravity is lowered slightly while the legs compress in preparation for the delivery action. The discus is still well back while the legs and hips are leading into the throw.

D. **THE DELIVERY** (Sequence Picture: Frames #5, #6, #7, and #8)

The main source of power throughout the delivery comes from the legs, hips and entire body, not the throwing arm. The hips, legs and feet continue to race ahead of the discus. The action of the hips is around and up while the plane

119

of the discus is becoming more horizontal. As the side of the body opposite the discus blocks, especially the front foot, leg and free arm, the discus swings out in a wide arc to maximize the radius of rotation producing great linear velocity of the discus. The chest is up and square with the hips which are facing forward, but the discus still trails slightly behind the shoulders. At this time, the thrower is up on the balls of the feet. At release, the front foot should be in contact with the ground.

E. **THE REVERSE** (Sequence Picture: Frame 9)

The reverse should be a natural consequence of proper technique. Generally, it should not be taught. It is the result of maximizing the lifting and rotating forces along with the whipping action of the discus arm. These must be so great that it makes a reverse necessary to check momentum and prevent fouling.

III.TRAINING OBJECTIVES AND TEACHING PROGRESSIONS

There are two major training objectives for discus throwers:

1. The development of strength and size.
2. The mastery of technique.

Other factors are involved in discus throwing (See Figure 2 factors of discus throwing.)

The development of strength and size is produced by application of a scientific functional weight training program. Some guidelines will be presented later in this discussion.

In the following section, the specifics of technique are presented along with some teaching progressions and drills. Some collateral exercises and training

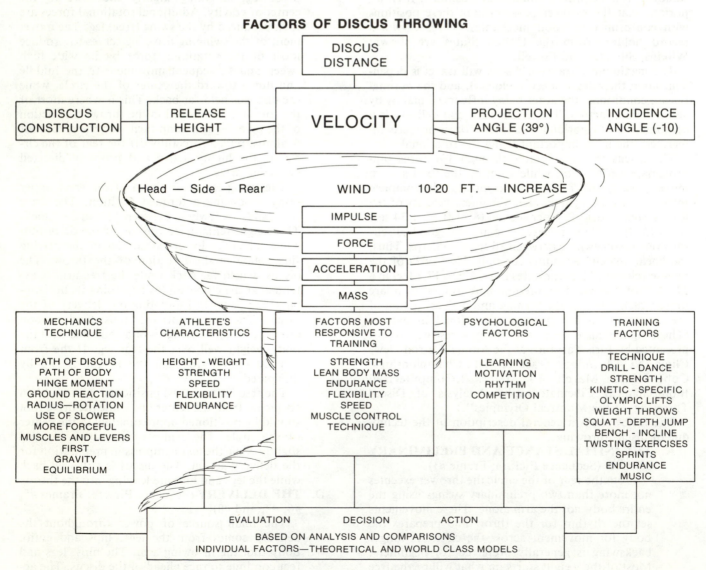

FACTORS OF DISCUS THROWING

Figure 2.

devices, along with a list of common form faults and corrections, are also presented.

Discus Technique and Teaching Progressions

It is of prime importance that basic fundamentals are learned correctly from the start. Advanced technique cannot be built upon a weak foundation of throwing fundamentals. Therefore, a great amount of time should be spent in drills teaching good delivery technique and proper turning mechanics.

I. The Grip and Release

A. Explanation

Each individual's grip will vary slightly in accordance with the size of the hand. The discus is held so that its circumference rests on the last joints of the fingers, the fingers are spread, and the thumb is on top for control. When the discus is released, it rotates clockwise out of the hand (for right handed throwers) and exits the hand via the index finger. It is important to develop a good release, one that imparts a smooth spin on the discus. A good smooth spin stabilizes the discus in flight. Figure 3 shows two styles of discus handholds.

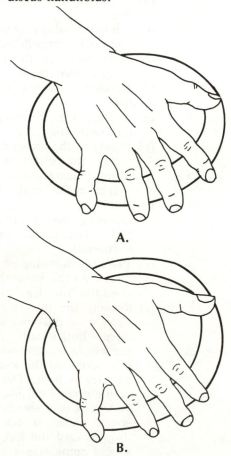

A.

B.

FIGURE 3. Two styles of discus handholds.

B. Drills

(1) **GRIP**

Purpose: This exercise teaches the proper method of gripping the discus.

Action:

(a) Place the discus on the palm of the non-throwing hand, about chest height, with fingers spread.

(b) Place the throwing hand on top of the discus, fingers spread, with the tips of the four fingers lipping the discus.

(c) The wrist of the throwing hand should be straight and firmly down on the discus. Note: at this stage the joint and the thumb only lies on the discus surface.

(2) **RELEASE: (BOWL THE DISCUS)**

Purpose: This drill is designed to teach proper technique in releasing the discus.

Action:

(a) Assume a stride stance.

(b) Place discus in hand with arm at the side, the palm facing the leg, and the discus between leg and palm.

(c) Maintain arm in a completely straight position.

(d) Swing the arm like a pendulum backward. On the forward swing bend at the waist and knees and attempt to roll the discus like a bowling ball. (Discus should roll off the index finger.)

Comments:

(a) Keep arm straight.

(b) Do not allow throwing wrist to cock (flex). It should remain straight.

(c) Squeeze the discus out of the hand, the little finger applying force first, following with each succeeding finger in turn (like squeezing a bar of soap).

(3) **VERTICAL THROW INTO THE AIR**

Purpose: The objective of this drill is to teach proper technique in releasing the discus and spin control.

Action:

(a) Assume a stride stance, leg opposite discus forward.

(b) Place discus in hand with arm at the side, palm facing the leg, and the discus between leg and palm.

(c) Maintain arm in a completely straight position.

(d) Swing arm like a pendulum backward and then forward and upward. Just before the arm is positioned horizontally in front, start the squeezing action of the hand.

Comments:

(a) Throw the discus only a few feet overhead at first. As skill in handling improves, throw it higher.

(b) As more skill is developed, the knees and waist can be bent to generate more power for throwing.

(c) Keep arm and wrist absolutely straight.

(d) The discus should retain an an almost vertical position as it is released.

II. The Preliminary Swing and Throwing Position (Power Position) and Delivery

A. Introduction

The power position and preliminary swings are basically very simple. Restrict the prelimimnary swings to two and keep the movement simple.

A great deal of time should be devoted to this one aspect of the throw. For the beginner this is an extremely important phase of training. Advanced throwers will throw 90% of what they throw with the full turn from this power position.

B. Explanation

Note: For effective coaching and training the circle should be divided into quadrants. Ordinary blackboard is desirable for marking. A line bisecting the circle should be marked with a short line perpendicular to this line being marked at the middle of the circle. (See Figure 4). This device is an invaluable coaching aid at all skill levels.

(1) **THE STANCE.** (See Figure #5)

(a) Place rear foot in middle of ring at an angle of approximately 45° or less.

(b) The front foot should be comfortably spread in direction of throw (a little wider than shoulder's width).

(c) The front foot can range from being on the bisecting line to approximately 8 inches off the center line. The toe of the front foot should be in line with the heel of the rear foot.
(Heel/toe relationship)

(2) **DESCRIPTION OF THE PRELIMINARY SWINGS.**

The preliminary swings establish the rhythm of the throw. They should be free, continuous and smooth flowing. The discus should sweep through the widest orbit around the body and as far back as possible. If the swings are too fast and forceful, rhythm, balance and position are destroyed. The purposes of the preliminary swings are:

(a) Overcome the inertia of the discus.

(b) Get the missile as far behind the body as is controllable.

(c) Give the body the maximum range of movement.

(d) Develop some rhythm.

Action:

(a) Assume the throwing stance (power position).

(b) Rotate to the forward position facing the direction of the throw, placing most of the body weight on the front leg.

(c) Hold the discus in the non-throwing hand about chest high. The discus should be horizontal.

(d) Place the throwing hand on the discus. At this point the weight is on the front leg.

(e) Keeping the throwing arm as straight as possible, swing the discus horizontally rearward, the weight is transferred to the rear foot and the knee of the rear leg is bent. The trunk is semi-erect and the discus should be swung in a somewhat horizontal plane. It actually will drop toward the hip, but one should emphasize a horizontal swing holding the discus high. As the discus swings to the rear,

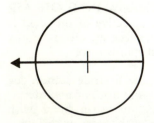

Figure #4

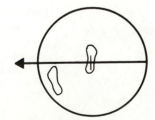

Figure #5

there is a tendency for beginners to let the discus slip out of the hand. This can be avoided in two ways:

1). A slight supination of the hand holding the discus at the end of the backswing.

2). Maintaining the movement of the discus arm in a cirular path.

(f) On the swing forward the discus should remain as far back as possible, while the weight is transferred from rear foot to front foot, and the hips and trunk rotate ahead of the discus. As rotation begins, the feet must rotate on the balls in order to allow the hips to rotate freely. When the hips and shoulders are facing the front, the discus arm is bent and swings across in front of the body at chest level. The non-throwing hand catches the discus in front at chest level in the position from which it started.

(g) This sequence is then repeated. **Limit preliminary swings to two.**

(3) DESCRIPTION OF THE DELIVERY

The objective of discus technique is to maximize release velocity. This is obtained by using the legs and hips to generate most of the force while the throwing arm acts as a sling. The action of the hip is forward, around and up while the throwing arm drags behind. The throwing arm should remain straight and sweep through the widest possible orbit. At the right time, the throwing arm is forcefully swung forward to deliver the discus.

In the learning stages it is advisable to teach the delivery from the power position without a reverse. Many beginners use a reverse and end up throwing with the arm, leaving out the all-important legs and hips.

Action:

(a) At the end of the second backswing, squat down over the rear leg with the waist bent forward slightly.

(b) Most of the weight of the body should be over the rear leg.

(c) The discus arm is held high and as far back as possible.

(d) The free arm should wrap around the front of the chest.

(e) The delivery starts with an extension of the elbow of the free arm and a horizontal swing backward of the free arm. It sweeps around, extended, until the hips are half way turned forward. At this time it shortens, putting a great stretch on the front of the chest. From this stretched position the muscles of the chest can act more forcefully.

(f) A split second after the free arm starts its movement, the legs and hips start their drive forward, upward and around, dragging the discus behind.

(g) When the hips and shoulders are facing forward, the front foot extends while the throwing arm strikes. It is at this point that the hip action begins to rise; however, the thrower must think predominately of an around-and-up action.

(h) As the arm strikes, the discus should be elevated to approximately shoulder level and should be flat.

(i) In the release, the discus should rotate off the index finger in a smooth spinning flight (clockwise for the right hand throwers).

C. Drills

(1) POWER POSITION ROTATION DRILL (HANDS ON HIPS)

Purpose: To learn the proper foot relationship, and foot and hip action. (The foot, leg, and hip action can be mastered in a few repetitions).

Position:

(a) Feet a little wider than shoulder's width, with hands on hips, and knees just slightly bent.

(b) Rear foot should be placed at the exact middle of the circle.

(c) All the weight should be on rear foot.

(d) Toe of front foot in line with heel of rear foot.

Action:

(a) Transfer weight from rear foot to front foot. As the weight is transferred, there is rotation on the balls of both feet.

(b) The hips and shoulders should rotate with the feet.

(2) POWER POSITION ROTATION DRILLS (simulating discus in hand)

Purpose: To learn the proper foot relationship, and foot and hip action. (The foot, leg and hip action can be mastered in a few repetitions).

Position: Same as in above (1) Power Position, except the rear knee is bent.

Action:

(a) Free arm active. It extends at the elbow and then is swung horizontally backward until it is almost pointing in the direction of the throw, at which time it shortens by bending at the elbow.

(b) All other action is the same as indicated in (1) Power Position.

Comments:

(a) The drill should emphasize postion and power.

(b) It is helpful for the coach to hold the throwing arm while the athlete executes the action.

(c) Another variation might be the coach holding the free arm while the athlete executes the action.

(d) Hold discus arm up and back.

(3) THROWING FROM THE POWER POSITION

Purpose: To learn how to deliver the discus from a good throwing position. The throwing action from this position is rather uncomplicated and allows the thrower to concentrate on small details.

Action:

(a) Assume the power stance.

(b) Execute two preliminary swings and then deliver the discus. The left arm extends at the elbow and begins its swing horizontally backwards before anything else moves. It is followed by the rotation and upward lifting of the hips and legs with the discus arm trailing. Then the left arm bends at the elbow and stops at the left side concurrently with the blocking of the entire free side, producing a slinging action of the discus arm.

(c) Do not reverse the feet in the early stages of learning.

Comments:

(a) The neophyte should spend 60% of his technique time throwing from the power position.

(b) At first, concentrate on smooth and continuous application of force and a smooth spinning release. This will result in a stable discus in flight.

(c) As skill is developed the intensity of the throw should be increased.

(d) Leg and hip action should be emphasized.

(4) ONE STEP AND THROW

Purpose: To allow throwing with added momentum and force.

Action: (description for right hand thrower)

(a) Stand facing the direction of throw near the back of the circle. (See Figure #6).

(b) Use one standard preliminary wind. As the discus swings to the rear, step forward with the right foot. The right foot should land at the center. (See Figure #6b).

(c) As soon as the right foot lands, rotate it clockwise, shifting the body weight onto it. Bring the left foot into the proper power position. (See Figure #6c).

(d) Deliver the discus, without reverse.

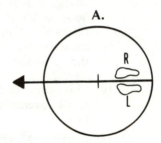

A.

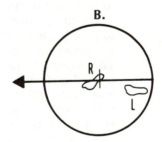

B.

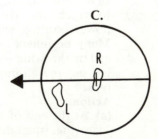

C.

Figure #6

III. Throwing with a Turn

A. Introduction

Discus technique requires the thrower to execute one and three-quarter turns. However, the beginner, should progress into this technique. The addition of the turn from the back of the circle contributes to the throw only when the thrower can achieve a good throwing position.

The predominant technique of the discus turn is called "running rotation." The technique of most of the top throwers is basically the same. The difference seems to be the swing of the driving leg and its timing from the back of the circle and the release. Wilkins and Schmidt use a wide sweeping action of the driving leg to generate more torque going to the center. Danek and Powell, on the other hand, arrive at the same basic power position but come from the back of the circle with a closer (narrower) bent driving knee. The delivery is around and up against a solidly planted front foot. Some throwers' delivery forces them to break contact with the ground before release, because of the great emphasis on the hip and leg action at the power position just before release.

B. The Footwork (For Right Hand Throwers)

The left foot should be on the center line, which—if extended—would bisect the foul lines. This permits the thrower to travel straight across the circle along the longest possible path to the release position. This foot position is preferred because it allows for application of force in a straight line and a longer distance in which to apply force. Beginners who straddle the center line frequently end up in the bucket, and consequently in a poor throwing position (See Figure #7, A and B).

C. Initial Stance and Preliminary Swings

The thrower should stand with back to direction of throw. A stance a little wider than shoulders width is desirable. The preliminary swings should be easy and uncomplicated and travel the longest path possible. The weight shifts back and forth from one foot to the other during the preliminary swings. The heel of the non-weight-bearing foot is allowed to come off the ground at the end of each swing. This enables the hips to complete rotation. During these swings the back should remain erect and shoulders level.

D. The Turn and Delivery (for right hand throwers)

At the end of the second backswing, the turn is initiated by settling (both knees bend), transferring the weight over the left leg, and unwinding. This transition should not be forced but should be easy and smooth flowing. **Simultaneously, the left arm should extend at the elbow and swing horizontally backward at chest level.** Head and eyes lead into the turn, but not vigorously. The discus arm is held back and at shoulder height. The left foot is turned counterclockwise as the weight is transferred to the left leg. This is not merely a passive transfer but involves a driving right leg. The right leg is removed from the ground as early as possible. The right leg's path, whether it is bent or straight, is around the left leg and then forcefully down and in toward the center line. It is important to remain in a semi-squat position over the left leg. Beginners frequently stand up and thus have difficulty making the jump-turn to the center of the circle. The correct action of the right leg (rear-driving leg) produces the necessary torque for the throw.

By executing a jump-turn off the left leg, the body is projected to the front of the circle into throwing position. The right foot should land first and immediately begin turning in a counter-clock-wise direction. This helps prevent a delay at the center. As the right foot lands, the right leg is bent. The left foot should land as soon after the right foot as possible. It should land in a heel/toe relationship with the rear foot. If it lands on the center line or to the right (facing the direction of the throw) it will block the hips. The front foot slightly in the bucket is a less serious error because it will not block the hips in delivery. From the power position the thrower should rotate on the balls of both feet.

The turn from the back of the circle must allow the thrower to land in an effective throwing position. The discus and shoulders should remain rotated clock-wise as far as possible while the hips move so that they are parallel to the direction of the throw. This con-

A. Correct Footwork   **B. Incorrect Footwork**

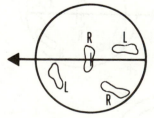
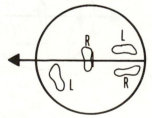

Figure #7

cept is known as "Crossing the X". From this point up to release, the action is the same as throwing from the power position only.

E. The Release and Reverse

As the rear foot hits the ground it immediately begins to rotate counter-clockwise. Before the front foot lands, the throwing action must continue with lead arm and driving hip and leg. This eliminates any possibility of a delay, which is common to many throwers. As soon as the front foot is planted, the right hip side should be vigorously rotated upward, counter-clockwise. Just prior to the completion of the hip and shoulder rotation, the throwing arm must strike with the discus release at shoulder height and relatively flat. The front foot and leg should provide a solid base against the ground. This will increase the radius for a longer power trasmission. If the hip rotation is correct, the reverse will follow naturally. **The reverse adds nothing to the throw and for beginners it is good to throw without a reverse.** The reverse will happen as a result of good technique.

F. Drills for Turning

(1) **BALANCE DRILL**

Purpose: To work on the balance and transference of weight in the transition phase.

Action:

(a) Without a discus, assume a position at back of circle, with pivot foot on the center line, feet spread a little wider than shoulder width.

(b) Start with one preliminary swing and execute a 360° turn back to starting position. Bend knees slightly and perform slowly, emphasizing balance and transference of weight over to the pivot leg. (See Figure#8).

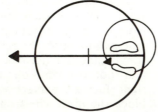

Figure #8

Comments:

(a) This drill can be utilized by all levels of throwers.

(b) It is best performed on a very slippery surface. Throw sand on the circle to facilitate the turning. (Remember to remove the sand when going on to other drills).

(c) This drill can be executed with a discus or without, as desired.

(2) **PHANTOM TURNS (HANDS ON HIPS) (RIGHT HAND THROWERS)**

Purpose: To master the technique of turning and arriving at a good throwing position. This drill can be used with beginners in a progressive manner to teach the turn.

Action:

(a) Assume the starting position dictated by the specific progression used. HANDS ON HIPS (See Figure #9, A, B, C).

(b) From a positon with weight on the left leg, rotate from left to right around the vertebral column. Execute only one of these rotations.

(c) Transfer weight to the left leg and execute a jump turn to the proper throwing position. Do not go beyond the power position.

(d) Check feet, hips and torso for proper placement.

(e) Repeat many times.

Comment:

(a) As soon as this skill is mastered go to phantom turns, simulating using a discus.

Progressions:

(a) Standing with left side toward direction of throw, execute the turn to the throwing position. (See Figure #9, A).

(b) The next progression has the thrower turned clockwise so that the shoulders are about 45 degrees to center line. Execute the turn into the throwing position. (See Figure #9, C).

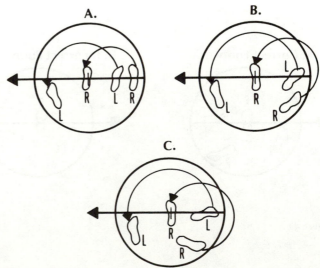

Figure #9

Additional Comments:
  (a) Place hands on hips.
  (b) It is important not to use variations A and B too much. The average beginner can progress to C in one or two lessons.
  (c) Go on to phantom turns, simulating using a discus.

(3) PHANTOM TURNS WITHOUT DISCUS (SIMULATION OF USING DISCUS)

Purpose: To work specifically upon the turning action and footwork.
Action:
  (a) Execute along a line on the ground.
  (b) Assume stance at back of circle, facing away from direction of throw, and feet spread a little wider than shoulder's width.
  (c) Execute preliminary swings transferring weight from left to right.
  (d) Execute jump turn into the throwing position. Do not go beyond this point.
  (e) Check foot and body position.
  (f) Repeat many times.

Comments:
  (a) This drill can be done with a discus for advanced throwers; however, since footwork and position are the objectives, it is better performed without the discus.
  (b) The preliminary swings are the same as described above; allow only two.
  (c) The transition from swing to turn is the same as has been described. There is a settling and shifting of the weight from left to right. The back is erect and shoulders level.
  (d) Throughout the turn, the discus hand should travel in a somewhat horizontal plane. In actuality, it goes up and down, but this should be minimized.

(4) ACTUAL THROWING

Purpose: To learn to throw the discus in a real-life situation. This is what it is all about.
Action: Same as described on previous page.
Comments:
  (a) Do not let beginning throwers throw for distance immediately. It is more important to master the basic fundamentals.
  (b) Work through progressions as described and shown in Figure #9 (A, B, C).
  (c) Strive for continuity and proper footwork.
  (d) 20 and 30 turns a practice is about the right amount. It is unwise to mass a great number of throws into one practice session until a good degree of skill is developed.
  (e) If possible, have throwers throw in different directions. This may assist in learning to throw in many different situations that are demanded by competition. A windy day gives them the experience of throwing in varied wind conditions.

(5) 3/4 TURN DRILL - SOUTH AFRICAN DRILL

Purpose: To work on the proper action of the discus arm and the power position action of leg, hips, trunk and arms.
Action:
  (a) Start outside the bounds of circle with pivot foot inside near throwers but pointing in direction of throw. The drive leg is outside circle. Body is slightly angled away from direction of throw. (See Figure #10.)

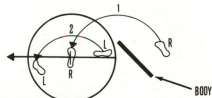

Figure #10

  (b) The free arm is pointing generally in the direction of the throw, with the discus arm in the opposite direction.
  (c) The body weight is moved onto the front foot and a jump turn is executed. Emphasize rotation more than linear motion.
  (d) As the weight is transferred, swing discus arm up and around toward direction of throw.
  (e) As the rear foot lands in the middle, attempt to place the front foot in place as quickly as possible. Proceed to the around-and-upward action of the hips and legs, ending with the delivery of the discus.
  (f) Emphasize rear leg and hip action, and a strong front foot and leg block.
  (g) Do not reverse.

IV. COLLATERAL EXERCISES AND TRAINING DEVICES

Weight training at all levels of skill should receive a great amount of emphasis in order to increase strength and muscle mass. A general development pattern is indicated with emphasis upon leg, back and rotary muscles of the trunk.

A. Use of Other Implements.

1. Sludderball (sling ball): A leather ball with a small loop at the top which weighs approximately 3 lbs. It can be thrown indoors or outdoors. Use the same technique as in discus throwing. It is a good off-season training device.

2. Light Discus: Used to master technique and specifically for working upon speed of advanced throwers. It should be used in the latter part of the season.

3. Heavy Discus: Used as a basic strength developer. For beginners, it should be thrown only from the power position without the turn. It should be used off-season and early in the season.

4. Hammer throwing and turning: Because the discus and hammer are rotational in nature, there is great carry-over. The hammer also dynamically loads the rotational muscle of the trunk in much the same manner as when throwing the discus. Recommended for boys and girls/men and women in all parts of the season.

5. 35 Pound weight throwing. (Not recommended for females).

6. Discus with a strap. Used for technique refinements.

B. Common Form Faults and Corrections

1. The grip on the discus should not be tense, nor should the discus be held with the wrist cocked. Keep the wrist straight.

2. Preliminary swings are often too many and too vigorous, upsetting body balance. They should be few and easily made in a smooth and continuous motion.

3. Keep hips under the trunk at all times.

4. Discus throwers are inclined to initiate the turn by a dropping of the leading shoulder, forgetting that the head is the balancing mechanism of the body. This will lead to a poor throwing position, and the thrower usually ends up in the bucket. The shoulders should remain level, and the head and eyes should lead the turning action. The gaze of the eyes is directed forward at all times. The turn should be initiated with the lead arm and lead knee almost simultaneously.

5. Many throwers have a delay upon landing in the center of the circle. It must be stressed that the actual throw should be started as soon as the rear foot has landed from the jump turn.

6. Allowing the thumb to rise, causes an improper release and flight of the discus. Throw flat (horizontally) with discus arm at shoulder level.

7. Some throwers place the front foot across the line of direction of the throw, thus stopping the hips from acting to full limit. This blocking of the hips will cause the discus to be thrown far to the right. Also, if the driving hip, leg and foot action stalls out and the lead foot is in the bucket, the discus will be thrown far to the right.

8. If the front foot is grounded too late or too far to the left side (for right-hand throwers), the action of the hips is not limited. When there is no resistance to their power, the body falls away and the discus swings wide to the left.

9. In the turns, if the discus is carried too close to the body, there is a tendency to "undercut" or "scoop" as far as should be allowed to swing well out, and the discus is released in line with the shoulder. The jump at delivery noted here is symptomatic of a too fast (and uncontrolled) turn. The discus being too close to the body allows it to spin very fast. To stay in the circle the athlete sometimes (wrongly) jumps. The discus thrower usually scoops the discus upon release if the slinging arm is allowed to drop too close to the hips.

10. At least one foot must be on the ground at the moment of delivery. If not, accumulated speed is dissipated at the moment when it is most needed.

V. INTEGRATION OF STRENGTH, TRAINING, AND TECHNICAL IMPROVEMENT

The most important developmental factors for serious discus throwers are strength, size, and technical proficiency. These factors can successfully be developed concurrently. To maximize development requires a year around approach. There can be no other pattern for the gifted and aspiring champion. For those who wish to participate in other sports, a compromise program has to be developed and coordinated between the coaches and the athlete. In many cases, the principles of training are exactly the same so that any number of sports performances can be improved with their application. The variable of program that will change the most will be the time factor. Weight lifting and technical cycles may be shortened for two sport track participants. Ideally, the gifted athlete should specialize in Track and Field.

Local environment, equipment, level of performance and coaching philosophy dictate to a large degree what the program can be. General concepts are presented for maximum flexibility in programming and structuring the training cycle.

The coach and athlete cooperating together are limited only by their imagination. Creativity can make training fun.

Table I contains information relative to Functional strength training and the integration of the total program.

TABLE 1. Example of a Yearly Training Cycle: Discus

12 Month Discus Training	Sept	Oct	Nov	Dec	Jan	Feb	Mar	Apr	May	June	July	Aug	Start Cycle Again
Weight 70-100%-													**Comments Testing**
Training 80%													1. 1.R.M.
And 60%											*=(1)	ACTIVE	2. Motor Performance VJ, SLJ, 50, RTA-RTV
Testing	*=(1, 2, 3)		*=(1)	*(1)	(1, 2, 3) *	*(1)		*(1)				REST	3. Body Fat

Season phases: Off Season (Sept–Nov) · Early Season (Dec–Feb) · Mid-Season (Mar–May) · Late Season (June–July) · Off-Season (Aug: Low Intensity, Fun and Games)

Technical Activities
1. 35 Lb. Wt.
2. Hammer 12 + 16
3. Discus
   1 KG
   3.7 lbs.
   4.6 lbs.
4. Sling Ball
5. Metal Bars or rings- Variable weight
6. Shot 8, 10, 12
   16
7. Run + jump, stairs
8. Sprints
9. Tramp/Diving
10. Ballet
11. Misc. Sports Activities

Off Season
1. Fall-Low/Key Competition (All Comers)
   a. Shot
   b. Discus
   c. Hammer
   d. Throwing Wt (male only)
2. Technique Training (Variable Wts- Emphasize heavier implements)
   a. Shot
   b. Discus
   c. Hammer
3. Weight Training
4. Run/Jump/Diving Ballet/Tramp/Gym
5. Misc. Sports
6. Competetive Wt Lifting (Power Lifting)

Early Season
1. Low/Key Competition- shot/discus/ hammer/throwing wt
   a. All comers or
   b. Indoor
2. Technique Training (Variable Wted Implements) Emphasize heavier
   a. Shot
   b. Discus
   c. Throwing Wt (male only)
3. Weight Training
4. Run/jump/Diving Ballet/Tramp/Gym
5. Misc. Sports
6. Competitive Wt Lifting (Power Lifting)

Mid-Season
1. Competition
   a. Shot
   b. Discus
   c. Hammer (optional)
2. Technique Training (Variable Weighted Implements)
   a. Shot
   b. Discus
   c. Hammer/Optional
3. Weight Training
4. Competitive Wt Lifting (Olympic Lifting)

Late Season
1. Competition
   a. Shot
   b. Discus
   c. Hammer (Optional)
2. Technique Training (Variable Weighted Implements) (Emphasize Standard and Lighter)
3. Weighted Training
4. Competitive Wt. Lifting (Olympic Lifting)

Technique Analysis
Film (Oct) · Film (Dec) · Film (Jan) · Film (Apr) · Film (June)

SAMPLE TRAINING PROGRAMS

Tables II, III, IV, and V are presented as general guidelines for an integrated program. Specific drills and weight training exercises are not given. Each training environment and coach's/athlete's philosophy will dictate the specifics.

TABLE II. OFF SEASON		
(SEPTEMBER, OCTOBER, NOVEMBER)		
MON, WED, FRI	TUES, THURS, SAT	SUN
1. **TECHNIQUE** (Large volumes & Low Intensity) STANDING THROWS ⎱ REGULAR AND SHOT ⎰ HEAVIER DISCUS ⎰ IMPLEMENTS 2. **CONDITIONING** WEIGHT TRAINING LOW INTENSITY AND LARGE VOLUMES	1. **TECHNIQUE** (Large Volumes Low Intensity) SHOT ⎱ FULL/PART DISCUS ⎰ ACTION-Varied HAMMER ⎰ Implements 2. **CONDITIONING** JUMPS SPRINTS AEROBIC WORK MISC SPORTS	O F F R E S T

TABLE III. EARLY SEASON			
(DECEMBER, JANUARY, FEBRUARY)			
MON, WED, FRI	TUES, THURS, SAT	SAT	SUN
1. **TECHNIQUE** (Large Volumes and Moderate Intensity) STANDING THROWS SHOT ⎱ REGULAR AND DISCUS ⎰ HEAVIER IMPLEMENTS 2. **CONDITIONING** WEIGHT TRAINING a. High Intensity and Low Volume (6 weeks) b. Moderate Intensity and Moderate Volume (6 weeks)	1. **TECHNIQUE** (Large Volumes Varied Intensities) SHOT ⎱ FULL/PART DISCUS ⎰ ACTION-varied HAMMER ⎰ Implements 2. **CONDITIONING** JUMPS SPRINTS AEROBIC WORK	ALL COMERS COMPETITION	O F F R E S T

TABLE IV. MID - SEASON				
(MARCH, APRIL, MAY)				
MON, WED	TUES, THURS FRI*		SAT	SUN

1. **TECHNIQUE** (Moderate Volumes and Varied Intensity)
 	
PART OR FULL ACTION
 	
SHOT   { REGULAR AND
DISCUS { LIGHT
        { IMPLEMENTS
 	
*Friday - Optional
    Easy Work or Rest Day
	1. **TECHNIQUE**
	(Moderate Volumes and Varied Intensity)
	
	PART OR FULL ACTION
	
	SHOT { VARIED
	DISCUS { IMPLE-
	HAMMER { MENTS
			C O M P E T I T I O N + Weight Training	O F F R E S T

TABLE V. LATE SEASON				
(JUNE, JULY, AUGUST)				
Note: The complete month of August should be active rest. That means no competition but a low intensity, highly active fun period.				
MON, WED	TUES, THURS FRI*		SAT	SUN

1. **TECHNIQUE** (Moderate Volumes and Varied Intensity)
 	
PART OR FULL ACTION
 	
SHOT   { REGULAR AND
DISCUS { LIGHT
        { IMPLEMENTS
 	
*Friday - Optional
    Easy Work or Rest Day
	1. **TECHNIQUE**
	(Moderate Volumes and Varied Intensity)
	
	FULL ACTION
	
	SHOT { REGULAR
	DISCUS { OR LIGHT
	        { IMPLE-
	        { MENTS
			C O M P E T I T I O N + Weight Training	O F F R E S T

The most critical aspect of the javelin throw is the velocity of the javelin at release.

16
The Javelin Throw

by
Ken Shannon, University of Washington
C. Harmon Brown, M.D., California State University, Hayward
Janis Donins, Unattached

Introduction

The javelin throw is one of the most complex events in track and field. It requires tremendous speed, agility, coordination and explosiveness. Due to the aerodynamic nature of the implement and its relative light weight (800 grams for men, 600 grams for women), the event does not require great strength. The event does require flawless technique in order to achieve high level results.

Contrary to what it appears to be, the javelin is not thrown with the arm. It is a total body action with the summation of the forces of the body resulting in a final whiplike fling of the throwing arm.

The main goal of the javelin throw is to achieve maximum distance. This is accomplished through awareness of the fundamentals of the biomechanics of the throw, refined technique, and proper training methods. This chapter will focus on these components.

Mechanics of the Javelin Throw

The distance a javelin travels on any given throw is determined by the velocity of the javelin, the angle of applied force and the angle of the javelin.

The most critical aspect of the throw is the velocity of the javelin at release. The velocity at release is a result of the velocity of the run-up plus the velocity of the body rotation or body torque. The run-up velocity has a limiting factor in that it can only be as fast as the thrower can run and still be able to control his/her body position at release. Body torque should be generated or initiated by the hips. At the final release step or plant, the weight of the body is transferred from the drive leg to the stop leg or plant leg. This action produces a high velocity torque of the hips and subsequently of the torso. This rotation occurs about the vertical axis of the arm from the shoulder. The final velocity is then attained at the hand on release. The greater the velocity, the farther the javelin will travel.

The next aspect of the throw is the angle of applied force. From rough calculations, about 24° is the optimum angle for force application. Thus, the path of the hand should be along a line that forms an angle of 24° with the ground. The farther away from (either up or down) this force angle, the shorter the distance the javelin travels.

The last aspect of the throw is the angle of the javelin itself. The javelin should be lined up basically with the line of force, although an angle slightly less is optimal. The effect of the javelin attitude or angle is that the farther away from the force angle, the greater the drag force (air resistance). The result is a decrease in the distance the javelin travels.

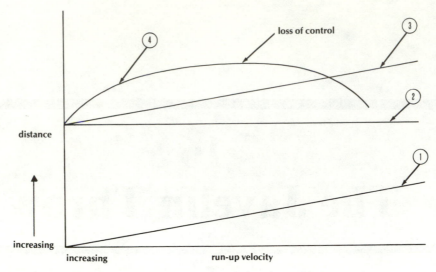

Line 1 represents the distance the javelin would travel from only the velocity of the run.
Line 2 represents the distance the javelin travels from only the body torque velocity. (standing throw)
Line 3 represents the theoretical distance the javelin would travel adding the run-up and body torque velocities.
Line 4 represents the actual distance the javelin travels. The discrepancy between this line and the theoretical lies in the fact that the run aids body torque through the hip rotation. The distance will decrease however at the point where control cannot be maintained.

FIGURE 1: Velocity Considerations

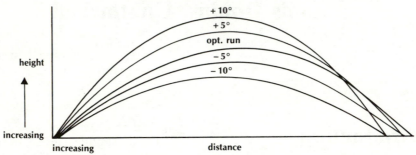

Theoretically the optimum force angle would be 33°, however, due to the shape of the javelin the optimum is lowered to 24°. Being off ± 5° results in about a 2% loss while being off ± 10° results in about a 6% loss.

FIGURE 2: Optimum Force Angle

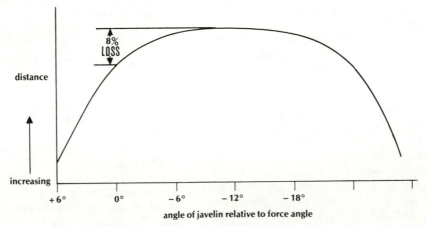

FIGURE 3: Javelin Attitude

Technique of the Javelin Throw

The technique of the javelin throw can be analyzed in four basic areas. These are the run-up, body torque, force angle and javelin angle.

The Run-Up

The function of the run-up is to impart as much velocity to the javelin as possible. The run-up, however, is one aspect of the javelin throw which throwers frequently abuse. Many coaches and throwers think that the faster the thrower runs, the farther he/she will

The javelin throw.

throw. But what happens is that the thrower either goes too fast to get his/her feet in proper position to make the transition to body torque, or the thrower has to slow down so much to make the transition that he/she makes virtually a standing throw. In either case the velocity of the run-up is not used advantageously. The limiting factor of the run-up then is not maximum velocity but the control the thrower will have at the final throwing position.

Even though the velocity of the run-up does contribute to the total velocity of the javelin, the greatest asset of the run-up is the amount of increased speed of body torque produced by the feet being on the ground at the right time and in the right place. When the feet are on the ground properly, a tremendous rotation of the hips is achieved which can accelerate the upper torso rotation much faster than normal. Therefore the run-up must incorporate a means for the body to get into a throwing position, i.e., the feet in the right place at the right time.

There are two basic methods to get into the throwing position from a run. The most common technique is known as a "cross step" or side step. This method entails turning the upper body parallel to the runway then crossing the leg and foot in front of the body. The foot comes through at a 90° angle to the body and lands at a 45° to 90° angle. At the same time, the opposite leg is moving under the body to get in front of the thrower to be used as a pivot. Two negative aspects of this side step technique are that it does not aid acceleration and linear alignment is difficult to maintain. Both the acceleration into the plant leg and alignment are critical to the javelin throw.

The other basic method of getting into a throwing position also incorporates a cross step. When the body rotates parallel to the runway, the leg and foot cross in front of the body, just as in a normal running step. The foot, however, lands pointing straight down the runway. This technique requires the thrower to be more flexible in the torso but allows acceleration and straight alignment into the throw. There are few throwers who are able to side step and still get the foot around to land straight.

The run-up speed should reach its maximum just prior to the throw when the feet are in the throwing position. The best way to accomplish this is for the thrower to start at a slow speed and accelerate on the last three steps into the throw. Some throwers run about half speed to the mid-point of their run-up and then drop the javelin back and begin to accelerate gradually. The athlete should stay on the balls of the feet to achieve "ankle snap" which maintains acceleration into the throw.

The last step or cross step should be "exaggerated" in order to get the stop leg or plant leg in front of the body as soon as possible. It is desirable to have the plant foot on the ground immediately after the drive foot hits. This will allow the upper body to remain in correct position and get the full advantage of the velocity built up during the run-up. The plant leg should be as straight as possible on the plant for maximum efficiency. A bent plant leg will cause a cushioning effect on the hip torque.

The plant foot must be moving as fast as possible underneath the body during the cross step. The best way to accomplish this is to keep it as close to the ground as possible. Sweeping it underneath the body while keeping it straight in a pendulum motions seems to be the most efficient method.

In the throwing position the front leg is used as the stop leg or plant leg while the back leg is driving or pushing "into" the front leg. No lift or vertical motion should be occurring at this time. Many throwers try to drive up over the top of the plant leg rather than into it and in so doing lose most of the valuable hip rotation, in addition to creating other problems.

The key factors in the run-up are acceleration into the plant and driving straight down the runway.

Body Torque

It is commonly thought that the javelin throw is primarily an "arm" throw. This is not so. The velocity imparted to the javelin should for the most part come from body torque. This body torque is developed from the rotation of the torso about a vertical axis which runs through the center of gravity of the thrower's torso. There are two schools of thought on how much the body should rotate or wrap to get into the throwing position. One says to wrap as much as possible, i.e., turn the shoulders more than parallel to the runway and wrap the throwing arm even farther around than the shoulders. The other says to turn the shoulders parallel to the runway and have the javelin in a straight line parallel to the shoulder. The latter is recommended because it allows more acceleration into the throw and is much easier to control.

Body torque should be initiated just as the plant foot hits the ground. The torque or rotation should be started slow and relaxed. This will aid control of the throwing angle and also allow time for the hip rotation to couple with the upper body rotation. The vertical axis of the thrower should form an angle of 24° slanted back from vertical. (See pg. 141) This should be assumed in the cross step. The chest should be turned or rotated up and the back should have a considerable concave arch. The throwing arm should remain trailing the body rotation. In other words, as the shoulders rotate, the throwing arm should remain parallel to the runway. As the shoulders square up (rotate about 90°), the arm should be accelerated forward by the chest and back snapping back to normal position. This creates an effect called the body whip. The shoulders should not rotate more than 90°. At 90° the throwing arm shoulder should be whipped forward by the chest and back into the throw. The key factors for body torque are to start slow to allow time for hip rotation to accelerate the body and to keep the throwing arm trailing to allow for maximum leverage. These two factors will also determine the throwing angle.

Force Angle

The throwing or force angle is the angle that a line, along the path that the throwing hand travels, forms with the plane of the runway. This angle is determined by body tilt and arm position. Body torque contributes to the throwing angle by fixing the plane in which the rotation takes place. The shoulders must rotate perpendicular to the vertical axis. The best way to achieve this rotation is to keep the non-throwing arm in the horizontal plane of rotation of the shoulders (horizontal relative to the 24° tilt-back of the axis). During the cross step, the non-throwing arm should be in the plane of the shoulder and out in front of the plane of the body at a 90° angle to the line of the shoulders. As the drive into the plant leg is made, this arm should be rotating in the horizontal plane of the shoulders. (See pg.135) As the plant foot hits, it should be in line with the shoulders and relatively straight, and as the upper body begins to rotate, it should remain in the plane of the shoulders. It may in fact lead the shoulder rotation from this point on. Many throwers have a tendency to "drop" or lower the non-throwing arm below the horizontal plane of the shoulders and cause the non-throwing shoulder to dip. This creates a lower throwing angle.

The throwing arm must be slightly above the horizontal plane of the shoulders and not bend more than 30° at the elbow while the throw is made. As the arm is accelerated past the shoulder, it should turn so that the elbow rotates up and away from the body. The rotation and 30° bend facilitates the next action, the passing of the arm over the shoulder. This will help to eliminate "javelin throwers elbow".

The key factors in the throwing angle are twofold: body torque takes place in the relative horizontal plane and the throwing arm passes above the shoulder and does not bend until it is accelerated.

Javelin Angle

The last aspect of the throwing technique is the javelin angle or attitude, which is controlled primarily by the wrist. This angle ranges from 28° (the jawline) for the advanced thrower to 33° (eyebrow level) for the beginning thrower. With the throwing arm slightly above the horizontal plane of the shoulders, the point of the javelin should be placed at the jawline of the thrower, almost touching it. The head should be slightly tilted in front of the plane of the body. The wrist must bend as the arm is brought past the shoulder to maintain the established angle. The palm should be face up as the throw is made (Figure #4)

The hold on the javelin is not critical in that any grip which is comfortable can be used. However, the edge of the cord grip should be used as a lever point. It is also recommended that the thrower use an adhesive on the hand to aid control and diminish friction losses. The javelin should not be held tightly but in a semi-relaxed hand. The key factor in controlling the javelin angle is

to control the javelin with the wrist in order to maintain the initial angle throughout the throw.

The overall effect, then, is a whip-crack effect of the body by a sudden, active checking (block) of the left side allowing and assisting the right side to drive forward and around to whip the javelin arm, i.e., before the body reaches the vertical. This imparts the proper trajectory to the javelin's flight. The follow-through off the left toe occurs after release.

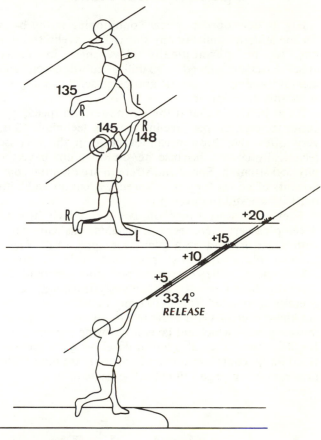

ANGLE OF RELEASE:	33.4°
RELEASE VELOCITY:	86.59 FPS
	26.39 m/s
HEIGHT OF RELEASE:	7' 2½''
BODY LEAN AT	
RIGHT FOOT TOUCHDOWN:	25°

FIGURE 4

Athlete Selection

Speed, ballistic explosiveness, flexibility and strength are all import factors in javelin throwing. Because of the need for more speed and explosive qualities and less pure strength, greater variation in body type and size is found among javelin throwers than among other throwing event athletes. Consideration must be given to sprint speed, jumping ability, explosive quickness, and agility. The ability to throw a ball may be a helpful indicator of throwing skill but long years of ball throwing may lead to patterns of arm orientation which may be difficult to adapt to the more passive whip action of the javelin. Some of the best javelin throwers have been horizontal jumpers or discus throwers. ("Javelin throwing is horizontal jumping while holding a stick in the hand.")

Physical Conditioning Special Exercises

Highly developed physical conditioning is the basis for the athletic results in any sport. The javelin thrower has to be harmonically developed in many areas—strength, speed, flexibility coordination and mental training. Systematic and purposeful training ensures this development.

It has been said that if there is power and speed, it is easier to learn proper javelin throwing technique. But, very often the thrower cannot perform the exercise technically correct because he/she does not have the physical strength. Speed and strength are essential components of power (power = speed x strength) and both must be worked to develop it.

There is a vast range of exercises which help to develop power: exercises with weights, medicine balls, with a partner and on a gymnastic apparatus. Weight training plays the most prominant role in power development. The exercises performed should be carefully chosen for each athlete's physical ability. Each exercise is repeated from 7-10 times in two or three sets. All these exercises are designed to strengthen specific muscle groups which aid javelin throwing performance. Besides power, they also aid in developing the areas of flexibility, coordination and mental training. The illustrations on page 139 are self-explanatory.

Teaching the Javelin Throw

The basic factor in achieving high level results in javelin throwing is technical readiness. In order to develop and improve javelin technique, it is necessary to establish a sound and technically correct base. Experience proves that learning a new movement correctly is much easier than relearning an incorrect one.

In teaching correct javelin throwing technique, it is advisable that the athlete first begin to throw without the javelin. Rocks of different weights, shots, medicine balls, baseballs, tennis balls, etc. are very good implements for this purpose. This method takes longer but in reality is the most effective because it emphasizes correct basic technique and avoids mistakes which may occur when teaching with the javelin.

When the beginner is taught with the javelin first, his/her attention is distracted from the total performance in the throwing exercise. The athlete may focus solely on the release of the javelin without concentrating on correct body mechanics.

In the early phases of teaching javelin technique, the concept of the general throwing movement should be developed. It is essential that in the throwing process the largest muscle groups should be utilized beginning with the legs, abdomen, back and shoulders and that this action be transferred to the torso and arm. This is developed by throwing medicine balls, rocks from different positions, as well as running, jumping and weight training.

In the training of the javelin thrower, the range of exercises is vast. Along with the usual track and field events, running, jumping hurdles, shot put, participation in swimming, gymnastics, ball games, weight lifting, etc. should be encouraged. This broadens the range of movements as well as reinforcing psychological strength.

All exercises should be viewed in relation to the complete throwing technique. For example, running over the hurdles enhances the rhythm of the javelin approach steps. The shot put has the same general body motions. Swimming develops flexibility which is important for the javelin thrower. The same could be said about many other different groups of exercises and sports.

The sequence in teaching the javelin throw is as follows:

TASK #1: GENERAL THROWING MOVEMENTS.
Exercises: Different jumps for distance and height, sprinting, exercises with weights, and, especially, exercises with medicine balls, shots, and rocks of different weights. In throwing the medicine balls, the throwing movement should begin from the active extension of the legs and the thrower should be in a stable position until the implement leaves his/her arms. It should be emphasized that the general throwing movement has a low range and is "explosive."

TASK #2: JAVELIN THROWING FROM A STANDING POSITION.
Exercises: Different throws with medicine balls, imitation throw (without javelin), rocks, balls, javelin throwing from standing and from different positions. To better learn the sequence of muscle interaction during the throw from the standing position, it is advisable that the medicine ball (4-5 pounds) be thrown with both hands over the head forward as shown in the pictures and in the same order.

In performing the throw from the step position, attention should be paid to the fact that the throwing movement begins with a right leg (for right-hand thrower) extension with the left leg blocking transfer of momentum to the upper part of the body. This creates a "bow" position of the whole body.

To better experience the action of the legs, it is essential that the thrower stay on both legs after the throw and not allow the weight to shift forward away from the right leg. The throwing movement, when it begins with the legs, gradually involves the rest of the body in a whiplike manner: muscle groups should be activated gradually and then sharply stopped, thus stimulating the next muscle group's action in the total throwing movement.

The standing throw.

The javelin throw from two steps

The medicine ball throw with both arms from these steps.

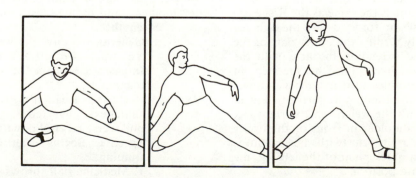

Imitational exercises for the javelin thrower with emphasis on leg work.

TASK #3: THROWING THE JAVELIN FROM TWO OR THREE STEPS.

Exercises: Throwing from three steps serves as the transition between the standing throw and the throw from the approach run. The sequence of exercises should be the following:

1) Medicine ball throwing with both hands over the head forward with one step, then two steps then the three steps approach run. Analyzing that exercise, the following should be noted:

   a) "Running away" from the implement is done smoothly, right from the first step.

   b) Steps should be "springy," but not "jumpy."

   c) Planting the right foot (third step) on the surface, the thrower should attempt to move his/her left foot ahead as fast as possible for the block, thus maintaining the "running away from the implement" position.

   d) Transition from the approach and into the throw should happen without delay. The throw begins with a very explosive right leg extension up through the chest and over an extended left leg.

2) Javelin throw from three steps without turning the upper part of the body to the right. The first step (cross-step) should be performed with an exphasis on the left leg's push-off and the right leg's swinging forward. In learning this kind of throw, attention should be paid to the planting of the right foot (on the toes) and a very quick push forward and plant with the left leg.

3) Javelin throw from three steps with the upper body turned (left side pointed into the direction of the throw) and the javelin in the extended right arm.

In performing the throw from three steps, the thrower should learn to develop an approach step rhythm and execute a quick cross-step without losing the "running away" position.

TASK #4: JAVELIN THROW WITH THE FULL APPROACH RUN.

Exercises:

1) Withdrawing the implement standing in the step position, left leg in front and javelin above the shoulder. Withdrawal occurs on the two count as it would happen during the run because the movement is completed in the first two throwing steps, before the cross-step and the release step.

2) The beginning position is the same as the first exercise. The athlete follows-up forward with the right leg ahead, simultaneaously turning the upper part of the body to the right and extending the arm with the javelin to the right and back. Then he/she steps in with the left leg and completes the withdrawal movement. The step (cross-step) should be performed in an accelerated manner with the weight on the right leg, and the left arm and shoulder in front of the upper part of the body. The right arm (with the javelin) is entended back. With a quick plant of the left leg, the thrower is in the release position.

At the beginning, when the thrower learns this exercise, it is suggested that he/she look back and observe him/herself to see the position of the throwing arm and the javelin. This gives visual feedback to correct mistakes. This should not become a habit because in competition it slows down the approach run and negatively affects rhythm. With multiple repetitions of the exercise, the thrower develops muscle awareness that will give him/her knowledge of the positions of the arm and the javelin without looking back.

3) The thrower performs the second exercise, but with the actual throw. Gradually, first two steps' length and speed are increased.

4) The throw with the short approach run. Before the actual throw, the athlete assumes the step position—left leg in front. He/she then moves two big steps back and assumes the same position as in the beginning. At the beginning of the throw, the thrower holds the javelin above the shoulder, performs two running steps, hits the mark with the left foot, withdraws the javelin on the first two steps, performs the cross-step and a quick last step, and throws.

Depending on the progress of the athlete, the approach run should be increased by two steps each time. When the preparatory approach run reaches 6 to 8 steps, it is considered to be throwing from the short approach run. The length of the approach run should not be increased for awhile.

Even a mature athlete should leave considerable time for the throws from a short approach. These will allow him/her to develop all technical elements of the javelin.

The learning process of the javelin throwing technique is not always smooth. To enhance its success, coaches and athletes must be innovative. The exercises should be related to each other in order to complement one another.

Training Program

Building a Base

A base of endurance, strength, flexibility, and general conditioning should be emphasized for 10-12 weeks, depending upon the maturity and fitness level of the athlete. This includes running, strength training, power development, and basic skills training.

   I. **Strength**

     a. General.   3 days per week, alternate days.

     Volume.   4-6 sets X 8-10 repetitions.

     Intensity.   60-65% of the single repetition maximum.

     Exercises.   Dead lifts, squats, power cleans, snatches, inverted situps, bench press, pullovers, lat. pulldowns.

     b. Specific. Begins after 6 weeks of general training.

       1. Medicine ball throws for trunk and shoulder girdle.

       2. Overweight implements or weights: for

specific throwing muscles and throwing action. Stubby javelins, rods, balls of 1.5 to 2.0 kg used.

II. Running

Athlete jogs 2-3 miles, 4-5 X per week.
Stride-accelerations 5-8 X 60-150m.
Hill running and bounding.
Stride and pullbacks with spear or stick.
600-800m run timed every 2 weeks.

III. Ballistic Training—Horizontal Bounding

a. Double leg hops 24-40m X 5-10.
b. Alternate-leg bounding 30-50m, twice weekly.
c. Stadium steps or hill bounding once weekly.

IV. Technique

Athlete throws stubby into net or spear with short approach once or twice a week 30-40X.

V. Flexibility

15-20 min daily on gradual (Yoga) stretching of shoulder girdle, trunk, hips, legs.

Power Training Phase

I. Strength

a. General. Every other day.
Volume. 5 X 5 at 80%, or pyramid from 70-90%.
Exercises. Snatch or power cleans, squats, incline pullovers with bar or dumbbell, bench press, inverted situps, horizontal trunk twists on bench, lat. pulls, quarter squat "pops."
b. Specific
Athlete throws balls, rods or stubbies in ratio 2 heavy (1.5-2.0 kg), 1 standard weight (600 or 800 g), 1 light (500g). 75-100 throws twice weekly.
c. Medicine ball drills X 20 min.

II. Running

1-1.5 mile jog warmup each day.
Cariocas 5 X 100m.
Sprints 60-100m X 5 twice weekly.
Pull-back accelerations with stick 10-15 X 30-40m.

III. Ballistic Activities. 2 or 3 X weekly.

Horizontal bounding 5 X 30-40m single and double legged. Boxes, cones, or hurdles— double and single leg hops, 5-10 reps once weekly.

IV. Technique

Focus on various technical points—relaxation, hips and trunk drive, leg speed and acceleration into throws. The athlete throws 3-4 X weekly; throws rocks on weekend.

Competition Readiness (6-8 weeks)

I. Strength

a. General.
Circuit training X 1 week at 40-50%. Athlete resumes 5 X 5 at 80% 3 X weekly for 4-6 weeks, tapered to twice weekly, reduced to 4 X 4 and 3 X 3 at 90-99% prior to major meets.

b. Specific
Throwing exercises with rods, balls or stubbies in ratio 2 light, 1 standard, 1 heavy.

II. Running

Sprints 30-80 m X 5-6 at full effort.
Approach runs on runaway with spear X 10-15.
Controlled Cariocas 3-4 X 100m.

III. Ballistic

Horizontal bounding 4-5 X 10 once weekly.
Jump cones or hurdles 5 X 10 once weekly.
Omit jump training for 2-3 weeks before major meets.

IV. Technique

Focus on refining skills, concentrating on the whole movement pattern. Upper body relaxation. Athlete throws under-weight implements for relaxed, explosive effort. (Men can use women's spear) 15-20 throws at full effort with recovery between, once weekly. Smaller meets are used to rehearse for major competitions.

Post-Season—"Active Rest"

Athlete maintains fitness base, relaxing with other sports activities. Maintains base of strength by training every 3-4 days using sets of 3-4 repetitions X 4-5 at 75-80%.

Drills for the Javelin

The following list presents various drills for the javelin throw. Some of these drills were examined in the previous section.

1. Hopping—both feet or on one foot or alternate back and forth.
   Hopping over hurdles or boxes.
2. Bounding—as in the triple jump.
3. Skipping
4. Carioca
5. Standing long jump and triple jump
6. Vertical jumping
7. Depth jumping
8. Medicine ball exercises
9. Throwing weighted balls
10. Grass drills: with javelin
    a) Carioca with javelin
    b) Groin drill
    c) 2 step cross-over
    d) Bounding cross-overs
       (1) Left leg lift
       (2) Right leg cross
11. Standing throws, 3 step,.etc.
12. Stomach Drills
    a) Incline bent knee situps
    b) Side bends
    c) Seated twists
    d) Leg raises from horizontal bar
    e) Skin the cat
    f) Schreiber transverse exercise

17
The Hammer Throw

by
Stewart Togher
Scotland

If it is the wish of the American hammer thrower to compete with the world's best, he must change his methods and attitude to training. Long-term, year-round training methods are required to develop all the abilities needed to produce a top thrower. Heavy weight training has been used for rapid strength gains because of the short preparation periods. However such short-term methods do not enhance the development or the learning process of an event as complex as the hammer throw. It is obvious that heavy weight training has been implemented for quick results to the detriment of hammer technique.

Adaptation to Training

In training, impulses of variable nature and extent should be applied regularly. Since the system or organism is self-adapting, the output or the response will be as complex as the input. The initial state of unbalance will be transitory and the eventual issue will be adaptation by learning, provided that the training impulse has been regular, but not so strong as to damage the system. Adaptation is always general as well as specific. General adaptation means that the system has learned to cope with the imposed training in every possible way. Specific adaptation means that the unit most exposed to the impulse will adapt to that impulse.

Regular training brings about an increase in the accuracy and efficiency in dealing with motor tasks related to the one used as an impulse, both with regard to general and specific adaptation. If the training input is incorrect either in quality or in quantity, due to mistakes in designing the training schedule, there is bound to be a distorted output. Damage and injuries arise and faulty nerve patterns are developed which ultimately lower the possible limits of development.

With the growing athlete, general adaptation is very sensitive to one-sided, or biased training, while in specific adaptation, the risk resides in the competitive nature of the developing abilities and skills. Training can elicit an increase as much as 200% in strength, but mostly at the expense of flexibility, accuracy and skill.

Speed and Strength Development

Speed development is efficient only when it takes place in combination with the training of other abilities. The imaginative power of the coach in employing or even inventing exercises of a versatile and dynamic character is essential. Care should be taken that the intensity of speed training varies in a planned manner to avoid the development of speed barriers. Such barriers are mainly due to relative monotony in training and not to be confused with genetic limitations.

Muscular strength depends on manufactors: the physiological cross section of the muscles involved, the number of the fibers activated during the effort, the efficiency of the nervous regulation adjusting muscular tonus and antagonistic muscle contractions, the coordination of posture and body balance, and the interactions between the time series of the different mechanical effects of muscle contraction. Strength development has to exploit all these possibilities. When training brings about an increase in the cross section of the fibers, when it helps mobilize more fibers in the execution of a task, strength will increase. When suitable patterns of muscle contraction and relaxation are developed by training coordination, the conditions of overcoming the resistance in the respective phases of the movement will improve. As coordination and tonus distribution grow better, the efforts become more efficient and economic. In order to insure this, it is necessary to employ a broad range of methods in the development of strength.

Research suggests that a child's speed of movement reaches a zenith at approximately eleven years of age (male) and that the development of static strength must be handled with care in the developing child so as not to interfere with coordination of movement. Speed and accuracy can also be impaired by the overemphasis of static strength development such as the 35 lb. weight and slow squats.

The development of dynamic and explosive strength is, on the other hand, of great importance at all ages. Dynamic strength occupies the largest domain of strength, its characteristic being the resistance against which the effort has to be carried out repeatedly. In practice, exercises used to develop dynamic strength will improve strength endurance when they are of low intensity while sub-maximum intensities are useful to improve maximum strength. When dynamic strength is trained, muscular circulation and capillarization improve, and when strength exercises are coupled with technical tasks, coordination improves.

Structuring a Training Program

The training year is basically divided into four main periods:

Oct.-Jan	Feb-April	May-Aug	Sept
General Preparation	Specific Preparation	Competition	Rest or Transition Period

This plan is only for one outdoor competition period and is ideal for the beginner since it allows for an extended build up period to establish mobility, fitness, strength, and technique in the general period, specific fitness and strength in the second period and readiness for competition in the third period. The first few weeks of the general preparation period are spent on mobility fitness (circuits) and simple drills (swings and turns with light hammers). This is followed by a gradual but progressive weight training program (extensive to intensive with decreasing load).

General Preparation Period

1) First 4-6 weeks of General Preparation Period. Typical week would be as follows:

Mon	Tues	Wed	Thurs	Fri	Sat	Sun
WU	WU	WU	WU	WU	WU	Rest
Circuits	Drills Inside	Circuits	Drills Inside	Circuits Outside	Throws	

WU:	Warmup - 1000 meter run followed by 10-15 minutes loosening.
Circuits:	Bodyweight related exercises: a) chinups, b) dips, c) pushups d) situps, e) back lifts

2) Twelve-week progressive weight period, November - January. Typical week would be as follows:

Mon	Tues	Wed	Thurs	Fri	Sat	Sun
WU	WU	WU	WU	WU	WU	Rest
Weights	Throws	Weights	Throws	Weights	Throws	

Weights in Intensity

2 weeks	5 x 8	50% of best
2 weeks	5 x 6	60% of best
4 weeks	5 x 4	60-75% of best
4 weeks	5 x 3	75-90% of best

Basic lifts are snatch, clean, front squat, back squat.

Starting poundages for beginners:	Fraction of Bodyweight
Snatch	1/2 (3/6)
Clean	2/3 (4/6)
Front Squat	5/6 (5/6)
Back Squat	1 (6/6)

These starting poundages which are fractions of bodyweight are taken as 50% of maximum. Therefore when testing for maximum in February, in the next period, the results should have reached the following norms:

Snatch	1xbodyweight
Clean	1-1/3xbodyweight
Front Squat	1-2/3xbodyweight
Back Squat	2xbodyweight

The basic ratio involved in the selection of these poundages is a 3, 4, 5, 6,. Therefore, eventually a top thrower following this lift ratio would achieve:

Snatch	300 lbs
Clean	400 lbs
Front Squat	500 lbs
Back Squat	600 lbs

Specific Preparation Period

A typical week during specific preparation period:

Mon	Tues	Wed	Thurs	Fri	Sat	Sun
WU	WU	WU	WU		WU	Rest
Weights	Throws	Weights	Throws	Rest	Throws	
	Hops		Hops		Sprints	
	Bounds		Bounds			

During the specific preparation period, the weights intensity is kept high but is cut to two sessions to allow the emphasis to switch to heavy hammer work. Hopping and bounding are introduced to improve the ballistic quality of the legs (action and reaction). Sprinting over 30-40 meters with fast cadence is also introduced from a standing start in order to reciprocate the fast start and turning speed in the throw.

Competition Period

Typical week during competition period:

Mon	Tues	Wed	Thurs	Fri	Sat	Sun
WU	WU	Rest	WU	Rest	WU	Rest
Weights	Throws		Throws		Compete	
	Hops		Sprints			
	Bounds					

If there is no competition on Saturday a light weights session can be done on Wednesday.

During the competition period weights (high intensity) are cut back to one session, heavy hammer throws to one. Minor competitions usually start in April, therefore May competitions are used to prepare the athlete for the National Championships in June.

Technique

General Statements:
1) Hammer is a rhythm event
2) It involves balanced movements in which the lower body parts predominate (hips and legs).
3) The concept of the throw as a whole must supersede that of the throw as a series of links in a chain, e.g., swings, low point, entry.

Swings

The speed of the swings is determined by the entry speed which the athlete can reasonably handle.

The function of the swings is five-fold:
1) To set the rhythm
2) To establish the correct plane of the hammer.
3) To set the correct position of the high/low points.
4) To establish correct balance prior to the entry (transition).
5) To establish the range at entry.

Correct rhythm is effected by direct countering of the hips opposing the hammer at high and low points. The hips are therefore used to create impulse to the hammer and, as the swings develop, the emphasis of the hips increase.

For maximum range the hammer plane should be kept fairly flat, the hammer not rising above head height at its high point. Correct countering of the hips forward in opposition to the high point will also allow for greater range behind the head.

Transition or Entry

The entry links the swings to the turns: As the hammer is swung up to the left in the final swing, the thrower turns under his hands to the right in anticipation of the hammer passing through the high point. The thrower should now be balanced to sweep the hammer frontwards. In the position at the top of the downswing, the shoulders are turned back to the right while the hips are held to the front. This displacement of the shoulders to the hips gives the athlete bodily contact (torque or slightly wound up feeling in the trunk). Three synchronized movements impart force to the hammer as it is swept forwards to start the first turn:

1&2) The thrower drops his mass vertically and horizontally by sitting back into the direction of the throw (vertical acceleration downwards and angular acceleration horizontally).

3) Unwinding the hammer to the front develops angular acceleration, however maintenance of contact with the hammer in the rotation of the lower body (hips and legs) will continue the acceleration past the low point of the swing into the throw.

This is obviously a critical stage in the throw, involving perfect timing with just the correct loss of balance (displacement) to direct the throw and yet maintain maximum effective radius into the first turn. This movement (transition) is mastered by displacement and timing rather than overemphasis of the arms when swinging or a sudden use of the hips and legs in order to achieve a greater torque effect.

Relaxation in the upper body (arms and shoulders) as the hammer swings to the left will allow the thrower to use the momentum of the hammer to balance over his left foot. (The left foot is effectively the center of rotation and the thrower should try to center the acceleration of the hammer about this central axis as it proceeds across the circle during the throw). Once the thrower has balance over his left foot, he can push off with the right foot after the hammer. Allowing the hammer to run to the left due to the fact that the shoulders are unwinding to the left means that to some extent the thrower is losing contact (torque) with the hammer. Therefore in order to be able to continue to accelerate the hammer, he must regain the torque he has lost. This is done by the hips and legs rotating past the upper body during the single support phase to catch the hammer in a wound up or torque position at the top of the next downswing.

Photographic sequence of the hammer throw.

By collapsing his weight over his left foot the thrower can use his mass (vertically downwards) to continue to accelerate the hammer in the next downswing. Then, as the hammer is swept through the bottom of this swing, the thrower can again continue the acceleration of the hammer by partially rising and sitting back as he pivots into the next turn. Arms are held out at all times to maintain maximum effective radius. The maintenance of this radius is aided by the thrower holding a fixed head position (looking at the hammer) during the first two turns. In the final turn the thrower again collapses over the left foot maintaining his weight over his left leg and, with the grounding of his right foot, executes a long sweeping release. The body lifts to full extension with the arms flailing after the hammer.

Extra range can be gained by leaning forward with the upper body in the first turn but this lean becomes less in the next turn as the pull of the hammer increases (to avoid piking and subsequent loss of rotation speed).

The four turn throw (toe turn and three heel turns) allows for a more gradual build up of acceleration. This throw is initiated by the first turn on the toe rather than on the heel. It is used mainly by the smaller more athletic type thrower.

It is noticeable that present top throwers (75 meters +) are beginning the throw with the feet placed slightly to the right of center (from the thrower's position) and that they tend to ground the right foot early (undercomplete). What appears to be undercompleting, helps the thrower to displace his mass more effectively in the direction of the throw thus increasing the acceleration of the hammer into the next turn.

Learning Progression for the Hammer Throw

Prepared by:
Carl Wallin
Dartmouth College

The following progression is intended for the novice hammer thrower: (right-handed)

WIND

1. Grasp the hammer handle in the left hand and swing it around the head. Straighten the arms out as the ball passes in front of the body and bend the arms when the ball passes in back.
2. Repeat the same movement with the right arm.
3. Now use both arms. Grasp the handle with the left hand under the right hand. Most throwers use either two or three swings over the head. This is called the Wind.

TURNS

4. Do a left face. Pivot on the heel of the left foot and push from the ball of the right foot. Begin with a 90° pivot and work towards having both feet facing in the same direction.
5. When both feet are facing in the same direction, take the body weight off of the heel and place it on the ball of the left foot. Pick the right foot off the ground and pivot 360° on the ball of the left foot. Throughout the whole pivot, keep the left leg slightly bent. This completes a turn.
6. Now combine two or three preliminary winds with an entry of the hammer and a turn. Enter the hammer at 12 o'clock.

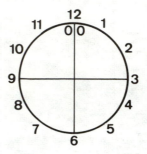

Figure 5.

7. Entry is the transition between the winds and the turn.
8. When turning with the hammer, keep both arms fully extended and keep the hammer with the body.
9. After mastering one turn, work for two. When two turns are mastered, work for three.
10. The delivery is done by stopping and bracing both legs at the completion of the last turn and lifting upward.

Part D
The Jumps

18
Fundamental Mechanics of Jumping

by
Jim Hay
University of Iowa

One method presented here is one which involves three simple steps to analyze technique in jumping events:

(1) the subdivision of the athlete's objective (distance in the horizontal jumps and height in the vertical ones) into a number of smaller parts.

(2) identification of the mechanical factors that influence or determine the magnitude of each of these parts, and

(3) discussion of the techniques needed to maximize (or optimize) each of these mechanical factors during the performance of the event.

Note: In the mechanical analyses which follow, steps (2) and (3) proceed simultaneously.

LONG JUMP

Assuming that the athlete abides by all the rules governing the event and that he does not touch the ground behind the line of his heels when he lands, the distance with which a long jumper is credited may be thought of as being the sum of (1) the horizontal distance which his center of gravity is in front of the scratch-line (i.e. the front edge of the board) at take-off, (2) the horizontal distance which his center of gravity travels while he is air-borne and (3) the horizontal distance which his heels are in front of his center of gravity at the moment they break the sand. These three distances—the take-off distance (L_1), the flight distance (L_2), and the landing distance (L_3)—are shown in Figure 1.

The take-off distance (positive, zero, or negative, depending on whether the jumper's center of gravity is in front, directly above, or behind the scratch-line at take-off) depends mainly on the "accuracy" of the run-up. If the jumper arrives at the board with the toes of his take-off foot close to the scratch-line (on the legal side!), his take-off distance is likely to act in his favor to the extent of perhaps 6-10 inches (15-25 cm.). However, if his run-up is not that "accurate" and he takes off some distance behind the board, his take-off distance will be negative. Under these circumstances the jumper operates under a self-imposed handicap—he must actually jump some distance in order to bring himself level with the scratch-line.

The take-off distance is also influenced to some extent by the physique of the athlete (tall, long-limbed athletes may obtain greater take-off distances than those less endowed) and by his body position at the moment of take-off.

The flight distance (which contributes some 85 to 90 percent of the total distance in good jumping) depends primarily on the nature of the take-off. Like the center of gravity of any other projectile whose flight is not seriously influenced by air resistance, the center of gravity of a long jumper follows a parabolic path. The exact dimensions of this parabolic flight path are determined by the jumper's velocity at take-off and, to a lesser extent, by the height of his center of gravity at take off. The jumper's velocity at take-off (about 30 feet per second [9.1 m./sec] for a 26 foot [7.92 m.] jump) depends on the horizontal velocity he obtains

Figure 1

from his run-up and on the vertical velocity he obtains by driving forcefully downward against the board. Because the jumper has a virtually unlimited time in which to build up horizontal velocity and only a split-second to acquire vertical velocity, it is the former of these two that makes by far the greater contribution to his velocity at take-off. For this reason sheer sprinting speed is of critical importance in long jumping.

The angle of take-off (which, strictly speaking, is included when one refers to the ''velocity of take-off'') is also greatly influenced by the differences in the times which the athlete has available to generate horizontal and vertical velocities. Although the optimum angle of take-off for a top-class jumper can be shown mathematically to be close to 45 degrees, in practice it is impossible for an athlete to attain such an angle unless he or she decreases his horizontal velocity markedly. While this slowing down gives the athlete more time to generate a vertical velocity near-equal to his horizontal velocity (something he'd need if he were to have a take-off angle approaching 45 degrees) anything he might gain from having a theoretically optimum angle of take-off is far outweighted by the huge losses he incurs as a result of decreasing his take-off velocity. In practice, therefore, long jumpers try to get as much vertical velocity as they can with the least loss in horizontal velocity. This generally results in angles of take-off in the order of 18 to 22 degrees.

The landing distance depends on the jumper's body position as he lands in the pit and on the movements he makes subsequently to avoid sitting back. The body position that the jumper adopts in preparation for landing is largely dictated by the nature of the rotation he acquired during the take-off and by what he does about it during the flight. (It should be stressed here that since the flight path of the jumper's center of gravity cannot be altered by his actions in the air—a well-established scientific fact—such actions serve only to aid in putting the jumper's body in the best position for landing.)

Although it is possible to leave the board with either forward or backward rotation about an axis through the center of gravity (all in-the-air rotations take place about an axis through the center of gravity) or indeed with no rotation at all, in practice most long jumpers possess some forward rotation at the moment they become air-borne. And, since the amount of rotation (i.e. the angular momentum) which an athlete possesses at this time cannot be altered in flight (the so-called Conservation of Angular Momentum Principle) all he can do is to try to make sure that his body does not rotate so far that he is unable to get his feet well forward for the landing.

To understand how this may be accomplished it is first necessary to have a good understanding of the Conservation of Angular Momentum principle. The angular momentum that a rotating body possesses is equal to the product of two factors—one is a measure of how the mass of the body is distributed relative to the axis of rotation (the moment of inertia) and the other is the rate at which the body is rotating about that axis (the angular velocity). It is the angular momentum, this product of the moment of inertia and the angular velocity, which remains constant throughout the air-borne phase of the jump. Now, if a jumper leaves the board with some forward rotation and then decreases his moment of inertia by assuming a tucked or piked position—as in the sail style of jump used by most beginners—his angular velocity is increased. (Because this is the only way that his angular momentum could possibly remain constant, the angular velocity increases when the moment of inertia is decreased and vice versa.) The net result is that the jumper's body generally rotates so far forward that he lands with his feet beneath, or almost beneath, his center of gravity. As a rule, therefore, jumpers who use the sail style only rarely achieve respectable landing distances.

Athletes who use the hang style are generally much more effective in controlling their forward rotation and ensuring an efficient landing. Once the jumper has left the board he sweeps his leading leg in a downward and backward direction. (In accord with Newton's law of reaction, this action produces a contrary upward and backward reaction of the athlete's trunk). Thus, as a result of the actions of the jumper's leading leg, the trunk is brought back to (and often slightly beyond) an erect position. In addition, since the athlete's body is near-fully extended as a result of these actions (and its moment of inertia is therefore almost as large as it can be), the athlete's forward angular velocity is reduced correspondingly. Exponents of the hitch-kick or "running-in-the-air" style employ basically the same methods as do those who use the hang style except that instead of sweeping the leading leg back and then, after some delay, bringing both legs forward for landing, they sweep each leg back alternately before finally bringing them together for the landing. In this way they are able to markedly increase the backward rotation of the trunk which such actions produce.

Once the jumper's heels have cut the sand, his main concern is to avoid falling back and thus lessening the distance of the jump. To this end, he allows his hip, knee and ankle joints to "collapse" (thereby decreasing his moment of inertia and increasing his angular velocity relative to an axis through his ankles) and, swings his arms forward (to give added forward momentum to his body).

The relationships between the distance jumped and the various factors which influence that distance are shown diagrammatically in Figure 2.

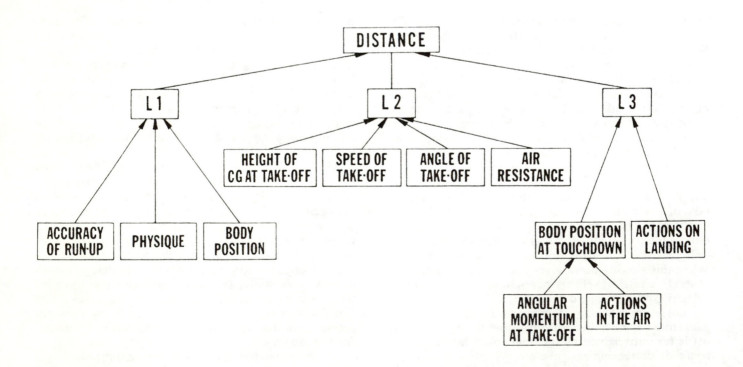

Figure 2

TRIPLE JUMP

For the purposes of analysis, the distance with which a triple jumper is credited may be subdivided in a manner similar to that already outlined with reference to the long jump. In this instance, however, there are three take-off distances, three flight distances and three landing distances which must be taken into account. Furthermore, since the length of the second and third phases in the sequence depend a great deal on what has taken place in the precedng phase or phases, the jumper is most unwise if he attempts to obtain the maximum distance of which he is capable in either of the first two phases. Instead he must strive for that combination of distances which will yield the greatest total for the three phases. In general this means keeping the first phase relatively low and short (i.e. compared with the maximum he could produce with just a single hop), the second phase near the best he can produce, and the third phase at the maximum possible under the circumstances.

HIGH JUMP

The height with which an athlete is credited in the high jump may be thought of as the sum of (1) the height of his center of gravity at take-off, (2) the height which his center of gravity is lifted during the jump, and (3) the difference between the height of the bar and the peak height attained by his center of gravity. These three heights are respectively designated as H_1, H_2, and H_3. *Note:* Since an athlete's center of gravity must almost invariably be lifted higher than the bar in order for him to make a successful jump, H_3 is generally negative.

The height of the center of gravity at the moment the athlete leaves the ground depends on just two factors—his physique and his body position. From the standpoint of physique, the fact that tall, long-legged athletes invariably have higher centers of gravity than short, short-legged ones explains in large measure why such athletes have tended to dominate the event. While the particular demands of the style being used (e.g. the need to initiate rotation about the long axis of the body in the Fosbury flop) may make it impossible to achieve or even unwise to attempt, the optimum body position in terms of H_1 is one in which the jumper has both arms extended overhead, his head and trunk erect and "stretched," his leading leg straight and as high as possible, and his take-off leg fully extended at knee and ankle joints.

The magnitude of H_2, the amount of lift the athlete gets, is governed simply by his vertical velocity at the moment he leaves the ground. This, in turn, is governed by (a) the vertical velocity of his center of gravity at the instant the heel of his take-off foot is planted prior to take-off, and (b) the change in the vertical velocity of

Figure 3

151

his center of gravity brought about during the take-off. In other words, his vertical velocity at take-off is equal to his vertical velocity at touchdown or foot plant, plus whatever change in vertical velocity he can effect during the take-off.

The vertical velocity of the athlete's center of gravity at the moment the heel of his take-off foot is planted is determined by his actions during the last strides of his run-up. If he simply maintains a normal running action, his center of gravity follows a fairly smooth undulating path, moving downward and forward at the instant each foot is planted and then upward and forward as he is driven into the next stride. Such a method of executing the last few strides of the run-up has the distinct disadvantage that, once the athlete has planted his take-off foot, he must first arrest the downward motion of his center of gravity before he can begin work on the critical task of propelling it upward into the air. In short, he must waste some of his effort to reverse the vertical direction in which his body is moving. To overcome this problem, most good jumpers modify their actions during the final stages of the run-up so that the last stride begins with the hip, knee and ankle joints of the supporting leg well flexed and the center of gravity low. From this position, the athlete drives his hips forward and upward and reaches his take-off foot forward so that, after a very short flight phase (as little as .01 second for some jumpers), the heel is planted *before the center of gravity begins to descend.* Thus, at the instant of touchdown, the athlete's center of gravity has either a zero or, perhaps, a small upward vertical velocity.

The extent to which an athlete can change his vertical velocity during the take off is governed by the product of the vertical forces he exerts and the time for which they act, i.e., by a quantity known as the vertical impulse. Although one's first inclination may be to suggest that the athlete should therefore strive to increase both the magnitude of the vertical forces which he exerts against the ground and the time for which they act (and, thus, the time of take-off), it has been shown repeatedly that the less time an athlete is in contact with the ground at take-off, the higher he goes. For some reason, which has yet to be adequately explained, the magnitude of the vertical forces that an athlete exerts increase at a greater rate than the time of take-off decreases. Thus a decrease in the time of take-off is generally accompanied by increases in both the vertical impulse and the vertical velocity at take-off.

The magnitude of H_3 (the height of the bar minus the peak height reached by the jumper's center of gravity) is governed mainly by the jumper's body position as he crosses the bar. If the jumper uses a simple scissors technique, his center of gravity may have to be lifted as much as 10-12 inches above the bar in order that he can effect a clearance $H_3 = -10$-12 inches). With more advanced jumping techniques—eastern cutoff, western roll, straddle, and Fosbury flop—the magnitude of the difference between the height of the bar and the peak height of the center of gravity gets progressively less until, with the last two styles listed, there exists the possibility that the center of gravity might actually pass beneath the bar while the jumper himself passes over it.

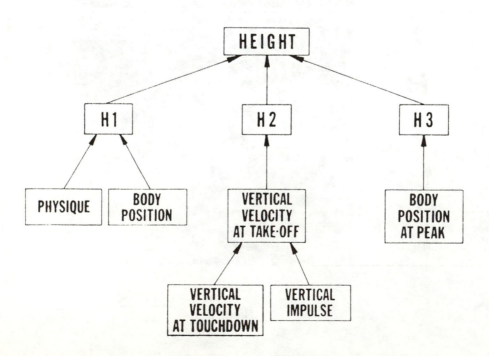

Figure 4. Relationship between height cleared and the various factors that influence that height.

POLE VAULT

The height with which a pole vaulter is credited may be thought of as the sum of (1) the height of his center of gravity at the instant he leaves the ground, (2) the height to which his center of gravity is raised while he retains contact with the pole, (3) the height to which his center of gravity is raised once he has let go of the pole and (4) the difference between the height of the bar and the peak height attained by his center of gravity. These four heights are designated as H_1, H_2, H_3, and H_4, respectively, in Figure 7.

The factors that influence H_1, H_3, and H_4 are the same as those that influence the corresponding heights in high jumping—namely, physique and body position (H_1), the vertical velocity at release (H_3) and the athlete's body position as he crosses the bar (H_4). In order to extract the greatest possible advantage from each of these separate heights, a vaulter would have to be tall, and would have to adopt a take-off position similar to that described for the high jump (to maximize H_1); would have to have as high a vertical velocity as possible at the time he releases the pole (to maximize H_3); and, would have to use the most tightly-draped

clearance position which would still permit him to clear the bar (to optimize H_4). In practice, however, a series of compromises is necessary because these conditions which serve to maximize one height often act to the detriment of the next.

Of the four contributions to the height which the vaulter clears, the height which his center of gravity is raised while he is in contact with the pole (H_2) is by far the most important—H_2 may contribute as much as 13 feet, 3.96m. (or 72%) in the case of an 18 feet (5.49 m.) vault.

While a complete analysis of the factors that influence the magnitude of H_2 requires a somewhat involved discussion of the interplay of energy between the vaulter and his pole, it is sufficient here to consider just three of the factors concerned—(a) the vaulter's velocity at take-off, (b) the energy he has "stored" in the pole at that time, and (c) the work he does as the pole rises towards the vertical.

The vaulter's velocity at take-off, determined by the speed of his approach and by the forces he exerts at take-off, is important in that it influences the amount of pole-bend he obtains and, partly as a consequence, his ability to bring the pole to the vertical (or desired near-vertical) position required for completion of the vault.

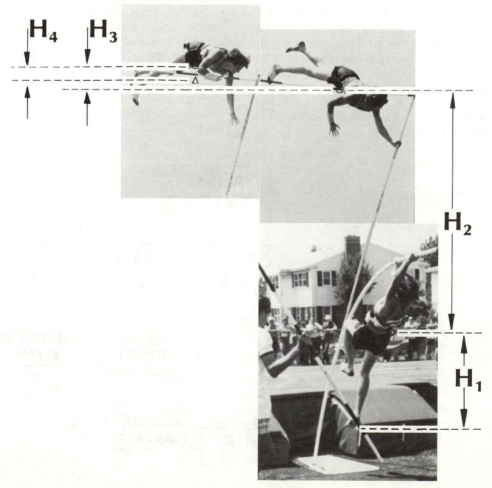

Figure 5

Because of this, the good vaulter tries to acquire as much forward speed in his run-up as he can control, to maintain it during the plant when there is a natural tendency to slow down and, finally, to exert forces at take off so that his body is propelled in the optimum direction. In vaulting with a metal pole (where pole-bend is generally not a significant factor) this optimum direction is approximately at right angles to the line of the pole—the direction which provides the best chance of the pole being brought to the required vertical (or near-vertical) release position. With a fiberglass pole, the need to bend the pole dictates that the vaulter direct his take-off somewhat more horizontally than if he were using a metal pole. Thus, present-day vaulters take off at angles of 15-25 degrees, angles similar to those used by top-class long jumpers whose take off they purposely try to emulate.

The energy that a vaulter is able to "store" in a pole prior to take-off—for any given pole, this may be thought of simply as the amount that the pole is bent at the instant of take-off—is governed by the forces he exerts on the pole once it is firmly "seated" against the back of the box. The forces involved may be divided into two categories—those that act across the line of the pole (the perpendicular forces) and those that act down the pole (the parallel forces). The first of these are due to the vaulter, intentionally or unintentionally, exerting an upward an forward force with his lower hand and a downward and backward force with his upper hand. This combination of forces (correctly termed a couple) exerted against a pole which is fixed at one end serves to introduce a bend into the pole. The main source of pole-bend at take-off, however, is the forces generated by the vaulter's forward driving action at take-off and exerted parallel to the long axis of the pole.

Although one normally thinks of a pendulum as a swinging body suspended from some fixed point, it is customary (and technically correct) to refer to the motions of the vaulter and the pole (once the vaulter has left the ground) in terms of a double pendulum—one pendulum consisting of the man rotating about a transverse axis through his hands (the man pendulum) and the other, the man and pole rotating upward about a transverse axis through the base of the pole (the man-and-pole pendulum).

Because any change in the body position of the vaulter inevitably alters the moment of inertia of each pendulum and thus the rate at which it is swinging upward (i.e. its angular velocity) it can readily be seen that the motions of the two pendulums are interdependent. For example, if a beginning vaulter pulled-up on his arms and assumed a tucked body position immediately after take-off—as beginning vaulters all too frequently do—he would simultaneously increase the moment of inertia of the man-and-pole pendulum, slow its rise toward the vertical, decrease the moment of inertia of the man pendulum and speed its forward upward swing. Such a sequence of events completely reverses that sought by the skilled vaulter who deliberately keeps his body extended during the early stages of the vault, thus keeping the pole moving quickly towards the vertical and his body behind the pole in position for an efficient swing-up. Then, as the pole nears the vertical, the vaulter quickly swings his legs upward and momentarily assumes a tucked position prior to pulling on his arms and driving his legs upward in front of the bar. This series of actions, which slows the upward motion of the man-and-pole pendulum at the same time as it speeds the man pendulum, carries the vaulter into that position from which he finally projects himself into the air and over the bar.

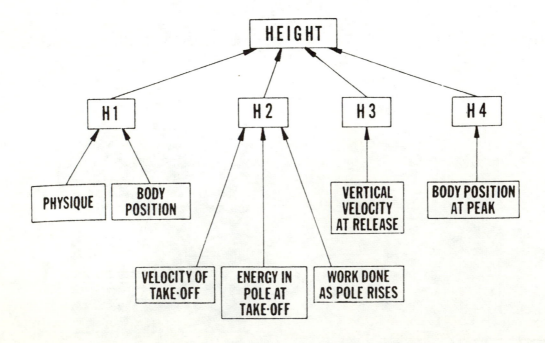

Figure 6.

19
The Long Jump

by
Bob Teel
University of Missouri

Introduction

The long jump is one of the most simple and natural events in track and field. Despite its apparent simplicity, a great deal of skill and conditioning is required to run full speed down a runway, consistently hit an eight inch board, and take off and land. For this reason it is imperative that the coach and athlete treat the long jump as a technique skill that can be improved only through proper training and conditioning.

The Approach

The approach should be long enough to reach (maximum controllable) speed and take-off. It should begin with a gradual acceleration rather than from an explosive start. An explosive start will cause several problems: inconsistent stride pattern, excessive deceleration at the end of the run and at take-off, and a general falling apart at the board.

Before beginning serious work on the approach, it is imperative that the athlete be well conditioned. Running is natural but sprinting is not. Proper sprinting form needs to be learned and practiced. There must be enough running and sprinting to develop a consistent, fluid stride pattern. It is well to note here that horizontal velocity (speed) is more important (by 2 to 1) than lifting in long-jumping. That is not to say that lifting is not im-

portant—it is, but not at the expense of velocity! Frequently an athlete is admonished to get more height off the board in order to get a better jump. This is true only if the athlete can gain more height without sacrificing velocity off the board. The athlete's usual reaction to such an admonition is a deceleration of the final two strides in order to get more lift. The jump appears better in the air, but the end result is less distance.

The length of the approach is a great contributing factor to the total success of the jump. The factors to consider when determining length of the approach are physical maturity, stage of conditioning, strength, and rate of acceleration of the athlete. A high school jumper might very well profit from a 14 or 16 stride approach but as he or she improves in the above mentioned areas, it should be lengthened.

Depending upon whether or not the athlete takes the first step with the foot that hits the board or with the foot of the free leg, the number of strides should be between 18 and 22 or 19 and 23. Since sprinters are within 1% of their maximum speed at 60 yards, it is reasonable to assume that even longer approaches could result in better jumps. Obviously this would be true only if the athlete was strong enough and conditioned enough to handle six approaches and jumps of the lengthened run-up.

The approach should be started in one of three ways: (1) both feet together and falling off the first check mark; (2) rocker-step-one foot touching the mark and the opposite arm flexed and forward as in running form. The other foot is back and the opposite arm is back in a proper running position. The athlete merely rocks back onto the rear foot and then takes off; (3) if the athlete experiences a great deal of tension in either of the first two styles, he or she can profit from a walk-on to the mark. Avoid running or jogging into the mark or extraneous moves such as skipping, jumping in the air, etc. These will all lend themselves to inconsistent early strides.

From the first stride to contact with the board, the run must be a relaxed, smooth accelerating sprint. The body should come up into an erect running position between 6 and 4 strides from the board. The tempo of the run emphasizes quickness. The athlete uses short angles with the arms and high knee action—a "pop! pop! pop!" action. Long strides and open arm angles cause the athlete to be slow off the board with accompanying dissipation of forces. The eyes should be on the board until four strides out; then they are lifted. The jumper mentally prepares to jump from three strides out but there is no change in running form until the penultimate stride. On the next to last strike the heel leads and the foot lands flat. This causes a lowering of the center of gravity. However, there must not be any effort to slow down on this stride! The foot also lands flat on the last stride, then goes onto the ball of the foot and then up on the toes. The effect of the flat footed last two steps is to prepare for the jump. The center of mass is on the rise which theoretically makes the jumper weigh less at time of take-off. If the center of mass is not lowered until the final stride, too much time is spent on the board making it more difficult to get into the proper take-off position.

It is imperative that the athlete have confidence that his or her approach will finish with the correct foot on the board in the proper position. An aid in establishing this confidence is the use of check marks. It is obvious that one mark be used at the beginning of the approach (as already mentioned). Research has shown that the first two strides are the most inconsistent ones. Therefore, it is recommended that a check mark be used for the second stride, and a final check mark at the sixth stride. The second stride check mark is the most important. To have a check mark any closer to the board than six strides from the beginning mark distract the athlete when he or she should be concentrating on attacking and hitting the board. If the athlete has a consistent stride pattern, the sixth stride check mark can be eliminated.

A coach's check mark should be established four strides from the board. This should be hit with the take-off foot. The mark for men should average between 30′ and 33′ and for women 26′ to 29′. The purpose of this mark is to let the coach know if the athlete is overstriding or backing off from the board in this area rather than having a quick cadence. The coach may want to place a shoe or some other reasonably large object down at this mark in order that he/she may easily see it from the stands or at a distance. Again, this is the coach's mark and not the athlete's!

The Take-off

It is difficult to separate the final two strides from the take-off. These and the ensuing action off the last stride constitute the heart of the jump and are the key to its success. The take-off foot strikes the board slightly in front of the body applying force underneath and a bit behind the center of gravity before breaking contact. If the foot is planted too far in front, it results in a check—the foot remains in contact with the board too long with the result being a loss of velocity and a high trajectory. If it is too far under, it will not have time to work against the board. The result will be not enough lift and accentuated forward rotation. The center of mass should pass directly over the take-off foot, otherwise eccentric thrust will occur. Most athletes make the necessary compensatory movement or movements without realizing that they are doing so. Unless the athlete's flight from the board to the pit is from left to right or right to left, landing near the outside boundaries of the pit, he or she is making the needed adjustment. The adjustment is made in one of two ways or a combination of both: Some jumpers, on the final stride, step toward the center line of the body. Others merely shift or slide the upper body over the take-off foot. It is this authors opinion that most jumpers do a little of each.

The jumper strives for full extension of the take-off leg. The free leg is vigorously driven forward and upward with the knee flexed as in a running stride. The key to height is the free leg and it must come through fast. The thigh or upper free leg should approximate a parallel position to the ground. A common error is to start the lead leg back too soon. It should not be rushed.

The arm opposite the free leg is driven up to chin or eye level. The conventional action of the arm opposite the take-off foot has been down and back and around. This action has been taught historically and is still being taught by most coaches. A better technique, however, for the 1 1/2 stride and particularly for the 2 1/2 stride style is as follows: When the arm starts down and back it stops when the hand is even with the hip. It is immediately thrust straight up over the athlete's head fully extended and continuous on its forward, downward, backward trajectory. The advantage of the non-conventional arm motion is twofold:

(1) The arm more quickly synchronizes with the opposite leg.
(2) Because it is more quickly extended above shoulder level, it is in position **earlier** to check forward rotation as it moves forward and downward.

The athlete runs off the board with a natural, quick, running action and a slight forward rotation—never backward. The chest and hips are up, the eyes and chin lift slightly. The jumper leaves the board at an angle of somewhere between 17° and 25°. However, the angle at which the jumper leaves the board is not nearly as important as the velocity with which the jumper leaves the board. The shorter the period of time on the board, the more horizontal velocity is maintained.

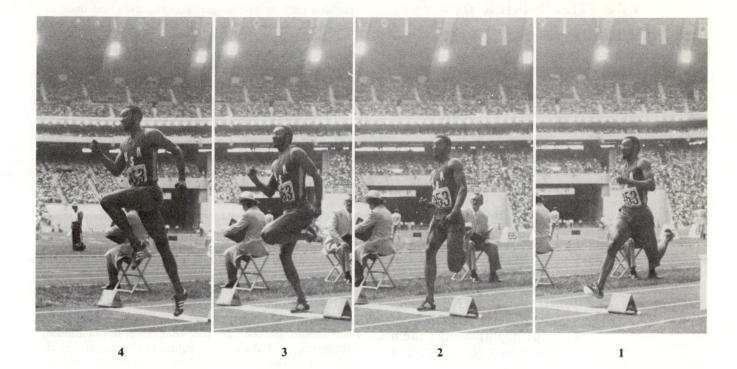

4   3   2   1

Long Jump (Hitch-Kick or Running-in-Air Style): Last stride and takeoff.

Flight in Air

There are three distinct in-the-air styles of long-jumping.

(1) Sail
(2) Hang or hip-swing
(3) Hitch-kick or running-in-the-air style

The easiest to do and the least effective style is the sail. The sail style jumper usually decelerates more at the board, and by assuming the landing position early, the forward rotation becomes more pronounced. For this reason it is not recommended.

The Hang or Hip-Swing Style

Advantages: (1)   Relatively easy to learn
                   (2)   Delays forward rotation
Disadvantages: (1)   Many jumpers tend to prepare too early to get into the arched position causing backward rotation off of the board with resultant deceleration.
                   (2)   Tendency for a premature snap into the landing position.

In the proper technique, the free leg comes through flexed and vigorous with a forward upward punch. The opposite arm is flexed with the hand about chin level. The arm on the side of the free leg is driven down and back. The take-off leg fully extends and then drags in the air only slightly flexed. The free leg continues its running stride, extends fully below the body and then joins the other leg in its extended dragging position. A word of caution here, if the legs are greatly flexed early, forward rotation will be accelerated. The arm opposite the free leg drops down where it becomes synchronized with the other arm in a backward, upward circular motion until fully extended above the back of the body.

The back is arched, the head up, and the body resembles a reversed C (Ɔ) in flight. This position is maintained momentarily which accounts for the name "hang" being given to this style. After this momentary pause, both arms fully extended, continue on overhead, sweeping down with fingers reaching toward the toes, and then on back behind the body as far as possible just prior to the heels hitting the sand. The legs, working with the arms, begin flexing until they become tightly flexed underneath the hips. They continue on through together and assume the landing position. Some jumpers bring the legs through in more of a circular action with seemingly good results.

The Hitch-Kick or Running-in-Air Style

(2 types; 1 1/2 stride and 2 1/2 stride)

Advantages:
  (1) Is a natural extension of the run.
  (2) Puts the athlete in a better landing position.
  (3) Reverses forward rotation for a brief instant.
  (4) Most efficient.

Disadvantages:
  (1) Most difficult to learn.
  (2) If using 1 1/2 strides there is a possibility of completing them too soon, thus getting into the landing position too early.
  (3) If using 2 1/2 strides there is a possibility of not completing them soon enough for a proper landing.

More top flight jumpers have used the hitch kick than any other style. It can be learned and used effectively by jumpers at all levels.

1 1/2 Stride

The free leg comes through vigorously and is flexed in a forward upward direction. The more drive with the free leg at this point, the more force that will be exerted against the board and the more that will be returned to the jumper. The thigh should reach the horizontal. The athlete should delay going into the backward running action for a split second. A common error is to begin the hitch kick too soon resulting in too early completion of the action. The leg is extended, goes beneath the body fully extended, flexes behind with the heel near the buttocks and comes through flexed and into the extended landing position. The take-off leg extends, then flexes with the heel near the buttocks and comes through forward into the landing position. The lower legs (from the knee down), in the running action, help reverse forward rotation.

The arms operate independently of each other in a windmilling fashion, but in synchronization with the opposite leg. For example: when one is walking or running, if the left leg is forward, the right arm is forward. The arm on the side of the free leg, if following the conventional action, will drive down and back extending. It continues on behind the body, up and around fully extended above the jumper and on down into the extended landing position. If using the unconventional arm action, the arm starts back in a flexed position. When the hand is along side of the body it is immediately pushed directly over head, arm fully extended. If the technique is sound, the athlete will get into the landing position at the proper time. The arm opposite the free leg, after reaching chin or eye height, comes down and back extended. It continues on behind the body, on up, and around fully extended above the jumper and on down to join the other arm in the landing position.

2 1/2 Stride

The free leg and the opposite arm action is identical with that used in the 1 1/2 stride style. The take-off leg completes one more cycle. The arm opposite the take-off leg also completes one more cycle. Strongly recommended is the unconventional action of the arm on the side of the free leg at take-off. This action was described earlier. The arms play a most significant role in reversing forward rotation. The higher they are elevated above the center of mass, the more effective they are. As long as they move in a clockwise direction, about shoulder level, they will produce a counterclockwise reaction on the trunk. It is true that the arm action below shoulder level produces a clockwise reaction on the trunk. But since the arms at this stage are close to the center of mass, the adverse reaction on the trunk is negligible.

It should be pointed out that several outstanding jumpers have used a combination of the hang and hitch-kick styles. They usually follow a pattern of the hitch kick leg action and the hang arm action. So long as the arms operate fully extended there is only a little loss of effectiveness. Some jumpers using the 2 1/2 stride style go to the hang leg action after the first stride.

The Landing

Whatever method is used when the athlete is in the air, it is only a means to achieve the best possible landing position. The most effective landing position has the feet as far ahead of the jumper's center of gravity as possible at the time of landing—without subsequently falling backwards into the pit. The most common error in landing is getting into position too early. The forward rotation can only be delayed or reversed momentarily—just as soon as the action in the air ceases, it reappears. This is mostly bad, but not all bad! Without any forward rotation, the athlete would likely fall backwards. The major problem, particularly with the early positioning, is the body's forward rotation around the center of gravity. The athlete may be told to hold his or her feet up longer, but this is an impossibility, for all parts of the body are rotating forward and dropping at the same rate of speed. The feet just happen to be the most visible result of this. Incidentally, the strength, or lack of it, of the stomach muscles plays no part in holding the feet up of a freely falling body. However, the wise coach or athlete develops a well conditioned mid-section, for it is essential for any successful athletic endeavor.

Just prior to the landing, the legs are extended as far as possible at the horizontal, toes up. The head, chest, and arms are thrust forward—the arms are reaching forward extended and are sweeping downward. The reaction to this downward sweep of the arms brings about

Long Jump (Hitch-Kick or Running-in-Air Style): Flight phase.

| 20 | 19 | 18 | 17 |

Long Jump (Hitch-Kick or Running-in-Air Style): Landing.

an opposite one for the legs. They rise slightly. The arms continue backward, extended outside the legs until, at the instant the heels touch the sand, they are as far as possible behind the body. This arm action results in the body's center of gravity moving backward and in essence causes a forward movement of the feet. The arms are then brought forward.

The knees relax just as the heels hit the sand (they are virtually locked until then). The feet should be about 8" apart. If much wider, distance will be lost and if much closer, loss of balance can be a problem. With the aid of the forward moving arms, the athlete should fall forward into a compact tuck position. There are other landing positions used such as the pivot to the side or the scoop landing where the hips are thrust forward at the last instant, and the athlete strikes the sand with the buttocks as well as the feet. Observation of these methods has been that unless the athlete is very technically sound, there is an early anticipation of the landing position.

When the athlete's take-off foot breaks contact with the board, the parabolic curve of his or her center of mass has been established. Nothing done by the jumper in the air will change this curve or where it will bisect the sand. the athletes with very good technique will have the heels hit beyond the parabolic curve juncture. The good technicians will hit close to the bisected point and the poor technical jumpers will break the sand behind the point.

Drills for "In-The-Air" Technique

These drills can be used with a two or three stride approach off the runway and into the pit. However, for teaching purposes, this author prefers getting the athletes well airborne so that the movements are not rushed. Apparatus to use are incline boards, gymnastic boards and spring-boards. The springboard works especially well for after only a few times off of it, the athlete feels comfortable with even faster and longer approaches and reaches a good teaching height. Whichever method is used, the landing should be in a high jump or pole vault when learning.

A. Hang or Hip Swing: Left Footed Jumper

Use a three stride approach first and move back as the athlete becomes more proficient.

Step I   (1) Drive the right knee up flexed until the thigh is parallel to the pit.

        (2) The left arm is driven up flexed. Hand even with the chin or eyes.

        (3) Right arm is driven back and down.

        (4) Left leg fully extends then folds up until the lower leg is parallel to the pit.

(5) Land on the right foot, knee flexed, and the knee and lower part of the leg and toes.

(6) Upper body is in an upright position.

Step II (1) Assume same position in the air as in Step 1.

(2) The right leg extends as in a running action and passes below the body fully straightened. It then folds up behind, joining the take-off leg.

(3) The left arm drops down, back and around till it is behind and above the body fully extended.

(4) The right arm continues its downward, backward, around movement until it is behind and above the body fully extended.

(5) The head is up and the back is arched.

(6) Land on the knees, lower legs and toes.

Step III (For step three the athlete can take a three stride approach if desired.)

(1) Merely go through Steps I and II in the air.

(2) Bring both legs through, tightly flexed into a front extended position.

(3) The arms sweep over the top of the head reaching forward and downward and continue outside the legs until they are extended behind.

(4) Land in a sitting position.

Do not rush from one step to the other. The athlete should develop confidence in each phase before progressing to the next one.

B. 1 1/2 Stride: Left Footed Jumper

Step I (1) Drive the right knee up flexed until the thigh is parallel to the pit.

(2) The left arm is driven up flexed. The hand is even with the chin or eyes.

(3) If using the conventional arm action, the right arm is driven down and back. If using the unconventional arm action, the right arm is flexed at the elbow with lower arm and hand up.

(4) Left leg fully extends then folds up until the lower leg is parallel to the pit.

(5) Land on the right foot, knee flexed, and the knee and lower part of the left leg and toes.

(6) Upper body is in an upright position.

Step II (1) Complete step one in the air.

(2) The right leg extends and straightens as it passes below the body and flexes behind with the lower leg parallel to the pit.

(3) The right arm is straightened above the head or comes around from behind to an over-head straightened position depending upon which arm action is being used.

(4) The left leg comes through flexed, heel near buttocks, and continues till the thigh is parallel to the pit with the foot below the knee.

(5) The left arm is driven down and back.

(6) Land in this position on the left foot and the knee, lower leg and toes of the right leg.

(7) Upper body is in an upright position.

Step III (1) Complete Steps I and II in the air.

(2) The left leg extends and the toes are up.

(3) The right arm continues on forward and downward extended passing the right leg just before touch-down and extending behind the body.

(4) The right leg comes through tightly flexed with the heel near buttocks, extends and joins the left leg.

(5) The left arm continues on around and over the top of the head joining the motion of the right arm in its forward, downward, backward sweep.

(6) Land in a sitting position.

C. 2 1/2 Stride: Left Footed Jumper

All of the airborne steps of the 1 1/2 stride drill are completed, plus the following:

(1) The take-off leg or left leg goes through one more stride and then joins the right leg in its extended landing position.

(2) The left arm action is the same as for the 1 1/2.

(3) The right leg action is the same as for the 1 1/2.

(4) The right arm goes through one more cycle: down, behind and over the top, extended forward, down and behind the body.

D. 1, 2, 3 and Jump Drill

This is a drill to teach the proper technique for the final two strides of the approach. It has already been pointed out that the athlete should land flat footed on the last two strides. With that in mind, the new jumpers should start in the following manner: (Assuming the jumper has a left foot take off).

(1) First step with the left foot at an easy jog pace landing on the ball of the foot

(2) Right foot on the ball of the foot

(3) Left foot on the ball of the foot

(4) Right foot landing flat

(5) Left foot landing flat

(6) Continue on up on to the ball of the foot, then toes and finish with an easy take-off using the proper arm action and lead leg action.

This is a 5 stride drill (L, R, L, R, L). The "AND JUMP" provides the proper rhythm for the last two strides. The athletes verbalize as they perform the drill. When they become comfortable with the drill, speed it up. Then add two strides: 1, 2, 3, 4, 5 AND JUMP. Continue to add two strides as long as a definite change in rhythm can be observed on the last two strides when performed at normal runway speed. With most jumpers the point is reached quickly. Drill from that point until the jumper can handle the rhythm, then move back again. When adding strides, perform first at a jog pace then increase the pace until the athlete is running at maximum or near maximum speed for the distance covered. The drill is continued back until the athlete is running the number of strides he or she is capable of at that point and time of training for a full approach.

E. Box Drills*

I.   8 Boxes 12″ High and 2′ x 2′
  (1) Place the boxes in a straight line.
  (2) Leave enough space between so that the athlete can comfortably bound up on top, down to the ground, back up etc.
  (3) Do 4 sets of 4 with double leg support from a standing start. After the athlete is better conditioned, do the same drill with single leg support.
  (4) As the training season progresses, place the last 4 boxes on top of the first four (making 4 boxes 2 feet high). Do the same drill and same number of sets progressing from double leg to single leg.
  (5) Occasionally intersperse a few boxes of differing heights 12″, 18″ and one 3′. Emphasize quickness off the ground!
II. 8 Box Hopping Drill
  (1) 12″ high boxes spaced farther apart than for drill I
  (2) Athlete takes a 4 or 6 stride approach and leaves the ground from the left foot, left on top, left down etc.
  (3) Repeat with right foot.
  (4) Later on some of the athletes move to the 18″ boxes and a few to the 2′ ones.
  (5) 4 sets of 4
III. Hurdle Hopping Drill
  (1) Set 5 to 10 hurdles at low hurdle height in a straight line.
  (2) Space so athlete can land and take off again comfortably and without any adjustment on the ground.
  (3) Double leg bounds over
  (4) 4 sets of 4
  (5) Single leg bounds later

  (6) As the training period progresses the hurdles can be advanced to the women's setting, high school highs, and collegiate height—As long as the athlete can handle the additional height.
IV. Varied Height Hurdle Hopping
  (1) Place 5 hurdles in a row at a comfortable distance.
  (2) Hurdle one is at low hurdle height; two is at women's height; three at intermediate height; four at high school high hurdle height; and five at a collegiate high hurdle height..
  (3) 4 sets of 4 double leg bounds over, taking off instantly upon landing. Some athletes can handle this drill with single leg support

F. Depth Jumping**

After a period of general conditioning, it is possible to begin doing depth jumps. First use a 2′ box and later use a 3′ box. The drill is used once a week and discontinued ten days before the first competition and not resumed as long as there is weekly competition. It is best done on a relatively soft grassy area or on a mat. Do not do on a hard surface.
Procedure:
(1)   The athlete stands on top of the box and drops off of it to the ground. He or she should not jump up off of the box!
(2)   Immediately upon hitting the ground, explode into the air with maximum effort.
(3)   Quickness off of the landing surface is paramount.
(4)   The drill is performed in 2 sets of 10. Early do both sets off of the 2′ box, then 1 set off the 3′ box and finally both sets off of the 3′ box. Add 1 set of single leg off of the 2′ box.

G. Standing Long-Jump Drill (2 types)

I.   This drill is used primarily to work on the proper backward arm action at landing. The athlete stands at the edge of the pit, executes a standing long jump, the arms extend forward, down and are all the way back of the body when the athlete lands in a sitting position.
II. This drill emphasizes the importance of a leg extension at landing. Again the athlete executes a standing long jump, gets the legs up, and hits the sand with the heels as far as possible from the take-off spot. The athlete lands in an extended position.

---

* The athlete must be well conditioned before using these drills. They are not for the beginning athlete.

** This drill should not be used until the athlete can leg press 2 times body weight or squat 1 1/2 times body weight.

H. Complimentary Triple-Jump Drills

I.   Bounding—left, right, left, right, etc. with thighs coming parallel to the ground. Either time or measure 10 bounds to check progress.
II. 20 meter and later 40 meter consecutive hops. The thigh of the hopping leg should reach the parallel plane.
III. Hop, Hop, Step, and jump into the pit.
IV. Ratio Bounding—Do this drill on a football field. Put 11 chalk lines down every 8', 9', or 10', etc.—whichever the athlete can handle with 10 consecutive bounds after a six stride approach. Lengthen the marks as the athlete becomes more proficient. The thighs should come to the parallel position.

I. Harness Drill—Use a gymnastic harness or an inner tube cut in half and tied at each end with 3 feet of rope.

I.   Athlete places the harness around the waist. Parner grasps ropes and offers moderate resistance for 20 meters. 3 × 20 meters.

J. Squat Jumps

I.   Athlete assumes a squatting position, then jumps upward and forward, with the arms going above the head, landing again in a squatting position. 3 × 10 consecutive jumps.

K. Pop Ups: Heading a Ball

I.   Place a pole vault standard, adjacent to the pit, where the athlete should reach maximum height. Tape a broken cross bar to the standard and suspend a ball or piece of sponge over the center of the pit. The athlete uses a 6 strides, takes off and tries to hit the ball or sponge with the head while executing good technique. This is good to check the upright position of the body. Increase the approach as technique improves. **This is not a drill for height.** It is a form drill to observe the execution at the high point of the normal trajectory. A danger of using this drill to see how high the athlete can go is that it will produce too much of a plant, reducing speed at take-off.

L. Hill Drills (4 kinds)

I.   600 meter hill—moderate incline—used during the conditioning period. Start with a minimum of one run up and progress to 10. Walk or jog back down.
II. 200 meter hill—steep—start with minimum of one run up and about 70% effort. Progress to 10 increasing the effort. Walk back down and take a maximum of 2 minutes rest at the bottom.

III. 80 meter hill—relatively steep. 3 sets of 3.
     1. High knee—moderate speed
     2. Bounding—Left, right, left ect. lift knees
     3. Sprint
IV. 40 meter hill—3% grade down
     6 × 40 all out with running start and full recovery between runs. This workout is never run until the athlete is in good shape. The down hill runs are followed by an equal number on a flat surface. We sometimes combine #3 and #4, doing #4 first and eliminating one of the sets of #3.

Structuring a Training Program for The Long Jump

Many collegiate coaches enjoy the luxury of having the athletes all fall and for the early winter prior to the opening of indoor competition. This allows for a broader and more extensive conditioning and teaching base than possible at the junior high or high school level. At the junior high and high school level many track and field athletes are involved in one or more sports before reporting for track. If participating in state basketball playoffs, the athlete may report for track the week of the first outdoor meet. The dilemma is how much work should be given—what should be left out or what should be added.

The athlete reporting from another sport is usually well conditioned, but not necessarily in top jumping shape. More mistakes are made in overtraining or overworking these athletes than in undertraining them. If they are overloaded, they will regress and probably will just be coming back when the most important meets are over. Technique work should be stressed. If box drills are used, cut them in half, if hill running is used, cut it in half. If the athlete has not been in a strength training program in the other sports, start at the beginning level. The intensity in all of these areas can be gradually increased over the next few weeks. Use good judgment and improvise. Also, if the athlete is a multi-event athlete, the major part of his/her conditioning may have come from the events other than the long-jump. In this case, stress the technique aspects of the long-jump.

Sample Workouts

All workouts are preceded by the warm-up described below. Each workout concludes with a half mile jog.

Daily Warm-Up

I.   3/4 mile jog
II. 20 minutes of stretching and flexibility exercises. Local warm-ups are of little or no value. All stretching movements should be static rather than ballistic. Static movements are done slowly.

III. Four 80 to 100 acceleration sprints—walk back interval

IV. (1) 100 meter high knee, staying on the toes—not fast

(2) 100 meter leg extension, staying on the toes—not fast. Come to the high knee position and exaggerate the extension of the lower leg. Do not lean the upper body backwards.

(3) 60 meter fast arm—fast leg. Cadence is as quick as the athlete can move in 15 meter segments with a breather after each 15 meters. The steps are short—almost running in place! High knee action.

(4) 2 × 100 meters. Relaxed form runs. All of the above are done with a walk back interval.

When the competitive season begins, it becomes necessary to adjust the weight training workout in order to keep from lifting the day before a meet. If possible, perform the Thursday weight workout after the meet. If a team competes mainly on Fridays, it would be better to go to a three day a week pattern—Monday, Wednesday, Friday. Incorporate the same lifts into the three-day program but each session would be of longer duration. Friday's routine would be done after the meet or on Saturday.

Pre-Season

Mon. 1, 2, 3, 4, and jump drill as athlete becomes more proficient)
10 to 15 pop-ups off a springboard or box, into the high jump pit, working on the in-the-air technique
6 × 6 stride jumps
10 × 1 step jumps
10 × 2 stride hop, hop, step, and jump
7 × 75 meter sprints at 85%—full recovery between
Weight training

Tues. 1, 2, 3, and jump drill
2 × 10 standing long jumps
5 × 60 meters easy form runs (check running fundamentals)
Hill run
Weight training

Wed. 6 to 10 pop-ups off of a box, at the pit, stressing lead knee drive
5 minutes of ratio bounding
5 minutes of a hopping drill
Box drills—select 2
Depth jumping
6 to 10 × 200's easy with a 200 walk interval, speed is increased as conditioning increased.

Thurs. 1, 2, 3, and jump drill
6 pop-ups, stressing proper knee and arm action at take-off
5 × 60 meters form runs
Hill workout—after a month to six weeks, this run is replaced by another day of drills
Weight training

Fri. 1, 2, 3, and jump drill
6 to 10 times off of a springboard or box into high jump pit (Each time work on a different phase of the in-the-air technique)
2 × 10 squat jumps
6 × 6 stride jumps
5 × 5 low hurdles 10 yards apart. Be aggressive—no striding or loping between hurdles
6 × 150 meters
Weight training

Sat. 3 mile cross-country run on own

Middle-Season

Do one hill workout every two weeks.

Mon. Continue with 1, 2, 3, 4, etc. and jump drill if necessary
6 to 10 springboard or box jumps into high jump pit stressing a different aspect of the in-the-air technique each time.
Land with the arms back
5 minutes of ratio bounding
6 run throughs away from the pit
6 to 8 × 200's—26-27-28 sec. range with a 200 walk interval
Weights

Tues. 5 × 5 low hurdles
6 full approaches with proper technique on the last 2 strides
On the last 2 run throughs, take-off but do not complete the jump
6 short approach pop-ups off of a box emphasizing the knee drive of the free leg and proper arm action
5 to 8 × 75 meter springs or 3 × 30 meters, 3 × 40 meters, 3 × 50 meters, with full recovery
Weights

Wed. 6 × 6 stride jumps
6 × 1 step and jump
6 × hop, hop, step and jump
2 × 10 squat jumps
2 box drills
2 × 300 meters, full recovery

Thurs. 6 full approaches as on Tuesday
5 × the springboard or box drill
6 to 10 pop-ups heading a ball
40 meter hopping drill
5 × 150's (speed increases as the conditioning increases), full recovery
Weights

Fri. Warm-up
A few easy 60 meter form runs
2 to 3 run throughs

Sat. Compete
Weight training after the meet, if practical

Sun. Rest

Late Season

Before the most important meets it is beneficial to take two days of rest and adjust the weight training workouts. Do the same lifts and at the same weight but cut down on the repetitions. With some athletes it is wise to eliminate the weight workouts the week of the most important meet. It is important that the jumpers have fresh, rested legs!

Mon.   4 to 6 full approaches
        A few easy pop-ups
        5 × 75 meters—full recovery—emphasize speed
        Weights
Tues.   2 to 3 × 6 stride jumps
        2 to 3 springboard or box jumps into high jump pit
        4 to 6 pop-ups off of a box at the pit
        Weights
Wed.   1 bounding drill
        1 hopping drill
        1 box drill
        3 × 150 full effort and full recovery
Thurs. 3 or 4 approaches
        A few easy pop-ups
Fri.   Warm-up or rest
Sat.   Compete
Sun.   Rest

For better performance, make every effort to have to first jump a fair one.

Hints for Better Performance

- Test the consistency of the pit before taking a run through. This can help to prevent injury.
- Make every effort to have the first jump a fair one. It will take a lot of pressure off of the following ones.
- Work on technique when fresh and work on only one aspect of technique at a time.
- Use heel cup or protective padding in the shoes. A heel bruise can put the athlete out of commission for weeks.
- Concentration on the run-way must be stressed. Many athletes have inconsistent approaches because of a lack of concentration.
- If the athlete consistently fouls by a small margin, he or she is probably keeping eye contact with the board too long. It is impossible to synchronize the eye and the foot at the speed the jumper is traveling.
- Time and record jumper's full approach periodically. Timing the last 4 strides is difficult to do but it can be quite revealing. Compare these times from training period to training period and meet to meet.
- Be discerning when studying the technique, on film, of top flight jumpers. Many of them excel in spite of their technique rather than because of it! They may have been blessed with exceptional talent.
- Take film of the athletes and analyze it with them. A word of caution: Don't over coach or over analyze the athlete. He or she can get "Paralysis by Analysis." A time comes when the athlete has to get out and do it unencumbered by worrying about what he or she looks like in the process!
- Do a "Consecutive Pop Up" drill as a conditioner and change of pace. 3 sets of 10 × 10 stride pop-ups quickly one after another.
- Run the stadium steps sometimes as a substitute for hill runs.
- Also do some double and single leg hops on the stadium steps.
- Take-off at least once as if jumping before competition begins.

20
Triple Jump

by
Steve Simmons
Gavilan Community College
Dean Hayes
Middle Tennessee State University

Introduction

The triple jump is a unique technique event requiring a combination of speed, strength and balance. It is composed of three distinct phases (parts) that must flow into one another. They are the hop (take off and landing on the same foot), the step (landing on the opposite foot), and the jump (performed similar to the long jump). The hop and jump are relatively easy to master but the link between the two, the step, is the difficult skill. The triple jump was previously called the hop-step-jump but the name was changed to emphasize the equal importance of each phase.

The double arm method of triple jumping was developed by the Russians in the 1950's. The Russian jumpers of that period as well as today are famous for their "moving statue" body position in the step and their great leg strength. In 1968 at the Mexico City Olympics, the Russian jumper Victor Saneyev set a new world's record of 57' 3/4" using the double arm technique. In the last twelve years this method of triple jumping, with its emphasis on leg and body strength, has proven itself superior to the more conventional single arm or natural method. For this reason, this chapter will focus primarily on the double arm technique.

Triple Jump Technique

The double arm technique requires the jumpers to make an unnatural movement with the arms: The jumper draws both arms behind his back while in the air in the hop and step phases so that they can be used to gather himself, forcefully, in preparation for the next phase. Through the use of the double arm technique, he can generate more straight-ahead power, drive, and lift with his body than with the single arm method. The lift especially is greater to that in the single arm action, because, in the latter, the arms are used more for balance than as an aid to momentum.

Approach

The approach should be from 100 to 135 feet in length with two check marks, the first, 8 steps down the runway, and the second mark, 4 to 6 steps from the board, depending on the jumper. Emphasis should be placed on a fast, controlled, rhythmic approach to the board with acceleration in the last 6 strides.

When the double arm jumper hits the board, he must have his arms in front or close to the front of his body.

The beginning jumper should exaggerate this action by having both arms chest high as he leaves the board. More experienced jumpers do not have to bring the arms this high. The reason for having the arms in front of the body is that the jumper can then take them behind his body smoothly without any break in his forward drive. Any other method of getting the arms behind the body will cause at least a small break in the jumper's rhythm. The jumper can either take the arms behind him in a sweeping circular motion or push them straight back with the elbows bent. It is recommended that the jumper use the circular method first for two reasons: 1) It gives him better balance and 2) The arms can be taken further behind the waist and brought through more forcefully.

The Hop

Just as with the single-arm method of jumping, the double-arm jumper must keep his hcp controlled. But he should have more height in the hop than the single-arm jumper. The increased height in both the hop and the step is an important characteristic of the double-arm technique.

In preparation for landing in the hop, the jumper should place his arms behind him and start to bring them forward in combination with a reaching action of the free leg before the hop foot hits the ground. (The action of the hopping foot is a heel-ball-toe landing common to triple jumpers). It is important that the arms be behind the body and brought forward before the hopping foot hits the ground, so that the jumper can use the arms to lift and drive his body into the step. As the jumper leaves the ground going into the step, he should bring the knee and thigh of the stepping leg up above waist level with the thigh parallel to the ground. The arms are then drawn out in front of the body, then down and back, in the same circular motion as used in the hop. The free side leg is flexed deeply at the knee. This is the "moving statue" position for which the Russian triple jumpers have been famous.

The hop.

The step.

The Step

It is the step phase of the triple jump that the double-arm technique varies the most from the single-arm. First of all, the jumper using the double arm will have a higher bounding type step than the single arm jumper. Secondly, when using the double arm in the step phase, the jumper bends forward slightly from the waist to meet the step thigh and lean toward the side of the hopping leg. He does this because of the position of his arms behind him. He must lean forward to keep his momentum and to maintain balance as he holds the stepping thigh up. This upper body lean is contrary to single arm jumping technique which requires the jumper to hold his upper body erect with the chest and shoulders square to the runway.

In the double arm method, the "moving statue" position in the step phase is an asset in a number of ways. Because the arms are brought forward from behind, the jumper can use them in combination with his step leg as a lever to send his body forcefully into the step. The arms are also used in this manner at the end of the step and into the jump. Another asset of the double arm is the heel-ball-toe landing that the jumper gets when executing the double arm step correctly.

When completing the step using the double arm, the jumper in the "moving statue" position, who has a good thigh split in both the hop and step should reach out with the lower leg and heel. The leg should be at an angle of about 45° at the knee. The heel hits the ground just a fraction of a second ahead of the sole of the foot. As the heel and then the full foot hit the runway, the jumper should sweep the arms forward, bring his center of gravity over the step leg and go right into the jump. This extended lower leg, heel first landing allows the jumper to shift his body forward and drive up and over the stepping foot with no loss of momentum. The jumper should reach out and bring the leg back under the body while the arms and free leg come forward and up.

The jump.

The Jump

As the athlete leaves the ground from the step, he takes the arms up and goes into a "hang style" jump. In this jump, the double arm jumpers have a greater tendency to "sit back" in the pit than using the single or natural arm action. This sitting back happens because the hang-style jumper so extends himself that he cannot bring his center of gravity over the knees when he lands and therefore comes to rest in a sitting position.

Teaching the Triple Jump

Establishing a Take-off Leg

The first two phases of the jump, the hop and step, are performed from the same leg. This makes it imperative that the jumper decide early what leg to use in beginning the action. The leg does not necessarily have to be the athlete's strongest. It is more important that the athlete feel comfortable on this leg so that he can execute the required coordinated movement.

Standing Triple Jump

The standing triple jump allows the athlete to get the feel of the whole movement without adding the complicating factor of the speed of approach. The athlete should not jump for distance but rather emphasize evenness of each phase and rhythm. The jump is executed in the following manner (assuming a left foot take-off):

The athlete places the take-off foot forward, swinging the opposite (free) leg forward and landing on the take-off foot for the hop. Next he steps forward, landing on the opposite foot. He then executes a jump landing on both feet into the pit.

LEFT (take-off)	LEFT (landing after hop)	RIGHT (landing after step)	BOTH (landing after jump)

Points to Emphasize:
1. The athlete should land flat footed in the hop and step phase, not up on the toes.
2. The athlete should bend the hop leg knee before landing in the hop. This will help to lessen the shock of landing.

169

3. In the hop phase, he should not swing the free leg straight.
4. Rhythm should be even during all three phases.

The Hop

Here the athlete walks three strides and executes a hop. After doing this three or four times, the athlete emphasizes the circling action of the hopping leg in the air and an active flat footed landing.

When this is accomplished, the jumper begins performing a series of five continuous hops from a three walking step approach (LLLLL or RRRRR). Emphasis should be on a flat footed landing, circling the hop leg, and an erect upper body.

The Step

The athlete can accomplish this skill by doing a series of continuous steps on the grass, landing each time on the alternate foot (L-R-L-R-L). It is essentially overexaggerated, bouncing, running steps. A simple method to use in placing these steps is to mark lines on the ground in a grid pattern starting at 8 feet apart and gradually increasing the distance between them.

As the distance between lines is increased, there should be a greater emphasis on the driving action with the knee at each take-off and a slight pause or freeze in the air.

Complete extension of the ankle, knee and hip joints at each take-off are important. The trunk should be upright and the feet should land flat footed or slightly heel first.

Hop and Step Combination

The athlete should perform this on the grass. The emphasis is on carrying the momentum from a flat forward take-off into the hop, immediately followed by a step. This can be performed in combination for learning and conditioning.

Jump with the Short Approach

The jumper starts with three running strides and adds strides as he masters control of the added speed. These strides generate momentum which give the jumper the feeling of carrying speed through all three phases. Lines or other markers should be placed on or near the runway to insure equal distances for each phase.* A good progression is to place a grid on the side of the pit:

Start with 9 or 10 feet for each phase. Add a foot to each phase as running strides are added until the athlete is up to 12 or 13 feet per phase.

---

* Note: The jump can be longer, but the coach should emphasize evenness of the hop and step.

The Arm Action

Double arm action is recommended for the reason detailed under the description of triple jump technique. It should be pointed out that many jumpers use a single arm action off the board in the hop in order to maintain speed. They then go to double arm action in the step and jump phase.

It must be remembered that in proper double arm action, both arms go forward each time a leg goes forward until the final part of the jump phase. This must be practiced continually during all the drills in order to learn proper coordination of the arms and legs.

Special Exercises for the Triple Jump

1. Skipping with weights on the shoulder (use barbells, sand bags or steel bars) from 50 to 100 yards, 5 to 20 times. Start beginners very light and add weight as the athlete rounds into shape and gets stronger. This drill builds strength in the lower back and legs of the jumper. Make sure the athlete is pushing off the ground with the foot and extending the ankle, keeping the back straight.
2. Hopping the length of the football field, alternating legs every 25 yards. As the jumper gets stronger, he should hop further on each leg; for instance, hop 75 yards on one leg, turn around and go back on the other leg. Beginners should start with 50 yards and gradually increase.
3. Hopping for distance. The athlete takes 3-5 hops on one leg. Measure. Try to increase the distance covered in each workout. Make sure the jumper does not forget to use the free leg correctly.
4. Hopping up stadium steps on one leg and hopping up the steps on both legs. Emphasize the weak leg in this drill.
5. Hopping down steps with a pop-up. The athlete simply hops down two or three steps; upon landing he springs back into the air and onto the step jumped from. This is a form of depth jumping that overloads the muscles of the jumper and is imitative of the triple jump. Stadium seats, especially wooden ones, should be used. This is not recommended for the beginning jumper.
6. Box Work - Use 2 to 3 boxes and develop variations or routine desired. The boxes are from 12-18 inches high and 2 feet x 2 feet wide. High Box = 18 inches. The athlete should perform the drills as follows:
   a. Stand on high box, hop off onto the ground, go into the step and jump into the pit.
   b. Stand on the high box, hop off the ground, hop again, go into the step and jump into the pit.
   c. Stand on the high box, hop onto the ground, step up to a high box and jump into the pit.
   d. Stand on the high box, hop onto the ground, step up to a high box and jump into the pit.
   e. Use a 5-7 step run up to a high box, hop up on

the box, go into the step and jump into the pit.

f. Use a 5-7 step run-up to a high box, take one hop before reaching the box, then hop once onto the top of the box, go into the step and jump into the pit.

g. Using a 5-7 step run-up to a high box, hop off onto the ground and step up to a high box and jump into the pit.

h. Stand on a 3 ft. high box, hop onto the ground and spring back up to the 3 ft. high box placed 3 ft. away (depth jump). This is not recommended until the athlete can squat 1½ times body weight or leg press 2 times body weight.

There are other ways the boxes can be used, and each coach should advise his/her own favorites. Box work is mainly a combination of depth jumping, rhythm, co-ordination work and strength training. The overload aspect of weight training and exercise is applied in the use of the boxes, and the imitative actions of triple jumping are easily incorporated into box training. One of the more positive aspects of the box work exercises is that the jumper must bring his free leg and foot through strongly and correctly. If he does not, then the free foot will hit the side of the boxes and remind him of his error. The use of the boxes can also get the jumper to develop the good thigh split that a triple jumper must have. Hopping and stepping from box to box forces the jumper to reach out and bring the box to him.

7. Running Scissors High Jumping. The jumper used both legs for take off and works from each side of the pit. He should make a strong effort to keep the body weight moving forward at all times, getting hips up and staying on his feet as he goes through the pit. He should not attempt to gather in the last few steps before reaching the bar. This drill can help develop forward drive in a fun manner. The bar should start at 3 feet and go up to 4 feet. The jumper should take 5 running steps on each leg at each height.

8. Triple Jumping Into the High Jump Pit. The athlete takes a short 6 step run-up and goes into a double arm hop and step and jump over the bar and into the pit. The hips must be brought up for bar clearance—the jumper is forced to get some height on his jump. The bar should start low and gradually move up. Five jumps should be taken at each height. This drill can be used with the long jump also. It is also a relaxed, fun drill.

9. Hop and Stepping in the Sand. This drill is a resistance exercise: As the sand gives way to the jumper, he must exert more force to come out of the hop into the step and out of the step into the jump. Upon landing in the sand the jumper's foot will sink and he must exert more power and strength to keep his momentum going.

The athlete can do the drill by hopping off the runway, landing in the sand on the hopping leg and then going into the step. Another option is for the athlete to perform the hop on the runway, land in the step in the sand and go on through into the jump. A third option is to use boxes: The jumper stands on either one of these

boxes and hops or steps into the pit, or takes 4-6 steps running approach to run off the box into the pit. The added height of the boxes adds a different dimension to the sand workout, that of increased stress on the legs. Here the overload principle is blended with the imitative principles of triple jump training. This drill is one which will be of great value for a jumper who has a injured heel, ankle, etc. The sand will cushion the landing and the injured jumper will be able to get in a workout.

10. Hopping over Hurdles. Line up 7-8 hurdles spaced to fit the jumper and have him hop over the hurdles using both feet in succession.

11. Triple Jumping With a Weight Jacket. The athlete starts with a 10 lb. jacket and moves to a 20 lb. jacket over a period of months.

12. Triple Jumping from Stairs. The jumper starts on the second or third stair of a staircase. The step should be about 18 inches high. A mark should be put on the floor to note the distance needed to cover on the hop, and the same for the step. The athlete takes 3-4 jumps from that step and moves up 1 or 2 steps and repeats. He should go as high as he can up the steps without putting the hopping leg under too much stress. The purpose of this drill is to progressively overload the hopping leg by jumping from higher steps and thus build strength in it.

13. Running up hills or steps with the upper body held erect and the knees lifting high.

14. Bounding on the grass with and without a weight jacket or weights on the shoulders.

15. Repeated bounding hops on the grass or track - over 50-300 yards.

16. Repeated bounding steps using the double arm 50-300 yards on the grass or track.

17. Thigh pushes. Use two men. Resistance work: one braces himself on a wall, etc. and raises his thigh to waist level as another athlete pushes down on the thigh.

18. Leg Flings from Prone Position. The athlete lies on his back with his body bent at the waist and his legs raised perpendicular to the ground. He then grasps the ankles of a partner who is standing with his feet on either side of the jumpers head. The partner then reaches forward and attempts to forcefully push the legs of the athlete down to the floor. The jumper must keep the legs straight and not let them hit the floor. (A good strength drill for the abdominal area)

19. Long jumping off the weak leg strengthens the weak leg.

20. Triple jumping into the pit.

Weight Training for the Triple Jump

1. Three quarter and half squats (strength builder for the lower back and legs). A typical workout would be 3x15 or 4x10 at whatever weight the athlete can handle.

2. Jump squats (builds leg strength and spring). A typical workout would be 2x15 or 3x10. The athlete picks the weight.

3. Heel raises (builds leg, ankle, and arch strength). Do 3x15 or 4x10 in a workout.

4. Leg press on the Universal (good for leg strength and stretching the hamstrings). 5x10 or 4x15 at the weight the athlete can lift.

5. Jump thrusts with weights (builds strength in the lower back and legs, stretches and adds strength to the hamstrings). Start the beginner at 40 lbs. and work up to 130 lbs. 2x20 or 3x15.

6. Leg swings from a box or bench. A weight boot or plate is tied to the foot, the leg swings up with the thigh parallel to the ground; very good for working on the thigh split and adds to the ability of the jumper to hold the legs up through the hop and step. 4x10 or 3x15, start at 20 and work up to 60.

7. Thigh lift. Place weight plate on thigh, raise thigh until parallel to the ground, hold thigh up for 10-15 seconds, let thigh down and repeat. 3x10 or 2x15, start at 10 lbs. and work up to waist level, 2x20 on each leg.

8. Skipping with weights (discussed in special exercises).

9. Reverse one leg press on the Universal. Jumper pushes backward on the leg press station. This exercise builds strength in lower leg and hamstring. 4x10 or 3x15, start the jumper at 80 lbs. and build up to 160 lbs.

10. Leg press on the stationary leg press. While lying on his back, the athlete pushes the weight up. 3x10 or 2x15.

11. Leg curls on the Universal. 3x15.

12. Bench press and military press for the upper body strength which is needed especially when using the double arm technique.

13. Fly-a-ways from a bench (essential in using the double arm method). Use dumbbells and start at 10 lbs. 4x10 or 3x15.

14. Knee extensions on the Universal (develops the quadriceps which must absorb much of impact of landing in the hop and step phase). 4x10 or 3x15.

15. Towel pulls (for building strength in the arch, ankle and toes). Add weight to the towel as the jumper becomes stronger. The exercise calls for the jumper to pull a towel to himself with his toes and bunch it up under his foot.

16. Pull downs with the foot. Hand a knotted towel down from the pull down bar, place the foot in the towel loop and push down with the thigh parallel to the floor, use the arms for balance by holding the ends of the bar. Do 2x5 or 3x4 to start.

17. Pull downs with the heel. Use the same towel rig as in the above exercise, but the athlete must sit on the ground with his leg straight out and leg in the towel; he then presses downward with his heel and leg, using his arms for balance on the bar.

18. Step ups. Place a barbell on any short of weight on the lifter's shoulders; the jumper then steps up on a bench or box 18″ high. The athlete must keep his back straight. Do 3x10 or 2x15 on each leg.

19. Polish pulls: Two athletes sit on opposite sides of a barbell and hook their feet under the bar and pull on the barbell at the same time. This exercise builds strength in arch and toes and ankle. 3x10 or 2x15. As the athlete gets stronger, increase the weight and reduce the number of repetitions.

Common Faults in the Triple Jump

Too Short a Step
Causes:
1. Hop normally too high or too long.
2. Too much forward rotation.
Corrections:
1. Use marks in practice to encourage evenness of phases.
2. Emphasize length of hop, not height.

Deceleration at the Board
Causes:
1. Improper arm action.
2. Looking at board in last two steps.
Corrections:
1. Keep head level and eyes up.
2. Emphasize running off board.

Dropping Feet too Early in the Jump
Causes:
1. Too much forward rotation in step phase.
2. Loss of balance can occur when shoulders are not kept perpendicular to line of flight.
Correction:
1. Do not let center of gravity get too far forward over step leg.
2. Keep shoulders square to the runway.

Too High in the Hop
Causes:
1. Lowering center of gravity last two strides of approach.
2. Driving arms and lead knee too high.
Corrections:
1. Do not lower center of gravity in last step (like a long jumper). Run off the board.
2. Do not allow hands to go past the chin.

Poor Arm Action in the Hop Phase
Cause:
Arm begins too soon.
Correction:
No adjustment of arm action until last step of approach run.

Not Active in Hop Landing
Causes:
1. Trunk not kept upright in hop.
2. Too much forward rotation. Plant foot too near center of gravity at take-off.
Correction:
Keep head up and lead with the hop knee more.

21
The High Jump*

The Flop High Jump
by
Don Chu
Cal State University, Hayward
Sue Humphrey
Arizona State University

Introduction

Since Dick Fosbury "backed" into a gold medal at the 1968 Olympics, high jumpers on every level, male and female, have taken up his unique back-to-the-bar flop style.

With so many athletes working on a revolutionary style, changes are inevitable. And so it has been with the flop. Some of the refinements stem from biomechanical analysis, others from individual adaptations.

The question continually asked of coaches is: "Is there a right way to do the flop?" It is these authors' opinion that there is, but that allowances can be made for individual variations so long as the jumper knows what he/she is doing.

Flop High Jump Technique

The Approach

Coaches, athletes, and especially spectators marvel at the consistency of top caliber high jumpers. Outstanding heights are reached meet after meet, competi-tion after competition. The key to success in high jumping may be summed up in one previously mentioned word, "consistency".

The definition of "consistency" includes a statement on the ability of the high jumper to engage in precise repetition of physical movement. Great jumpers do not "warm up" to great heights. They are, in fact, ready to perform maximal jumps from attempt number one until they finally fail on three attempts. In order to accomplish this, the high jumper must fully understand the meaning and importance of the approach to the bar.

The purpose of the approach is more than simply running to the bar and taking off. The approach is intended to place the jumper in the best position for take-off. This position is not a static point of balance as captured on film. It is a dynamic position representing not only balance, but speed of limb movement and the summation of physical forces.

Approach Shape: By the very shape of the approach in high jumping, certain mechanical advantages are gained which will aid the high jumper in attaining his potential height. The most often used approach in flopping is that of a "J" shape. Since it is begun in a straight line, it allows for the development of speed, built up, and then transferred to the slight curve at the end (usually three to five steps in length). Running through a

*This chapter consists of two articles: (1) "The Flop High Jump"; and (2) "The Straddle High Jump: Techniques and Training."

The flop high jump.

quarter of a circle allows the jumper to build "centripetal" force (the opposite, or release from this force is better known as "centrifugal") prior to take-off. It is this force which will throw the high jumper over the bar after he/she breaks contact with the ground at take-off.

The approach length is generally nine to eleven strides. Longer approaches tend to create too many variables for consistency and fewer strides do not allow the high jumper to develop enough speed for maximal forces to be applied to the ground. It is important to understand the following relationship: the speed of running an approach is the maximal speed which can be controlled. This will be further clarified in this chapter. Since the take-off spot is at the standard nearest the jumper the question of approach radius often arises. This distance will vary with the height and limb length of the jumper. Data from USOC Olympic Development camps tend to indicate that an arc radius of 18 feet is very comfortable and effective. This might range from 15 to 20 feet depending again on how tall the jumper is, and how effectively he/she can run the arc. If there are three to five steps within the arc itself, that leaves four to eight strides straight on. It is recommended that jumpers take a ten-step approach with a five-step lead-in and five-step curve.

First Step: The first step is the most underrated and overlooked portion of the approach. It sets the tempo of the whole approach because it is a result of how much force the jumper uses to initiate his/her approach run. If this step varies, it means the jumper is using a different amount of force to push off each time. This, in turn, means different stride length, speed and take-off point. To technicians, however, this step requires essence of consistency. It should be measured, marked and practiced.

Steps Two-Five: These steps are in a straight line. After pushing off, they reflect the tempo or pace established by the first step. The body position of the jumper should be balanced. His/her body should be over the foot when it contacts the ground. The jumper must not be leaning forward in an attempt to accelerate since this would place his/her hips in an ineffective position for take-off. Likewise, a position of leaning back while running will also result in an ineffective position, mechanically speaking, for take-off. Thus, the run is a "controlled" maximal-speed approach.

The Curve: A "turn mark" should always be placed on the approach surface during practice. This mark enables the jumper to develop a kinesthetic awareness of when to change the approach and start to "lean-in" on the curve and build his/her centripetal force. The lean position is vital. It is important to remember this will be what projects the jumper over the bar at take-off. If the jumper fails to lean-in, then he/she must actually apply an eccentric or off-center thrust at take-off, that will only detract from his/her potential height. Film studies show this angle to be approximately 10-15° of body lean to the inside of the curve.

The Last Three Steps: The final strides going into take-off must now change. A slight acceleration going onto the take-off mark is desireable. This is not to be mistaken with "changing gears". There is no hard, discernable change in approach speed. In actual viewing, it appears as a "smooth" and "quick" approach to take-off. Acceleration at the end of the approach allows the jumper to actually shorten the stride length slightly and "catch" the body's center of gravity on the rise. This is the **most important** aspect of the approach for any of the jumping events.

The Plant

The outside foot should be planted almost parallel to the bar pointing to the opposite standard. This will allow the inside knee to drive across the body to the opposite hip, in order to rotate it. Since rotation must begin with the plant foot on the ground, any improper placement of this foot will disrupt the jumper's ability to achieve the back-to-the-bar position.

The more the foot points toward the bar, the more difficult it will become to achieve rotation. In fact, the jumper can injure the ankle or knee in attempting to rotate over a foot that is almost perpendicular to the bar. Complaints of tenderness over the outside of the ankle or the inside of the knee after jumping may stem from an improper plant.

The body, due to the acceleration and position of balance in the run, should have its center of gravity 15-18 inches behind the plant foot. The 10° body lean should have been held to this point.

The plant should be a heel-to-toe action. The rock-up may not be as pronounced as it is in the straddle, but it is still essential.

Because of his/her acceleration during the approach, the jumper may require a stronger braking action with the rear spike in order to check the linear motion. But he/she must still try to run off the end of the approach and transfer linear speed into vertical velocity. This action is easier to achieve with the flop than with the straddle.

The jumper must avoid planting on the front part of the foot. That sort of plant would prevent the checking of linear speed and the development of vertical power with the ankle and foot. These members and the muscles around them must be fully extended to develop the maximal power from them. Planting on the forefoot will likely cause the athlete to drive into the bar as if he/she were long-jumping.

The penultimate stride with arm back.

Arm Action

The arm action should resemble the sprinter's, but not with the same rigid pumping action. The arms should be relaxed with the elbow bent enought to allow the thumb area to pass at hip joing level. On the second to last (penultimate) stride, the arms should gather and synchronize with what will be the lead leg.

For the athlete who takes off on the left foot, the sequence of foot strikes through the penultimate and last strides is left-right-left. Since the normal arm action in running is reciprocal, the right arm will be forward when the left foot strikes the ground.

The athlete must be taught to let the right arm remain forward as he/she moves to the right foot, and then bring the left arm together with the right. At this juncture, both arms are synchronized with the right or lead leg.

As the athlete moves through the last stride to the plant, both arms remain synchronized with the right leg so that they will be back on the body as the jumper makes the plant.

As the jumper begins the lead leg drive, both arms move forward at the same time. Considerable thrust can be developed with a double arm action. The arms should begin to bend as the athlete swings them through so that they remain in tight with the right knee. That is, as they swing through, they remain flexed until the force of the arm swing is directly vertical and in the same place as the knee drive.

The take-off.

The Take-Off

The take-off is a continuation of the plant. As the foot rocks to the toe, the drive leg begins to pass the take-off leg, with the knee driving upward.

Two points are essential in good leg action:

First, the ankle of the take-off leg must fully extend or plantar-flex. Anything less than a full ankle extension at take-off will result in a loss of power.

Second, the lead knee must be driven away from the bar (for rotation) to the opposite standard and rise to at least waist height for full power development. The lower part of the lead leg must be perpendicular to the ground at this point. Any action which carries the lower leg out

away from the vertical will cause the jumper to carry along the bar and fail to achieve enough height or rotation to clear it.

Coaching hint: Tell the athlete to keep everything "tight" and to drive the knee up, across the body, and away from the bar toward the opposite standard. The turning action of getting the back to the bar must originate on the ground.

By keeping everything in tight at take-off, the jumper will achieve a perpendicular position to the ground and develop all forces in a vertical direction, thus helping to attain maximum height.

The lead knee should continue to drive up after the take-off leg has left the ground. If the lead knee is driven properly, the legs should be spread as maximum height is attained over the bar. The athlete should attempt to drive the knee to the height of the bar. Whenever the athlete's knees are close together as they come over the bar, it indicates a lack of lead knee drive and a flight path that will not achieve full potential.

Measuring the Approach: Athletes have toyed with many ways to accurately map out their approach. The difference in facilities from week to week often plays havoc with high jumpers trying to "get their steps". The following is offered as a method of guaranteeing the measurements of an approach to be the same, regardless of where they are put down. "Triangulation" requires a single 200-foot tape. The measurements for an approach are then taken as follows:

1. From the base of the standard (shaft) out to a point 'A'. This measurement should be parallel or in line with the high jump bar as it rests on the standards. Record this distance e.g., 18′.
2. Run the tape out so that point B (starting point) is perpendicular to point A. Record the **total** distance on the tape e.g., actual distance from point A to B may be 50 feet, the reading on the tap measure will be standard A + B = 68 feet.
3. Finally, run the tap back to point C (base of the standard shaft) and record the total distance A + B + C = Total Measurement.
4. When remeasuring, lay the tape out to points A, B and C, e.g., 18, 68, 123′ 6″ and the jumper will have each point of his/her approach wherever and whenever. If points A and C are firmly held, the jumper merely has to hold the tape at the measurement for point B and adjust by pulling the tape until both sides of the triangle are straight. Then by dropping the tape at this point, he/she has the starting point.

On Top of the Bar

If, once the jumper has left the ground and has driven the lead knee properly and kept this knee up, he/she will find the back to the bar in a position to be arched.

The key to arching over the bar is the position of the head and legs. If the jumper drops the head back, the body will arch and the hips will rise in an

On top of the bar.

effort to clear the bar. This position is easier to obtain when the knees are spread.

The kinesiological reason for keeping the legs spread stems from the fact that the iliofemoral ligaments of the hips are tight when the thighs are close together (internally rotated). This limits the range of motion available for hip extension, which is associated with arching over the bar. Keeping the legs spread (externally rotated) allows the iliofemoral ligaments to slacken and permits more forward movement of the thigh on the hip joint and, thus, more arch.

Some coaches use verbal cues to teach their athletes to drop their head. They tell them to "look at the far corner" of the pit. This technique has its merits, but the body will tend to follow the head; and any tipping of the head to look back will tend to turn the body over on its side and cause one hip to drop. The best technique is simply to drop the head straight back and keep the legs spread.

The arms and hands may be permitted to come to a relaxed rest on or along the thighs as the athlete travels over the bar. Thus, a short powerful drive with the arms on the take-off will be followed by the arms coming to rest at the sides.

Some jumpers prefer to continue thrusting their arms up and to finally reach back with one or both. This is usually due to a lack of strength and timing in the arm drive.

The problem with this technique is that it puts the shoulder much closer to the bar early in the trajectory. Any dropping or reaching of the arms too early in the flight path will simply pull the athlete down by dropping his/her center of gravity earlier than desired.

Many athletes drill countless hours on flipping the feet up after clearing the bar with their hips. This movement is a result of the biomechanical

principle known as action-reaction. Anytime the athlete wants the feet to move up, he/she need simply move the head forward from the arched position over the bar. The feet will come up and put the body in a piked position.

Some coaches teach the athlete to drop the hips as he/she feels them clear the bar. Since the path of trajectory is already determined at take-off and since the athlete usually attains an arched position over the bar, the clearance really does not have to be a dramatic effort but, rather, a subtle curling up of the head and neck. That is all that will be required to elevate the feet.

It may be noted that every jumper, when approaching maximum heights, will have very little time to bring the feet up. Hence, gross movements such as pike position, cannot be carried out efficiently at maximum heights.

Summary

Although the flop has many subtle variations, the jumper must still observe biomechanical laws in order to be successful:
1. He/she must develop linear speed in order to exert the necessary force against the ground to achieve vertical velocity. The use of a curved approach is recommended.
2. The development of vertical force is a matter of proper plant and take-off technique. The biomechanical law of transfer of momentum from a part to a whole is best served by mastering the synchronized drive-leg and double-arm lift techniques.
3. The proper positioning over the bar is achieved by dropping the head back; this, coupled with the spread legs, forces the hips up. The reverse action-reaction movement forces the hips down and the feet up.

Careful utilization of this principle will assure the athlete of maximum height over the bar and foot clearance as the hips drop into the downward half of the flight trajectory.

An understanding of these principles and the application of them in coaching will allow the jumper to be fundamentally sound as he/she goes on to develop individual "style".

Training Methods

I. Strength Training

This is divided into five phases: first a base period devoted to quantitive work, and then later power phases for the development of maximal strength and its retention throughout the year.

A. Maximal Loading

This is an early pre-season period, usually July-Sept. During this time the jumper does a great volume of lifting, usually measured in total pounds (or kg). A larger number of sets and repetitions at moderate weight are utilized—i.e., 4-6 sets of 10-15 repetitions at 60%-70% of maximum.

B. **Power Development Period**

During this phase, emphasis is placed upon the maximal amount of weight which can be moved during a specific **time**, usually one second. This is the Russian "optimal load" concept, used to enhance faster movement response. Lifting is interspersed with jumping drills—bounding and box drills—twice a week, usually Monday and Friday. This phase generally takes place from October through January.

> Example:
> H a l f - s q u a t s
> 1 set × 6 reps @ 80%
> optimal load (O.L.)
> 1 set × 8 reps @ 90%
> 8 single-leg hops (each leg)
> 1 set × 5 @ 100%
> 1 set × 4 @ 110%

II. **High Jump Work-Outs**

Three types of high-jump work-outs are used to emphasize different aspects of the training program.

A. **Technique**

This is the commonest type of session, usually done twice a week. The bar is set 6 inches below the jumper's maximum jump. 15-18 jumps are taken. Adequate rest is taken between jumps so that the jumper can be fresh and go all-out with each jump. The bar is raised 1-2 inches after the first few jumps, if all is going well. The jumper must concentrate on the specific points to be stressed in the technique during this type of session.

B. **Endurance**

This is aimed toward making many jumps during a session—up to 30 when the athlete is well-trained. Start the bar 8 inches below best jump attained. The athlete should clear 3 times at this height, and raise the bar by 2 inches. Repeat this process until the jumper misses twice—then lower the bar by one inch, which he/she should clear.

C. **Maximal Height**

The athlete takes 12-15 jumps at his/her's lifetime best and continues to jump regardless of whether the bar is cleared. Stress concentration on each jump. The athlete should try to relax and allow technique to remain and carry him/her over.

Exercise Used:	
8 box jumps	Half-squat
1 set × 8 @ 70%	Inverted leg press
1 set × 10 @ 60%	Power-clean
8 in-depth jumps	Snatch
1 set × 5 @ 100%	Squat-jump

Train three times per week—M-W-F (no jump training on Wed.)

C. **Power Transfer Period**

These exercises are more specifically related to the jumping movements. They should be carried out at maximal speed. They are usually done February thru April and consist of 4 sets × 5 repetitions at maximal intensity (85-95% of single RM):

Double-legged jumps with barbell
Single legged jumps
Bounding split squats
Inverted leg press
Shoulder and biceps curl

D. **Transition Phase-Preparation For Major Competitions.**

This consists of two weeks of circuit training. Set-up 6-7 stations. The athlete does 40-50% of single RM-30 seconds work, 15 seconds rest. 3 circuits.

E. **Power Retention Phase**

This helps to maintain gains made earlier, and is used during late season championship meets. One day per week. 4 sets × 6 repetitions for major muscle groups.

Seasonal Training Objectives

Off Season—Active rest (August and September)
Weights 2-3 times a week
Jog and stretch daily
Active participation in other sports
(examples: volleyball, basketball)

General Fitness Tests—Test in early October and each month after during the season. It is best to test early in the week when the athlete's legs are fresh. Two attempts should be given with the best effort recorded for reference. Tests are standing start 50 yards in flats, standing long jump, standing start triple jump, and vertical jump.

Fall (October-December)

Long intervals of 660's-440's	Once a week
Short Intervals of 330's-150's	Once a week
2-3 mile run and hills	Once a week
Plyometric drills	Twice a week
Weights	2-3 times a week

In November start approach, technique work and curve 110's twice a week.

Early Season (January-March)

Weights	Twice a week
Technique jumping	Twice a week
Hills - Stairs	Once a week
Plyometrics	Twice a week
Curve 50's-100's	Twice a week
Short intervals	Twice a week
2 mile run	Once a week

In Season (April-June)

Weights	1-2 times a week

Technique Jumping — Twice a week
Plyometrics — Once a week (see notes on tapering this area)

Curve 50's — Twice a week
Short intervals — Twice a week

Sample Workouts:
Fall (October)
M—660-550-440, wts.
T—Plyometrics, 4 × 220's
W—6 × 330, wts.
TH—Plyometrics, 6 × 180's
F—2 mile run, 4 hills (300 yds long)
Weekend—Rest
Fall (November)
M - Plyometrics, 3 × 330
T - 6 × curve 100's, jump, wts.
W - Plyometrics, 4 × 220
TH - see Tuesday
F - 3 mile run, hills or stairs
Weekend - Rest
Early Season
M - Plyometrics, 4 × 330
T - 6 × curve 100's, jump, wts
W - Plyometrics, 8 × 180
TH - see Tuesday
F - 2 mile run, 7 × stairs or travel
S - Meet or rest
S - Rest
In Season
M - Plyometrics, 6 × 180
T - 6 × curve 50's, jump, wts.
W - 330-220-150-150-220-330
TH - see Tuesday
F - Jog-stretch-travel
S - Meet
S - Rest
III. Drills
   A. Training
      Examples of plyometric exercises are box depth jumps. Boxes should be 14″-18″ high to begin with. Variations can include jumping from one height box to the same height box off a double or single leg, off a low box to a higher one or a higher one to a lower one, or completely over the boxes landing on grass each time. Total recovery from these exercises range from 6-8 days, so the athlete needs to stop these 10-14 days before big meets. Other plyometric drills are hurdle hops off single and double legs, stair hops, bounding, a jump series of long jumps, triple jump, hop-hop-step-jump, 25 yd. hops off a single and double legs, hopping and bounding relays, high knee hops and skips, and rope jumping.

      There is also a series of tests the West Germans use. These different groups are done at separate times. Group 1-5 standing hops off right and left legs, 5 hops from a 6 stride approach off each leg. Group 2-10 hurdle jumps off double leg, 5 hurdle jumps double leg, 10 hurdle jumps off take-off leg, 5 hurdle jumps off take-off leg, and 4 step approach scissors H.J. Group 3-10 1/2 or 1/4 squats with 50% max total time, 3 squats 70% max total time, 10 squats 60% max total time. In all these squats the thighs should be parallel to the floor. Group 4-30m sprint with a standing start, 150m sprint with a standing start. Group 5—technique analysis (approach, take-off, clearance).

   B. Technique
    1. Back rolls on high gym mats from a standing start or a trampoline.
    2. Back pull-overs with a partner for flexibility.
    3. Circle runs in the direciton of the curve to sense what a true curve feels like, circle 8 runs.
    4. Mirror practice of double arm blocking and lead knee drive. This should also be walked and jogged through.
    5. Actual jumping (a) endurance training of up to 30 jumps, (b) technique training twice a week, 15-18 jumps each session and (c) maximum jumping 10-15 jumps at PR heights regardless of misses.

   C. Teaching Progression
    1. Determine the take-off foot—the athlete takes a running jump to see what foot is used to take off.
    2. Mark a curved approach on each side of the standard with tape.
    3. The athlete executes a scissors jump using a 5-step curved approach to a sitting landing position on the pit then a back landing position, and then a high back landing position.
    4. He/she then does a scissors jump as above working on a free knee drive up and across the body at take-off.
    5. The double arm action is started on the second to last step. For a right foot jumper, the left foot is forward on the second to last step and the right arm is back. The right arm is kept back as the athlete goes into the last step. The left arm then comes back naturally as the final step is taken. Both arms are now back and ready to punch upward. The hands should not go any higher than shoulder level at take-off.

IV. Flexibility Exercises
Jog 880 mile, do these varied flexibility and other stretching exercises, stride 4-8 × 110's before the main workout. After the workout, the jumper should warm down with 440-880 jog of easy effort.
   A. Hip Flexion (Bent Knee)
   Purpose: To stretch upper hamstring.
    1. **Initial position:** Lying on the back with one leg leg kept straight and in firm contact with the floor.
    2. **Exercise:** The other knee is bent fully and the thigh is raised to as close to the chest as possible. While still pulling with the thigh muscles, an additional stretch is provided

by grasping the knee with both hands and pulling slightly. The leg is then returned to the starting position.
   3. Repeat for a total of 10 times.
   4. Repeat with the other leg.

B. **Straight Leg Sit-Ups**
Purpose: To stretch the low back.
   1. **Initial position:** Lying on back with arms across the chest or behind the head and legs secured.
   2. **Exercise:** Tuck the chin, raise the head and shoulders, then upper and lower back in a curling fashion as far as possible in one smooth motion, without twisting or turning, and return.
   3. Repeat for a total of 10 times.

C. **Hip Flexion**
   1. **Initial position:** Back lying with one leg kept straight and in firm contact with the ground.
   2. **Exercise:** The other leg is raised, keeping the knee straight as far as possible. While still pulling the thigh muscles, an additional stretch is applied with the hands by grasping the thigh and pulling slightly. The leg then returns to the ground.
   3. Repeat for a total of 10 times.
   4. Repeat with the other leg.

D. **Trunk Hyperextension**
Purpose: To stretch trunk and dorsal spine.
   1. **Initial position:** Lie prone with arms at the sides and legs secured.
   2. **Exercise:** Contract the back muscles and raise the head and shoulders being careful **not** to twist or turn.
   3. Repeat for a total of 5 times.

E. **Heel Cord Stretch**
Purpose: To stretch calf muscles.
   1. **Initial position:** Sitting on the floor with knee extended, ankle relaxed and a strap under the metatarsal arch.
   2. **Exercise:** Contract the muscle on the front of the lower leg, bringing the toe toward the shin. At the end of the range, keep contracting this muscle and pull the strap with the hands for additional stretch. Return to initial position.
   3. Repeat a total of 10 times.
   4. Repeat with other leg.

F. **Hip Abduction**
Purpose: To stretch thigh abductors and groin.
   1. **Initial position:** Sidelying with the lower leg bent ninety degrees to aid in balance.

   2. **Exercise:** Raise the top leg straight up as high as possible and return, keeping the buttocks in and not allowing the leg to go in front or in back of the body.
   3. Repeat for a total of 10 times.
   4. Repeat lying on other side with other leg.

G. **Hip Hyperextension**
Purpose: To stretch the front thigh and hip flexors.
   1. **Initial position:** Lie prone with the knee of one leg flexed to approx. ninety (90) degree angle and grasp the ankle with the hand on the same side of the leg to be stretched.
   2. **Exercise:** Contract the muscles of the rear of the thigh and buttocks to raise the upper leg, keeping the leg from moving out or away from the body as it is raised the guiding (not pulling) with hand.
   3. Repeat for a total of 10 times.
   4. Switch to the other leg and repeat.

H. **Knee Flexion**
Purpose: Increases the amount of flexion at a joint by breaking down adhesions and restoring extensibility to the various tissues of the joint.
   1. **Initial position:** prone position with the legs out straight.
   2. **Exercise:** The knee is bent and the lower leg is lifted through the range of motion as far as possible by itself. Then the ankle is grasped by the hand on the same side and the heel is brought down to touch the buttocks, being careful that the front of the hip does not lift up off the ground, then the leg returns to a straight position.
   3. Repeat for a total of 10 times.
   4. Repeat with other leg.

I. **Foot Exercises**
Purpose: For use in the regular warmup and/or rehabilitation
   1. Plantar flexion and dorsiflexion
   2. Ankle rotations
   3. Arching of the foot
   4. Tendon stretch
   5. Heel raises
   6. Lateral stretch
   7. Resistance against a towel
   8. Marble pickup
   9. Towel gather
   10. Flexion and dorsiflexion against resistance
   11. Inversion and eversion against resistance
   12. Grip and spread toes

The Straddle High Jump: Technique and Training

by
Frank Costello
University of Maryland

There have been more changes in the high jump techniques over the years than in any other event in track. First came the scissors, then the eastern cut-off (a variation of the scissors style), next the western roll, followed by the straddle and finally the flop. Today only two styles are being used in international competition: the flop and the straddle. The two styles differ so much that they are almost two separate events.

In the United States the majority of jumpers use the flop, and many of them would have more success with the straddle. In Europe some of the top jumpers in the world use the straddle, and all have one thing in common—they use the standard type of Russian straight leg drive straddle. Certain things are necessary for an athlete to be successful with the straddle:

1) flexibility
2) strength
3) coordination
4) patience
5) coachability

The athlete also needs a coach who is willing to learn the event and spend hours of time on a one-to-one basis with him/her.

The straddle is slowly becoming a lost art in the United States. This article is written in the hope that it will interest coaches in this style of jump. The straddle method is a great technique, and it has a place in track and field today.

The Techniques of the Straddle

There are four main phases of the straddle high jump: the run-up or approach, the take-off, the bar clearance and the landing. All phases are closely interrelated so that one phase leads into the next.

The Approach

The purpose of the approach is:
1) to develop an optimum convertible horizontal momentum and to achieve a favorable take-off angle with as much speed as possible;
2) to develop a smooth rhythm in the run;
3) to obtain the proper angle of flight to the bar.

The approach run must be in a straight line—usually seven to nine hard running strides. Most straddlers use a heel-toe (photo 1-a) type of run. In the straddle, different parts of the body clear the bar one after the other. Near to the bar the flight path must, therefore, be longer to prevent the last parts of the body, particularly the trail leg, from touching the bar. For this style a flatter angle of approach should be chosen. It varies, as a rule, between 25 and 45 degrees. When Valery Brummel set his world record of 2.28 meters (7' 5-¾") in 1963 he used an angle of 28 degrees. Vladimer Yashchenko used an angle closer to 40 degrees.

The approach has two parts.

The first part emphasizes the development of speed, while the second part (the last three strides) serves as preparation for the take-off. The athlete must lower his center of gravity (settle) (photo 1-b) and have his body in position to use his arms and lead leg at take-off. The penultimate stride (next to last) (photo 1-c) is the longest, and the last step is the shortest. According to the most recent findings, the penultimate stride should be about 12 inches longer than the last stride (photo 1-e).

#1a #1b #1c #1d

#1e #1f #1g #1h

#1i #1j #1k #1l

#1m #1n #1o #1p

The straddle high jump.

The Take-Off

Before the take-off the jumper must lower his/her center of gravity. Many times this action will cause some loss of speed. The knees are deeply bent on the penultimate step (photo 1-d). On the last stride the jumper must already be starting the hips forward and upward. The kicking leg (lead leg) stays in a bent position (photo 1-f). It is recommended in this type of straddle to use a double arm action at take-off (photos 1-e—1-f). The arms go back as the plant leg moves forward. They then drive forward and upward with the lead leg.

The take-off should be understood, not as the instant at which the foot leaves the ground, but as a flow of movement of the pelvis through the take-off leg. The reaction to the compression and the forceful drive upward, the change in action of the take-off leg from resistance, and absorption of shock to that of exploding upward must occur instantly with great force. Both power and great strength are needed.

The take-off foot lands heel first and is immediately slapped down (photo 1-f). The hips continue their forward and upward movement, thus increasing the backward lean of the body. It is the hips coming forward, not the shoulders going back that causes the backward lean at take-off. The swinging leg is still well bent at the knee joint as it moves forward. As the center of gravity moves over the plant foot, the lead leg straightens out (this is referred to as the pendulum kick) and continues to drive upward (photo 1-g). At this point many young straddle jumpers make the mistake of letting the right hip collapse after the pendulum kick has taken place. The swinging movement of the arms and of the free leg is halted just before the end of the take-off. In the straddle the hips must be drawn into the forward and upward movement of the swinging leg to produce the required rotation impulse (photo 1-h).

At the point of take-off the foot of the plant leg must turn with a corkscrew action. This will give the athlete the rotation needed to clear the bar (photo 1-h).

Bar Clearance and Landing

In most cases the lead arm will be the first part of the body to cross the bar. The lead arm will be closely followed by the lead leg (photo 1-i). Reach down over the bar with the lead arm. A common mistake is to allow the lead leg to flatten out on top of the bar causing the jumper to lose control of the lead leg. To prevent this error the jumper should keep the toes of the lead leg pulled toward himself/herself giving him/her the necessary control of the lead leg (photo 1-j).

As a jumper's body crosses the bar he/she drops his/her head and shoulders down on the far side of the bar. This will help lift the hips into proper position for clearance (photo 1-k). At the same time the jumper should start to lift the trail leg out and up. To enhance this procedure, he/she should raise his/her lead arm up and turn the shoulders in the opposite direction to the direction the trail leg is moving. The reaction to this ac-

tion will be the lifting of the trail leg (photos 1-1—1-m). It is not necessary to kick the trail leg but merely to lift it in a bent position (photos 1-1—1-m). As the jumper clears the bar he/she continues on the path to the landing area. He/she will land on his/her side and then roll onto the back. If the jump was executed correctly he/she will land directly in line with the approach.

Special Preparatory Exercises

1) **Line Drill**—Place a bar on the ground and approach with a 45 degree angle. Kick the lead leg up and pass over the bar, landing on the far side of the bar on the lead leg. As the plant foot leaves the ground, rotate the plant foot with a corkscrew action. The jumper should land directly in line with his approach. This is an excellent drill for beginners to get the feeling of rotating off the ground to reach the straddle position on top (photo 2a #1 and 2a #2)

2a #1.

2a #2.

2) **Lead Leg Drill without Pit**—Place the bar about 1 meter high. Using three steps, approach the bar at a 45 degree angle. Jump over the bar and land on the ground on the lead leg. The action is the same as the line drill but because the bar is at 1 meter, it forces the athlete to be conscious of his lead leg (photo 2-b).

2b.

3)**Lead Leg Drill with Pit**—Same drill as No. 2 except the bar is placed much higher and the athlete lands on the lead leg in the pit and then rolls onto the back (photo 2-c).

2c.

4) **Trail Leg Drill**—In the front leaning rest position, the jumper brings the foot of the leading leg (as at the beginning of the bar clearance) to the hollow of the knee of the swinging leg, and turns the knee and toe well outward. The pelvis is then consciously introduced into this movement so that now a rotation and body torque around the spine takes place (photo 2-d).

2d.

5) **Walk and Hold Drill**—In this drill the jumper walks through the last three steps. He/she holds each step for 10 seconds, keeping the knee deeply flexed. This drill helps develop a feeling of the low position necessary before take-off. It is also excellent for strength development.

6)**Lead Leg Kick Drill**—Using three steps the jumper takes off and kicks an object with his lead leg at heights of 9 to 10 feet. This drill is excellent for developing a fast and powerful kicking leg. If done incorrectly it can be dangerous; so it should always be supervised by a coach (photo 2-e).

2e.

Training Schedule

Off-Season (Summer-Fall)

Workout Schedule

Monday
1) Warm up (easy ¾ mile jog)
2) Flexibility - 20 minutes
3) Simulation drills
4) Weight training
5) Simulation drills
6) Cross country - 3 miles

Tuesday
1) Warm up and flexibility
2) Simulation drills
3) Plyometrics drills
   a) Hurdle hop (5 hurdles at intermediate height)
   b) Double leg hops
   c) Standing long jump
   d) Standing triple jump
4) Easy Cross-country 2-½ miles

Wednesday
1) Warm up and flexibility
2) Full approach runs - 20 minutes
3) Simulation drills
4) Weight training
5) Cross country 3-4 miles

Thursday
1) Film study - 30 minutes
2) Warm up and flexibility - 10-15 minutes
3) Simulation and take-off drills
4) Plyometrics drills - 20 minutes
5) Cross country 3 miles - hard

Friday
1) Film study
2) Warm up and flexibility
3) Weight training
4) Simulation drills
5) Cross country 5 miles - easy

Saturday
1) Warm up and flexibility
2) Easy plyometrics drills
3) Film study
4) Recreation games - 1 hour (basketball, volleyball or soccer)

Sunday
1) Five miles easy run
2) Swimming for endurance and recreation

The off-season is a very important part of the jumper's training. The objective of the off-season training is to improve strength, endurance, overall conditioning and develop technique. The jumper must be highly disciplined during this period of time.

Simulation drills are all exercises that are performed at a very slow rate of speed. The athlete isolates a particular part of the jump. For example, in working on the last two steps, the jumper would walk through the last two steps, over and over again, getting the feel of the movement of the arms and legs. Simulation drills over the bar are done with the athlete stepping over a very low bar (1 meter) and slowly going through the action of clearing the bar (photo 2-f).

2f.

Off-Season Weight Training

Monday

1) Push press - 3 sets of 10 reps.
   Start with about ½ - 2/3 of body weight
   increasing 5 pounds every fourth or fifth lifting day.
2) Parallel squats - 3 sets of 10 reps.
   Start with body weight increasing 10 pounds every fifth lifting day.
3) High pulls - 3 sets of 10 reps.
   Start with about ½ body weight.
4) Curls - 3 sets of 10 reps.
5) Step-ups-2 sets of 20 reps. (alternating legs)
   Start with 2/3 body weight.
6) Sit-ups - 2 sets of 50 reps.

Wednesday and Friday

The same as Monday's workout except on Wednesday eliminate push press and substitute bench press - 3 sets of 10 reps. Start with about body weight, increasing 5 pounds every week.

Pre-Season Workout Schedule

Monday

1) Warm up and flexibility - 10 minutes
2) Weight training
3) 5 X 330 m. on track ½ speed
4) Film study

Tuesday

1) Warmup and flexibility - 10 minutes
2) Jumping
   a) Lead leg drills - 10 times
   b) 15 jumps at working height - use 3 or 5 step run
      (Working height is the height that a jumper can clear 60% of the time.)
3) Plyometrics drills - 20 minutes
4) Track work
   a) 5 X 60 m. - 2/3 speed
   b) 5 X 100 m. - 2/3 speed
   c) 5 X 150 m. - 2/3 speed

Wednesday

1) Warm up and flexibility - 10 minutes
2) Weight training
3) 5 X 400 m. on track 1/2 - 2/3 speed
4) Film study

Thursday

1) Warm up and flexibility - 10 minutes
2) Jump drills
   a) Work on full run-up
   b) Lead leg kicks at basketball rim

3) Plyometrics drills - 20 minutes
   a) Standing long jump for distance - 10 times
   b) Standing triple jump for distance - 10 times
   c) Bounding - 5 X 50 m.
4) Track work
   a) 5 X 50 m.
   b) 5 X 80 m.

Friday

The same as Monday's workout

Saturday

1) Warm up and flexibility
2) Jump training
   a) Work on full approach
   b) 20 jumps at working height
   c) Lead leg and trail leg drills
3) Easy distance run 3-5 miles

Sunday

Rest

Pre-Season Weight Training

Monday

1) Power clean - 5 sets of 5 reps.
2) Parallel squats - 5 sets of 5 reps.
3) Push press - 5 sets of 5 reps.
4) Split squats - 2 sets of 20 reps. (alternating legs)
5) Curls - 5 sets of 5 reps.
6) Sit-ups - 2 sets of 50 reps.

Wednesday and Friday

The same as Monday's workout except on every other Wednesday strive for maximum lift.

In-Season Workout Schedule

Monday

1) Warm up and flexibility
2) Simulation drills
3) Technique training
   a) Work on approach rhythm
   b) 10 jumps - place bar about 5 inches lower than best jump
4) 5 X 60 m. high hurdles

Tuesday

1) Warm up and flexibility
2) Plyometrics drills - 15 min.
3) Work out with medicine ball
4) Acceleration runs of 100 m. - 6 reps.

Wednesday

1) Warm up and flexibility
2) Speed work
   a) 5 X 50 m.
   b) 5 X 100 m.
   c) 5 X 150 m.
3) Approach work
4) Film study

Thursday

The same as Tuesday's workout

Friday

Flexibility and easy run

Saturday

Competition

Sunday

Recreation games (basketball, volleyball or swimming)

22
Pole Vaulting

by
Guy Kochel
Arkansas State University

Introduction

The pole vault is the most complex event in track and field. There has been a tremendous amount of research in the physiological, biomechanical and kinetic factors of the vault. But the real keys to good vaulting are mastering the basic elements of the vault and proper training.

The pole vault is the coordination between the athlete and the pole in a double pendular action. The athlete acts as one pendulum and the pole, the other. It is necessary to get maximum controlled speed transferred into the pole, creating pole speed (speed at which the pole pivots about the base). This is indicated by the vertical rise of the pole. There are many factors that contribute to pole speed and the projection of an athlete's center of gravity high above the top hand just as the pole reaches the vertical position. These factors are discussed through the next section. The following is a breakdown of the various phases of the vault and an analysis of each.

Phases of the Vault

Approach

The length of approach varies with the individual, but usually ranges from 100-150 feet. Most world class vaulters use an approach of 120 to 150 feet. It is very important that the approach run be consistent. It should be made with maximum controllable speed in an erect position: the faster the run, the more potential energy stored in the pole.

Checkmarks—Most vaulters use 18-21 strides and three checkmarks. The first checkmark is at the beginning stride, with two additional marks to double check the stride pattern. The second checkmark is the coach's mark, 30-50 feet away from the box. The third mark, at the take-off point, indicates whether the athlete is too far out or too far under.

Pole Carry

The most important element in the carry is that it is comfortable and suitable for an effective pole plant. The distance between the hands varies with the individual, ranging from 18″ to 36″. The planting end of the pole should be about head high and slightly to the left of the centerline of the runway. The pole should be carried in a position near the hip, with the back arm bent, and the front and back hands approximately the same distance from the hip.

Plant

The approach and plant are the most important phases of the vault. A good vault consists of a good approach and a good plant with a smooth transition between the two. The plant phase is where most of the problems occur. What goes wrong in the air is usually a result of what happens on the ground by a poor plant.

Learning the fundamentals of the plant is essential to the successful vault. Most experts say the plant starts at two strides out from take-off. It is this author's opinion that the plant is initiated 3 to 3 1/2 strides out. In the beginning of the plant, the vaulter shifts forward with a wrist curl press to overhead action, placing the right arm as high as possible above and directly over the toe of the take-off foot. There must be a smooth transition between the hands and arms to position the pole for the plant. The right arm then drives forward, upward in front of the head, while the left arm acts as a guide to direct the pole into the box. It is very important to have a **high** and **early** plant (the most common fault of all vaulters is the late plant), and to create the largest angle possible between the top hand and the box. The vaulter should make the plant **through the box, not to the box.**

The shoulders are kept square to the box at the plant. A common fault is to lean on the pole during approach, turning the left shoulder and causing a round-house plant. The overall sensation during the plant phase should be that of driving into the pole—but also of being behind and under the pole. It is important to experience both sensations. Remember, the key to a good vault is a high, early, aggressive plant.

The plant.

The take-off.

Take-Off

There are many variations of the take-off because of the differences in style, grips, speed and physique. The take-off should not require conscious thought, but through repetition in practice (which develops confidence), it should be an automatic action. During the plant the vaulter should be able to feel if he has planted too far under or too far out. Basic elements required for a good take-off are the following:

1. The pole should be directly over the take-off foot.
2. The right arm should be as high as possible.
3. The lead knee should have a quick hard drive in leaving the ground, driving forward and upward.
4. The left arm keeps the pole away from the body, but will collapse at a point to a right angle. The left arm then becomes the control point of the vaulter.
5. The left leg should be completely extended and pulled through to catch up with the right leg. The left leg, kept straight, will enable the hips to lift.

Swing and Rockback

The swing transfers horizontal speed into vertical speed. During this period the left leg begins to catch up with the right. This catching up process will continue into the rockback position.

The rockback phase maintans the momentum that was attained in the approach, plant, and take-off. The right arm should be completely straight with the left arm collapsing almost to a right angle, lined with the pole, while still keeping the pole away from the body. The vaulter should not pull down with the right arm and not pull or overpress with the left arm. This will cause a stall on top of the bar.

The right knee is driven forward and up. The left leg, which is kept as straight as possible, will catch up with the right leg in a smooth driving action. The rockback action continues until hips are between the pole and head. The vaulter must try to get his hips as high as possible and behind the pole. Momentum must dictate what the head does. The head must not be thrown back in order to get back on the pole. This will cause the vaulter to lose momentum and stall out of the top of the bar.

The vaulter should stay in the rockback position until the pole is almost straight, then begin the pull and turn. Most vaulters want to start their pull and turn too soon. The rockback is not a superquick action. The higher a vaulter is vaulting, the more patient he has to be in this position. He should keep his back to the bar as long as possible.

Pull-Turn-Release

The pull and turn start when the pole is almost straight and are almost simultaneous because the turn is started by the pull. This phase should be delayed as long as possible to achieve maximum vertical lift from the pole as it comes out of the bend. The vaulter should pull vertically and through the hips. The legs should go in an upward position and not out. The pull and turn is a very quick and powerful movement with the vaulter finally extending his arms straight down the pole. As the arms are extended downward, the left arm reaches its full extension first, then the right arm is released in a pushup action. The arms are quickly lifted away from the crossbar and the thumbs are rotated inward, causing the elbows to rotate away from the crossbar.

In releasing the pole, the vaulter gets off the pole and up and away from the bar, then lands in the pit. A premature release can cause incomplete extension of the pole.

The pull-turn-release.

Pole Progression: and Flex No.

Flex numbers are very important for the coach to understand. The lower the flex number, the stiffer the pole (6.0 stiffer than 7.0). The athlete weighing 150 pounds should be able to progress to stiffer poles (155-160-165) as he increases strength, speed and technique. The vaulter should know that a pole is too soft when he goes through the bar, lands too deep in the pit, or when the pole is not reacting properly.

Most vaulters feel it takes them two weeks to get on a new pole, but this author believes this is more of a psychological barrier than anything else. If the vaulter is ready to progress in poles, he should be able to get on the stiffer pole immediately if the pole is the correct flex.

The vaulter must learn to adjust to weather conditions. The following is a guide for vaulters in inconsistent weather conditions:

Tail Wind—Many vaulters go through the bar because they are moving faster, making the pole too soft. Good vaulters love tailwinds. A tailwind is a good time to move onto a larger pole.

Head Wind or Revolving Wind—Usually destroys the mind. Athlete could shorten run, get on a softer pole and/or lower the hand grip.

Rain—short run—low hand-hold. The vaulter should start at a low height.

Pole Vault Workouts

Workouts should be directed to fit the particular needs of an individual vaulter. All vaulters should be directed toward workouts which lead to consistent and maximum performance. The following areas should be developed:

1. Strength
2. Flexibility
3. Vaulting skills
4. Speed
5. Endurance (vaulting endurance)
6. Agility and coordination (gymnastics)
7. Air mindedness (gymnastics trampoline)
8. Rest (most important toward big meets)
9. Mental concentration

Pre-Season Week Cycle

Monday	Tuesday	Wednesday
Hard 2-4 miles easy	Flexibility-run Gymnastics Skills	Hard wts. Run drills or 2-4 mis. easy run

Thursday	Friday
Flexibility-run Gymnastics Skill	Weights Weather Drills

Set up two to four weeks of general conditioning and vault drills, then begin vaulting M-W-F with hard weights after vault practice.

Year Cycle

	Sept.	Oct.	Nov.	Dec.
Strength	60%	60%	60%	60%
Skills	20%	20%	20%	20%
Speed	15%	15%	15%	15%
Flex	5%	5%	5%	5%

Jan. Feb.	Mar. Apr.	May	June
Goes down	Goes down	R	R
Goes down	Goes up	E	E
Goes up	Goes up	S	S
Goes up	Goes up	T	T

Percentage of time spent on skill depends upon the fundamentals and experience the vaulter has during that period of time. The beginning vaulter needs to vault as much as possible.

Speed work is usually 6×165 under control or $2\text{-}3 \times 100$'s for time and followed by a cooldown jog. The vaulter should never run over $2\text{-}3 \times 330$ yards during a workout and never on the same day as the quick speed work.

The weight program is based on a percentage of maximum the first year. If the coach feels the athlete is mature enough and has picked up some other method that will help him, then he should try it. But new maximums should always be set every four weeks.

Common Faults

1. Inconsistency of Run
2. Moving the bottom hand up on plant
3. Pulling top hand toward body at take-off
4. Drifting to right
5. Stalling out on top of bar
6. Throwing head back
7. Press too hard with left hand
8. Swinging body away from pole
9. Vaulting into the bar

Drills to Correct Faults

Pop-ups: Jogging or running down the runway and planting in the box, through the plant, swing and rockback phases.

Short Pole Vault: Using 11-12 foot pole with regular vaulting technique, but the pole does not bend and emphasis is on pull and turn.

Towel Drill: This is done on the track, measuring steps from a towel (the towel is the box). The vaulter sprints to the towel and plants. This will increase speed and consistency of approach at the plant.

Short Run Vault: The whole vault is done but with a shorter run, in order to vault more in practice. Emphasize certain phases of vault and adjust steps or other problems. Good in inclement weather.

Apparatus: Simulate phases of the vault on rings, parallel bars or other gymnastic devices. Great for increasing specific strength.

Run Through: Drill on runway checking checkmarks for vault.

Vault for Height: Technique—vaulting as high as possible (usually film day).

Kick the Bar: Place the bar two feet over the vaulter's best height. A good drill to aid vaulter psychologically. Technique is to try and get ankle over the bar or kick the bar off. Helps vaulter get into an exaggerated inverted position, which is essential in gaining more height.

Imagination: Place bar on goal height which is desired for the year. The athlete lies under the bar (in the pit) and imagines every detail of the vault.

Rings: The vaulter on rings—high enough that feet will just touch, hits mat as take-off and swings on rings driving right knee hard—keeping left leg straight, catching up-swing to rockback position.

Weather Drills: It is important to practice vaulting in less than ideal conditions. The athlete should vault against the wind using a soft pole and a low hand hold and vault in the rain, again using a soft pole and a low hand hold. This will insure that he will know what to do in these situations in competition.

Teaching the Beginner

Step One: In learning the hand hold or grip, the athlete stands the pole vertically in front of him and places the right hand on the pole at the "top of the reach" and the left hand approximately 18 inches below the right hand. Maintaining this hold, the athlete drops the pole with the tip above the eye level in front of the left eye. The right hand should be "palm up" and the left hand "palm down."

Step Two: The beginner stands on a box facing the pit, with the pole in a vertical position in the vault box. The athlete holds the pole at shoulder height directly in front of his body and springs off the box with the left foot, passing to the right of the pole. He uses the pole and the arms for support and pulls up the knees as he goes forward, landing in the pit.

Step Three: The box is moved back two feet from the pit so that the pole is tilted back toward the vaulter. The beginner drives the right knee forward and up, and pulls up the knees in order to reach the pit. He should keep a very low hold in order to land in the pit.

Step Four: Gradually the box is moved back away from the landing pit and Step Three is repeated, adding a strong thrust of the left leg swinging up to catch up with right knee. The athlete should keep the left leg as straight as possible and begin to feel a lifting sensation.

Step Five: Repeat Steps Two, Three and Four with the vaulter and instruct him to execute a turn by driving the right leg toward the left standard.

Step Six: The beginner is now ready to get on the runway and use a standing plant (plant described earlier). The action is a forward wrist curl and press action. The athlete then progresses to a walking forward wrist curl press plant (four-step plant drill).

Step Seven: This is the "towel drill." Here the athlete gets on the track and places a towel 80 to 95 feet from the beginning of the run. The towel is the box. The vaulter runs through to get a consistent run and plants the pole at the towel. The take-off (left) foot should be at a point directly under the top hand. The athlete should run and plant at the towel until his plant and run are correct.

Step Eight: This step involves the "bend drill." The athlete needs to learn how it feels when the pole bends. Confidence is gained by knowing what is going to happen when the pole bends and what happens when the pole comes out of the bend.

The coach gets to the side of the box (left side for a right-handed vaulter) and holds the base of the pole in the box. The vaulter gets on the runway approximately 30 feet away, and runs towards the pole. He grabs the pole low (tape an area where vaulter is to grab). As the athlete grasps the pole, the coach pulls the pole toward the pit as hard as possible. The pole will bend and the athlete will fly through the air into the pit. Beginners love this "flying" sensation in the air! This makes them even more eager to vault.

Step Nine: The athlete is ready to start vaulting at low heights with a low hand hold. Light poles should be used for the beginners so they can get the feel of the bending pole. As the vaulter progresses the fundamental techniques should be learned, such as the correct run, pole carry, plant, take-off, swing, drive, rockback, vertical extension, pull up, turn, push up and clearance.

Part E
Special Events

No single event requires the same blend of athletic ability and versatility as does the decathlon/heptathlon.

23
Multi-Events:
The Decathlon-Heptathlon

by
Sam Adams—UC Santa Barbara
Vern Gambetta—UC Berkeley

Introduction

The decathlon/heptathlon are unique events in track and field. No other single events require the same blend of athletic ability and versatility. This blend presents a complex problem to the coach and athlete in terms of preparing for competition. The multi-events demand an intricate combination of speed, strength, and stamina. Technical skills must be constantly practiced and refined. Training for these events is more than hard work. It demands a systematic and progressive plan that encompasses all area of physical and mental preparation.

The premium in the decathlon and heptathlon is on the true all-around athlete. The world class multi-event specialist may have an outstanding event but rarely, if ever, does he/she have a weak one. The present scoring tables (revised in 1962) favor the all-around athlete. These tables tend to downplay outstanding single even performances, (except in the pole vaults), and reward consistency. (Figure #1, #2, #3) Balance is the key word and training should reflect this. Friedel Schirmer, former German national decathlon coach, has said: "Decathlons are usually never won on the strength of one outstanding event but often lost because of a weak one."

The decathlon, for men, consists of a two-day, ten-event competition. Five events are contested each day in the specified order. The first events are 100m dash, long jump, shot put, high jump, and the 400m dash. The second day events are 110m high hurdles, discus throw, pole vault, javelin throw, and 1500m run.

The heptathlon, for women, is a two-day, seven-event competition. Four events are contested the first day. They are, in order, 100m hurdles, shot put, high jump, and 200m dash. Three events are contested on the second day. They are long jump, javelin throw, and 800m run.

Philosophy of Training

The very nature of the decathlon/heptathlon suggests that training should be a slow methodical process. Training can be likened to putting together a large puzzle. Each piece (event) must be carefully prepared for. Through a thorough training program, the pieces will come together in a good score.

A proper foundation must be carefully laid in the first years of training. Progress should not be hurried. One must not think in terms of days or months, but in years.

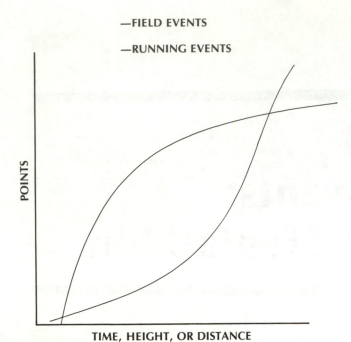

—FIELD EVENTS

—RUNNING EVENTS

POINTS

TIME, HEIGHT, OR DISTANCE

Running Events — Progressive
Field Events — Logarithmic

Example

100m	13.0 ► 12.5	88 pts
	11.0 ► 10.5	128 pts
High Jump	5'11" ► 6'3"	89 pts
	6'6" ► 6'10 3/4"	85 pts

Figure #1. Decathlon Scoring Table.

Figure #2. Decathlon Scoring

	500 pts	700 pts	1,000 pts
100m	12.5	11.5	10.3
LJ	18'2"	21'1"	25'11"
SP	34'7¼"	44'5½"	61'6¼"
HJ	5'3"	5'11½"	7'1½"
400m	57.9	52.5	46.0
110mHH	19.2	16.6	13.7
Dis	102'2"	133'7"	188'7"
PV	9'6¼"	11'9¾"	15'8"
Jav	133'2"	180'9"	265'9"
1500	4:44.0	4:14.5	3:40.2

Figure #3 Heptathlon Scoring

	500 pts	750 pts	1,000 pts
100mH	17.7	15.0	13.1
SP	28'8"	41'¼"	55'7¼"
HJ	4'3¼"	4'11½"	5'9¼"
LJ	14'1"	17'5"	21'1¼"
800m	2:47.5	2:23.2	2:05.1
7.00m	29.7	26.2	23.3
Jav	81'2¾"	127'10"	184'10"

Few decathletes have risen to national class in less than three years. East German experts feel it takes eight years to reach the top level in multi-event competition.

Compromise is an intergal part of multi-event training. There are times when it is necessary to sacrifice some immediate gains in an event in order to perfect a technique that will yield more permenent long term results. Excellence in the multi-events also means a compromise in the ultimate success in any single event. The decathlete/heptathlete cannot devote the time to specialized training that the single-event performer can.

The holistic approach must be used when setting up a training program. One must take into account the whole person, not just physical aspects of training. It is necessary to evaluate total life-style of an athlete including occupation, age, training facilities, coaching, competitive opportunity, etc. Not until all these unique characteristics have been considered can the proper program be designed.

Generally, the development of the multi-event athlete can be divided into two distinct stages: the **learning stage** and the **specificity stage**. The main objective in the learning stage is to balance performance by working on the weaker events. During this stage, the athlete should concentrate on good all-around physical development and sound learning of the technique events. The actual physical training is aimed at developing speed, general strength, and endurance. It would be advisable during ths stage, to compete each season in the number of multi-event competitions that allows adequate time to recover and train between each one. A good rule of thumb is for the athlete to compete in as many competitions as years in training. In other competitions, the decathlete should try to compete as often as possible in "key events", the 100m, 400m, 110mHH, and PV. For the heptathlete, these would be the 100m hurdles, high jump, shot put or javelin. This learning stage can last for three or four years until the weak events are brought up to a standard of good all-around performance.

The specificity stage of training should begin when the athlete achieves a certain amount of parity between the three groups of events (runs, jumps, and throws) (i.e. when there are no glaring weaknesses). The emphasis in this stage of training is on giving reasonably equal attention to each event. Training emphasis during this stage is aimed on sharpening speed, specific strength, more speed endurance and specific endurance. This is the stage of training when the athlete becomes a true multi-event specialist.

Training Components

A multi-event training program should include the following components:

1) **Speed** - The development of sprinting speed is an integral and important part of training from the very beginning. At least five events in the decathlon and four in the heptathlon are directly related to speed. Speed training should be carried out year round, not just as

pre-season and in-season activities. Methods used should be sprint form drills, starts, and sprinting over 30m, 60m, 100m, and 150m.

2) Speed Endurance - (It could also be called special endurance.) Essentially this is 400m training. The emphasis is on carrying the speed developed in the speed component over longer distances. Training consists of running 200m, 300m 500m and 600m at various speeds and combinations.

3) Technique - Sound (basic) technique is fundamental to the development of the athlete's potential. He/she should strive to develop good consistent nerve patterns in all field events. The challenge is to find a technique that is simple and mechanically sound. Through its formation, each athlete develops a personal style. Wilt and Ecker state it very well:

"The personal style depends on the individual's abilities—body structure, speed, strength, endurance, muscular coordination, sense of balance and rhythm. Top performances are the result of the application of the right technique expressed in personal style."

Each athlete should develop a framework for the events with a set of cues to remind him/her of the points of technique which he/she wishes to emphasize.

The learning stage should have the greatest emphasis on technique. This is when the fundamental concepts and sound motor patterns are developed. Technique is refined and sharpened during the specificity stage.

A very important aspect of technique that is often neglected by multi-event athletes is running technique. By this is meant running form, starting technique, relaxation, and strategy. The athlete should be aware of these factors and consider them potential sources of added points.

4) Strength Training - This can be divided into two sub-categories:

General strength training consists of the traditional weight training exercises including squats, snatches, cleans, clean and jerks and bench press. These exercises emphasize the development of total overall body strength. The younger or beginning athlete may initially confine his/her general strength training to a circuit on a Universal Gym. Later he/she can move to the more dynamic and competitive olympic types of lifting.

Specific strength training encompasses the more dynamic exercises to develop power for running, jumping and throwing. They include bounding, hopping, jumping over hurdles, depth jumping and medicine ball exercises.

General strength training dominates the learning stage. Once the athlete becomes more proficient and enters the specificity stage of training, strength training is divided almost equally between general and specific strength. It is important that strength training parallels technique work and does not take precedence over it.

5) Endurance training - The purpose of endurance training is to develop the aerobic base to run a good 1500m/800m and to provide the general endurance necessary to handle the long hours of competition. This running should be based on the need for general endurance while keeping in mind that the 1500m has a 50%-50% aerobic - anaerobic split and that the 800m is predominantly anaerobic. Endurance training can be accomplished by an off-season 20-30 min. steady run every other morning and a 20-30 min. Fartlek session once a week. During the season, several pace 800m or 1200m runs would be advisable.

6) Mobility (Flexibility) Training - This area is often neglected or downplayed as an important component of training. However, it is essential since it assists in injury prevention as well as aiding technique (by allowing greater range of movement and faster movement through a given range.) A daily 15 min. pre- and post-workout stretching session will pay large dividends.

Decathlon/Heptathlon Training Components

In a sound multi-event training program, each phase should include these components: 1) speed, 2) speed (anaerobic) endurance, 3) technique, 4) general endurance (aerobic), 5) strength, and 6) flexibility. The following table will give a clearer picture of the training components required in each event:

Table I. The Training Components Required for each Decathlon/Hepathlon Event

	Speed	Speed Endurance	Strength	Technique	General Endurance	Flexibility
100m	65%	10%	15%	5%*	—	5%
400m	30%	45%	10%	5%*	5%	5%
100mH-110mHH	30%	25%	5%	30%	—	10%
800m-1500m	—	45%	5%	5%*	45%	—
SP	10%	—	40%	45%	—	5%
DT	10%	—	30%	55%	—	5%
JT	10%	—	15%	65%	—	10%
PV	25%	—	20%	50%	—	5%
HJ	15%	—	30%	45%	—	10%
LJ	40%	—	20%	35%	—	5%

*Technique is defined in these events as running form, relaxation, starting technique, and sense of pace. This chart is adapted from a chart by Ron Witchey in "Year-Round Decathlon Training Schedule," **Track Technique, #64,** June, 1976.

This chart is not the gospel, but a framework to help set up a training program. The various percentage values have been assigned specifically with the multi-events in mind. For the single event specialist, the requirements could differ a great deal. They could also differ for each individual multi-event athlete depending on the varying strengths and weaknesses.

Training Organization

Once one has a grasp of the components of multi-event training, it is crucial that these are organized in the proper training sequence. On any given training day, the athlete should do sprint and technique work before any speed endurance training. Endurance and strength or power training should be at the end of the session.

In a sequence of training days, the same principle applies. Technique work should follow a rest or light training day. Speed and speed endurance should be in the middle of a training cycle with endurance and strength work towards the end.

Because of the sheer demands of the decathlon/heptathlon, the training load will be heavy. Workload should be evenly distributed over a period of time interspersed with an adequate number of rest days. Planned rest periods during a training cycle help minimize overuse injuries and ensure that a large buildup of fatigue does not occur.

Yearly Training Cycle

A yearly training cycle should be broken down into four phases: **Total rest** and **active rest** take up the month of September. **Off-season (Fall) training** (strength, speed endurance, endurance emphasis) occupy the months of October through December. The four-month January to April period **(Winter and early season)** takes in indoor and early season activities. Speed endurance and technique work dominate this phase. The work load should not be sacrificed for indoor competitive results. The **in-season** activities, May through August, ensure sharpening of speed and speed endurance and refining of technique. These are obviously crucial during the competitive phase of the yearly cycle.

There are a variety of **short-term cycles** which can be fitted into the three longer training phases of each year's activity. The holistic approach must be taken to determine the appropriate training load and format for each individual. The crucial element is the number of training days taken before a planned rest day. Experience will dictate the right combination.

Off-Season or Fall Training
(Oct.-Dec.)

The emphasis in training in the non-competitive season must focus on areas where the athlete can learn new events and correct weaknesses. Running background, endurance, speed endurance and mechanics should be stressed at this time, along with strength training, and fundamentals and concept work in technique areas.

A suggested three-week introductory cycle for beginning fall work is as follows:

Weeks 1 & 2

Monday	Tuesday	Wednesday
AM run	warm-up	AM run
warm-up	hurdle	warm-up
1 throw	drills	1 throw
weights	1 throw	weights
(circuit)	running	(circuit)
	ladder-1st wk	
	8 x 220-2nd wk	
Thursday	**Friday**	**Saturday**
warm-up	AM run	warm-up
hurdle	1 throw	hurdles
drills	weights	running
1 throw	(circuit)	2-3 miles
running		
hills		

Week 3

Monday	Tuesday	Wednesday
AM run	warmup	AM run
warmup	hurdles	warm-up
long	1 throw	1 throw
bound	running	weights
1 throw	5 x 330	(circuit)
weights		
(circuit)		
Thursday	**Friday**	**Saturday**
warm-up	AM run	warm-up
hurdles	warm-up	hurdles
1 throw	1 throw	1 throw
long	weights	running
bounding	(Max test)	timed run
running		1½ - 3 miles
hills		

All technique work in this cycle should be based on learning proper concepts and basic fundamentals. Long bounding is inserted after a reasonable level of running conditioning has been achieved.

Weight training in this introductory cycle should be of a high repetition, low resistance variety. Proper execution of the lifts, and general body conditioning are the goals. A strength test can be inserted on the final lifting day of the cycle for incentive purposes, and to help establish beginning weights for the strength program that follows. Novice lifters should continue the circuit training for an additional three-week cycle.

Running training is basically geared for background in the 200-400m, and 800-1500m. It is of relatively high repetition, moderate intensity when interval training is involved, and moderate distance and light Fartlek in the

AM runs. Once every three weeks a cross country, hard effort run of from 1½ to 3 miles can be used as an endurance test. Running mechanics should be emphasized in the warmup and in all running training.

Suggested running training sessions for the fall program.

1. Ladder—110-130-150-170-190-220—this can be run up, down, or up and down. Intensity and recovery can be varied.
2. Hill repeats—twice in each three-week cycle. 75-150 yds, moderate grade.
3. 8-12 x 220—moderate tempo, 220 recovery.
4. 5-6 x 330—moderate tempo, 4 min. recovery.
5. 550-440-330 + 4 x 220—good tempo, 8 min. recovery. Easy 220's.
6. 330-220-150 x 2—good tempo, 4 min. recovery.
7. 880 + 4 x 440—(decathlon) projected 1500 pace. Five min. recovery after the 800's, 440's on a 3 min. cycle.
8. 660 + 4 x 220—(heptathlon) projected 800 pace. Ten min. recovery after 660, 220 walk between 220's.
9. 6 x 440—projected race pace for decathlon, race pace + 10 sec. per 440 for heptathlon. Run on a 3 min. cycle.
10. 1½ - 3 mile cross country run—timed run, hard effort.

Suggested circuit weight training program for the fall program;

1. Sit-ups—15 reps.
2. Squats or leg presses—10 reps.
3. Curls—10 reps.
4. Bench press—10 reps.
5. Leg curls—15 reps.
6. Heel raises—15 reps.
7. Cleans—10 reps.
8. Military press—10 reps.
9. Flys—10 reps.
10. Pullovers—10 reps.

After this initial conditioning cycle, a different emphasis is incorporated into the training. A continued three-week cycle or a shorter cycle can be used. A three-week cycle has nine different running sessions which will be repeated at a higher intensity in the following three week cycle. It must be remembered that a multi-eventer does running activities in almost all other events, so these sessions need not be as lengthy as those of an individual event specialist.

Many events have carry over to other events. The sprints, hurdles, and jumps all complement one another, so specifics are more important in these events than general conditioning. The shot put and discus complement one another to some extent, particularly if the shot putter uses the rotational style. The javelin has it's own particular demands and must be treated with care. Injuries are common to multi-event athletes in the javelin, mostly due to faulty technique. Proper throwing techniques, extensive, progressive conditioning, and throwing activities are a must.

Jump related activities should not be incorporated into the training until a good level of running and strength conditioning has been achieved. Long bounding activities should be incorporated for several weeks before short, more explosive bounding is added, which should not be done more than once a week.

Long jump runway consistency is of prime importance to the athlete, so runway work should be done regularly, several times per week. Concept work on jumping mechanics will vary with the skill of the individual, but should be incorporated in all the athlete's training.

The pole vault is a key event in the decathlon due to the high point yield. All decathletes should do vault-related activities twice per week.

Running training is basically speed-endurance, with one day per week devoted to 800-1500m race tempo work. This does not have to be anything more than pace judgment, moderate quantity, short recovery work. The objective is to be familiar with the projected race pace, and efficiency when running at that pace.

Weight training must be based on the demands of the event, so the program should be a total body program. Extensors and flexors of all major body joints should be worked. Flexibility is of considerable importance and can be partially achieved through a proper weight training program. When lifting, the joint involved should always be put through a full range of motion. Development of leg strength is very important in multi-event training because of the explosive nature of most of the activities involved.

For beginning athletes it is very important to instill proper concepts of the events involved. All technical events should be introduced at the most basic fundamental level. Games and testing in related activities can be incorporated to maintain enthusiasm. Competition in the events should not be encouraged until a reasonable skill level has been achieved, particularly in the events where a risk of injury is involved.

The second phase of fall weight training is devoted to power development. A suggested program is as follows:

Monday-Friday	Wednesday
Mini-circuit—3 times	Mini-circuit
Sit-ups—15 rep.	Same as Monday-Friday
Leg curls—15 reps	
Heel raises—15 reps	
Power—80% maximum	Power—80% maximum
Bench press 3-5 x 6 reps	Behind neck press 3 x 6 reps
Squats 3-5 x 6 reps	Curls 3 x 6 reps
Incline press 3-5 x 6 reps	Cleans 3 x 6 reps
Mini-circuit—3 times	Mini-circuit—3 times
Pullovers—10 reps	Pullovers—10 reps
Curl—10 reps	Flys—10 reps
Flys—10 reps	

Winter and Early Season (Jan.-April)

The winter and early season training is characterized by an increase in the amount of emphasis on jump training and a blending of speed into the running program. Technique work and speed endurance are also emphasized. A sample two-week cycle follows:

	Monday	Tuesday	Wednesday	Thursday	Friday	Saturday
week #1.	AM run warmup long bnd. lg. jump shot high jump weights	warmup hurdles pole vlt (D) javelin running 8x220	AM run discus (D) shot (H) weights	warmup hurdles shot (D) javelin (H) high jmp. shrt. bnd. running 800-1500 tempo	AM run pole vlt (D) shot (H) weights	warmup hurdles long jump discus (D) javelin running 550-440-330
week #2.	AM run long bnd. shot high jump weights	warmup hurdles lg. jump pole vlt (D) javelin running 3 x 330	AM run discus (D) shot (H) weights	warmup hurdles shot (D) javelin (H) running 1320 or 660 + 4 x 220	AM run pole vlt (D) shot (H) weights	warmup hurdles lg. jump discus (D) javelin running 330-220-150 x2

D = Decathlon
H = Heptathlon

Suggested running sessions in this phase of training are as follows:

1. 3-5 x 60 from blocks. Done after warmup on non-hurdle days.

2. 6 x 150—medium-hard tempo.

3. 6-8 x 220—medium-hard tempo, good recovery.

4. 330-220-150 x 2—medium-hard tempo, good recovery.

5. 3 x 330—hard tempo, full recovery.

6. 550-440-330—hard tempo, full recovery.

7. 880 + 4 x 440-1500 tempo, 5 min. recovery after 880, 440's on 3 minute cycle. 440 x 3—800 tempo, good recovery.

8. 1320 + 4 x 220—1500 tempo, 220's easy. 660 + 4 x 200—800 tempo, 200's easy.

In-Season (May-August)

When competition gets heavy, it is very difficult to maintain cycles. This is especially true when the athlete has to compete in several meets per week. He/she should work on each event at least once per week, and incorporate a sprint or hurdle race, a jump, a throw, and a mile relay leg in competitive efforts in dual meets. Weight training will have to be modified during the competitive season to a twice per week basis.

Preparation for a decathlon or heptathlon competition includes a change of work load the week prior to the competition. A suggested pre-competition week follows:

Monday	Tuesday	Wednesday	Thursday	Friday	Sat-Sun
hurdles jump throw weights	starts runways throw 1 fast, sustained run	check runways light throws	active rest	active rest	competition

The week after after a multi-event competition should be basically a recovery week. No hard training should be attempted. Limited competition the following week is advisable.

Preparation for Multi-Event Competition

The actual time of competition in the decathlon/heptathlon is very brief. In the decathlon, the competition time totals approximately 7 min. and 30 sec. In the heptathlon, the approximate time of competition is 5 min. and 30 sec. The actual time on the field, warmup, cooldown, wait between events, and the time between jumps and throws can be between 8-12 hours. These time factors must be accounted for in workouts.

The key to a good performance is an even-tempered, consistent mental approach. It is important for the athlete to remember that the competition consists of 10/7 events. At the end of two days, all things begin to even out. A subpar performance in one event will not necessarily result in a poor score. Even at the highest levels, it is very rare for an athlete to have personal record performances in all seven or ten events.

In actual competition, the athlete should be prepared for all possibilities: weather conditions, timing and facilities. He/she should have all the equipment needed to cover these, such as extra shoes, spikes, sweats, shoe strings, or anything else that might disrupt concentration during competition.

When warming up before the start and between events, the following factors should be considered:

1) The size of the competitive field.
2) How performance will vary with weather conditions.
3) When the athlete's best throw or jump occurs. The athlete should not leave his/her best efforts in warmup.

Competition strategy is relatively simple. The athlete must know him/herself well so that he/she will, for instance, start at a height that can be cleared. The same goes for the throws. It is best to get a "safe throw" and then go for the big one. Gambling is not rewarded in multi-event competition. A no-height in an event or three fouls reap zero points. A subpar performance that yields some points is better than nothing.

Strategy in the 1500m/800m, the final events in the competition, can drastically effect the final placing and overall score. The athlete should know exactly what he/she has to run in order to score the necessary points and also be aware of what the competition will have to run. Often, to preserve a lead, the athlete may not have to beat another athlete, but may only have to maintain a certain time margin. He/she must be prepared to run as fast as needed to win.

Tips for Efficient Multi-event Training

If it is possible for short-cuts to exist in multi-event training, the following tips might be kept in mind when designing an efficient training program:

1. The athlete should not limit him/herself to 15 throws or 10 jumps in a workout (for example). He/she should keep throwing if still learning and not tired.
2. HJ and PV workouts require a good warmup. One good long session in each per week may be much better than two hurried ones.
3. Back layout high jumping (flop) requires less technical training time than does the straddle (once learned). Athletes who are presently straddling but who are suitable candidates for the flop should consider changing.
4. The athlete should do some of sprint work on the long jump runway while at the same time practicing the approach with check marks. With the high point yield, he/she cannot affort to miss the board!
5. In-season quality workouts for the 200m-400m-800m are crucial. There is not the time or energy for high repetition, slow training.
6. 1500m training can also act as a good, quick warmup for a daily training session. An 800m, 10 seconds slower than race pace (3 min. rest interval), followed by 3 x 200m at race pace (one min. rest intervals) twice a week will be helpful. The times will come down naturally as the session progresses. (This should not be too tiring as a warmup activity.)
7. Mental homework helps. The athlete should think through the essentials of technique and remember the cues. This will simplify things late in a competition when fatigue builds and the mind grows fuzzy.
8. He/she should train in the proper event sequence periodically, but not get hung up on it, and experiment and find out what works best.
9. The tables should be studied to find out where he/she can reap the biggest rewards and will benefit the most for a given amount of training time. This will depend on his/her own inherent abilities and stage of development.

Basic Concepts of Multi-Events

1. Decathlon/heptathlon is one event with 10/7 phases.
2. Consistency and balance are rewarded.
3. The athlete must be patient - success takes time.
4. Decathlon/heptathlon are speed-explosion orientated.
5. Strength and power training are the basis for sound technique.
6. The scoring table is the constant upon which training should be based.
7. Develop a sound fundamental framework of technique in each event.
8. The athlete must control his/her emotions and maintain concentration in order to maximize performance.
9. Incorporate fatigue into training periodically. Fatigue can influence technique especially on the second day of competition.
10. Properly used and timed rest is as important as training.

A total commitment is necessary to achieve success in multi-event competition.

Suggestions for Development of Multi-Events

1. More exposure at high school and junior high level.
2. More regional training camps for developing athletes and coaches.
3. More opportunities for multi-event competition. Include in big relay meets and indoor.
4. Fall and winter postal multi-event competition.
5. Decathlon classes in P.E. curriculum.

Conclusion

The multi-event athletes have no peers in the realm of sport. A total commitment is necessary to achieve success. Patience and persistence with a look to the long term are essential.

In no other event (except perhaps the marathon) can athletes with a wide range of abilities experience the same kinds of personal triumphs and satisfactions. The beginner and the world class athlete are not unlike one another in this respect. In both training and competition, the decathlon and heptathlon are generous with the amount of joy they provide.

Perhaps Bill Toomey, 1968 gold medallist and former world record holder in the decathlon, stated it most aptly: ''...you don't need cheers, headlines or even anyone to watch you perform... There's enough satisfaction just in doing it.''

24
Racewalking

by
Bob Kitchen

I. TECHNIQUE

A. DEFINITION OF RACEWALKING

Despite its sometimes odd appearance, racewalking is merely an extension of normal walking. There are two basic rules:

(1) One foot must be on the ground at all times. The lead foot must be in contact with the ground before the back foot leaves the ground. Thus, there is always a period of "double contact" when both feet are on the ground.

(2) The leg which is on the ground must be straightened at the knee during the support phase of the stride, i.e., when the leg is directly under the body. The leg may be straightened during other phases of the stride for reasons of speed and efficiency, but it must be straightened during the support phase in order to be legal.

A violation of (1) is commonly called "lifting" and is cause for disqualification. A violation of (2), when the knee is bent during the support phase, is commonly called "creeping" and is also cause for disqualification.

B. BASIC RACEWALKING TECHNIQUE

The surest method for teaching an athlete to racewalk is to have him/her walk normally on track or road and gradually increase speed. In order to keep increasing speed without breaking into a run, the athlete should find him/herself naturally doing several things.

(1) The arms will rise and swing back and forth over a wide arc. The angle at the elbow will approach 90°.

(2) Because of the more powerful drive that the arms give, the stride length will increase. The heel touches the ground first and as speed increases the angle of the sole to the ground increases from nearly 0° (flat-footed) to about 45°.

Racewalking action.

(3) The greater the speed, the greater force with which the leg and heel hit the ground. As this happens, the leg will tend to land straight at the knee.

Below is a sequence of the racewalking action. Note especially the position of the arms, foot placement, the straightening of the knees and posture.

C. ADVANCED TECHNIQUE AND CORRECTION OF FAULTS

1. POSTURE

The correct posture for racewalking, both for efficiency and legality, is from "perpendicular" to a 5° forward lean. (See opposite page)

Faults: Too far a forward lean leads to disqualification, as knees will usually remain in the bent position. Too far backward lean results in loss of power in the extension of the rear foot.

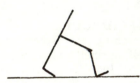
Too far forward.

Too far backward.

Corrections: Strengthen the stomach muscles in order to maintain proper posture. Increase ankle flexibility to enable forward lean.
Have coaches, teammates constantly remind the walker when he/she is leaning forward or backward.
An excellent antidote for backward lean walking up moderate hills.

2. FOOT PLACEMENT

The ideal foot placement is "walking on a straight line" (see below). Maintaining the power in the same direction as the line of direction results in the maximum distance covered for the same energy expended. Other foot placements result in loss of power and distance. In other words, one can have a longer stride with the same effort. A loss of 2 cm from poor foot placement equals approximately 400 meters (2 minutes) in a 20 km or 1 km (5 minutes) in a 50 km!

INCORRECT 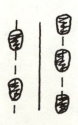 CORRECT

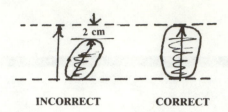
INCORRECT   **CORRECT**

Corrections: Increase hip flexibility for greater range of motion and length of stride.
Check to see if orthotics are needed; or if one leg is longer than the other (heel lift needed); or if other biomechanical problems exist. Develop proper roll: push off ball of foot and roll off tip of big toes. Do not push off the side of the foot.

3. KNEES

Each stride should ideally begin with a straight leg (not bent at the knee) for maximum power and legality, although this is not necessary under the rules. The knee may be bent upon the contact of the heel with the ground, especially in the longer slower races; but the knee must be straight underneath the body or the violation called "creeping" occurs. At the moment of contact with the heel to the ground, the quadriceps should be relaxed.

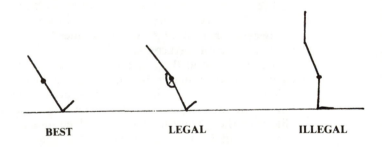
BEST   **LEGAL**   **ILLEGAL**

Corrections for creeping tendencies:
Strengthen and increase the flexibility of the hamstrings and the area behind the knee with standard weight and stretching exercises. Emphasize driving back with the knee and powering forward the opposing arm over the waistband of the shorts.

If the walker has trouble straightening the knee consistently, have him/her warm up thoroughly before doing any fast racewalking and avoid walking up steep hills.

Have the walker do repeat sprint walks at high speed with an exaggerated bend forward at the waist, letting the supporting leg collapse and relax underneath him/her.

4. HIPS

Proper rotation of the hips allows a walker not only to achieve the proper foot placement, but also to gain extra distance without overstanding. Diagram (a) shows a walker's foot placement with no hip rotation, while diagram (b) shows the extra distance gained with proper hip rotation.

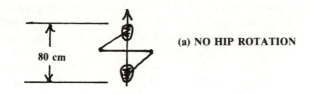

(a) NO HIP ROTATION

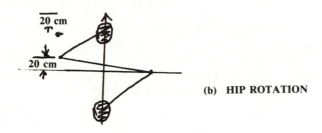

(b) HIP ROTATION

The proper hip rotation is actually made up of rotation in both the horizontal and vertical directions. Most of the rotation required is in the horizontal or forward direction. The vertical rotation or hip drop, as it is often called, should only be about one-third the horizontal rotation as shown below.

good proportion of horiz. & vert. rotation

poor proportion: many rotations but little forward progress

One of the simplest and most effective methods to develop proper rotation is to walk on a straight line. While doing so, purposely overstride and cross over (right foot on left side of line and vice-versa).

5. SHOULDERS AND ARMS

The shoulders and hips work together. The same work by the shoulders is transferred to the hips, so they are dependent upon each other. 50% of one's power comes from the shoulders (not the arms) and 50% from the hips. This power derives from the dipping or rolling of the shoulders in coordination with the dropping of the hips (see below). The proper shoulder roll can be developed by keeping the elbows low, especially when in front of the body.

The arms, naturally, work with the shoulders and should be carried at approximately an angle of 90°. Elbows should be kept in close to the body (no "chicken winging") with the forearm brushing the waistband of the shorts. The hands should reach no higher than the nipple line nor cross over the center line of the chest. Constant attention must be given so that the shoulders and arms remain relaxed and not tense for full economy and power.

BEST   **INEFFICIENT LOSS OF POWER**

II. TRAINING OBJECTIVES

Racewalking is an endurance event, physiologically akin to long distance running. The principle international distances are: 10 km (juniors), 20 km and 50 km. Training, therefore, is aimed at increasing cardiovascular capacity, both aerobic and anaerobic. Racewalking also requires the development of upper body strength and increased flexibility in shoulders, torso, hips and legs for efficiency and range of motion. In addition, attention must always be paid to developing legal technique.

III. STRUCTURING A TRAINING PROGRAM

Developing an individual training program for an athlete depends upon which skills are required and the distance of the event. Racewalking distances range from 1500 meters/1 mile all the way up to 50 km. The suggested programs are primarily directed towards 10 km, which is the national and international distance. However, the drills, workouts and principles can be extended to the needs of the world-class walker.

A. DRILLS

1. Backward sprinting: 10-12x60-100 meters.
2. Walking on a straight line. One foot directly in front of one another and crossing-over (left foot on right side of line, etc.).
3. Running action with dumbbells (5-10 lbs.) 5-15 minutes.
4. Static stretching (see article on flexibility) and "Mexican" exercises (see below).
5. Lots of racewalking. The extraordinary technique of racewalking requires a lot of practice in order to develop the specific muscles needed and acquire the necessary rhythm.

B. STRENGTH TRAINING

1. Weight Training

Because of the great demands that racewalking places on the upper body, some form of weightlifting is needed for every walker. What is needed and beneficial depends upon the basic strength and body type of the walker.

The goal for weight training in racewalking is increased muscular endurance as well as increased flexibility. Any weight training should be followed by some walking in order to release tightness and tension from the shoulders and arms. Relatively light weights should be used.

The following is a general program from which adaptation can be made, depending upon body type, basic strength and experience in weightlifting. Begin with 20-30 min of warmup—running and calisthenics-two to three times a week (Mon-Wed-Fri, etc.)

Exercise	Week 1-6	Week 7-10	Week 11-
1. Hook lying sit-ups add weight and/or incline	20-30	20-30	20-30
2. Military Press or Bench Press (best)	3 X 10	3 X 6	4 X 5
3. Upright Rowing	3 X 10	3 X 6	4 X 5
4. Parallel Squats	3 X 10	3 X 6	4 X 5
5. Toe Raises (In, Out, Fwd)	3 X 15	3 X 10	3 X 10
6. Bicep Arm Curls	3 X 10	3 X 6	3 X 5
7. Bent-over Rowing	3 X 10	3 X 6	3 X 5
8. Chinups	1 X 10	1 X 10+	
9. Leg Curls and Knee Extensions	3 X 10	3 X 6	4 X 5
10. Good Morning Exercise (Hold bar behind neck, bend forward)	3 X 10	3 X 6	4 X 5
11. Dumbbell Side Bending	3 X 10	3 X 10	3 X 6

2. Hill Training

Hill training (similar to the Lydiard method) is extremely beneficial in pre-competitive season for cardio-vascular development as well as increasing power in the hips, legs and arms. Try to find a long hill (440-1200 meters) with an incline steep enough so that one can straighten at the knees with some power exerted. When one is too tired to "straighten", the workout should be concluded. Begin with 1-2 repetitions until one can do 4-6 reps at a strong pace. Do this workout once or twice a week in the pre-season.

Hard, steady mountain or trail climbing in which one does not straighten is, nevertheless, very beneficial in off-season training.

C. FLEXIBILITY WORK

In recent years, a series of flexibility exercises performed while walking has gained a widespread acceptance. They are often nicknamed "Mexican exercises" due to their popularization by the world champion Mexicans.

These exercises' main purpose is to loosen the upper body and help the walker develop a well-coordinated flow with the shoulders and pelvic area. Try to work the entire series into every warm-up session and be aware of the coordinated movements which these exercises develop during all training sessions.

The following is a description of the three basic exercises:

1. Windmill

Swing first one arm back over the shoulder, then the other so that a "windmill" appearance is simulated. Remember to bring the arms back with the elbows as straight as possible, and keep a sharp angle to the body, not letting the hand swing freely as if it were a pendulum. Keep the head up, neck relaxed. One swing of the arm to one stride of the leg is the upper tempo.

2. Cross-Over

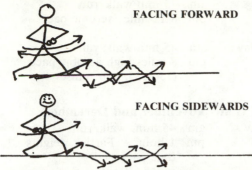

FACING FORWARD

FACING SIDEWARDS

The arms are held high, with the hands clasped in front of the chest, and the feet across over a straight line. Then turning the shoulders sideways and looking back over the rear shoulder at the trailing foot, the arms are again swung, elbows high, front and back. In these exercises, be sure to extend the hips well and go as slow as necessary to achieve the cross-over. Keep the neck relaxed.

3. Shoulder Roll

The arm is lifted up as a unit, shoulder to the ear, and then the forearm is dropped rapidly, shrugging the shoulder and relaxing the upper body. At the same time, walk in tight circles, crossing over slightly. The tempo should be slow.

These exercises should be interspersed with slow racewalking, i.e., a set of exercises, 100 meters walking, another set, and so on.

The more time spent on these exercises, the better walking coordination and relaxation one will achieve. Eventually, they should all feel natural and part of one's normal walking rhythm.

It is not suggested, however, that these be the only flexibility exercises used. See special section on static exercises.

D. ENDURANCE WORK

The basis of any walking program is a substantial endurance base. 90% of the walking done in pre-competitive season should be aerobic distance walks. These should include "long slow" (9-11 min/mi), Fartlek; and "long fast" (7:30-9:00 min/mi). The glue which pulls it all together is the "long long" walk. These should be included every week in pre-season and every other week in the early competitive season. The particular distance depends upon one's competitive distance and present condition. Speed should be from "long slow" up to "long moderate". For one milers, 10-12 miles; 10 km, 12-15 miles; 20 km, 15-20 miles; 50 km, 20-30 km.

E. SPEED WORK

Anaerobic speed work and pace work is just as essential to top class racewalking as it is to running. Basically, the same type of interval, Fartlek and pace work utilized for runners can be directly applied to walkers. (See sample training program below)

The basic principle to keep in mind is that walking takes longer to cover a given distance than running. Therefore, a 3 minute run at a high cardio-vascular effort roughly equals a 5 minute walk at the same hard effort. The body may not be moving as quickly, but the same strain on the system is there and lasts longer. As a rule, intervals should be a larger percentage of the racing distance than in running.

In all high speed walking, careful attention must be given to legal technique so that when the athlete is tired, faults do not inadvertently creep into his/her style.

F. RUNNING AND OTHER SPORTS

Whether a racewalker should include running in his/her training is a controversial topic, and several theories exist. The world champion Mexicans ban running from their training, but the Russians and East Germans use it to varying degrees. In running one pushes off the ground and lands on a bent knee, both actions counter to the requirements of legal walking. Yet many walkers have benefited from running cross-country. The cardio-vascular development cannot be denied, especially when the walker is young. Also the value of a season of fellowship for the "lonely walker" is a dimension often overlooked.

Cross-country skiing has also been popular for the walkers in the northern countries. The rhythmic, gliding motion of X-C skiing is very similar to racewalking. The cardio-vascular system, upper body and rhythm all benefit greatly. While there is substantial hip extension in X-C, it is different from racewalking. In X-C one skis in two parallel tracks; in racewalking one walks on a straight line.

There is no definitive answer yet, for "the jury is still out." The key to watch is how any non-walking activity affects the technique and rhythm of one's racewalking. In any event, during the early and mid-competitive season the serious walker should only walk. That is the period when one wants to specialize.

G. BASIC DIFFERENCES BETWEEN TRAINING FOR WALKING AND RUNNING

1. In walking one must develop and train different muscles from those used in running. The center of gravity of the walker must stay much lower than the runner's. The quadriceps remain loose or isolated rather than tensed in running.
2. There is greater stress in racewalking on the upper body than in running. The "average" walker is considerably more muscular in the upper body than his/her running counterpart.
3. The walker spends a longer time on his/her feet than the runner, taxing all systems that much longer. a top-class marathoner may run sub-2:20, but a top-class 50 km walker will walk approximately 4:00.
4. There is always the problem of legal walking technique to be concerned with.

IV. SAMPLE TRAINING PROGRAM
(10km Walk)

A. Phase I (August-September)

Sunday am 45 min walk or run aerobic (pulse 140-150)

    pm 3 hours slow aerobic pace (140-155/min pulse)

Monday am 45 min walk/run

    pm 2 hour moderate to slow pace; weights

Tuesday am 45 min walk/run

    pm 1½ hour high aerobic pace (150-155 pulse) static stretching

Wednesday am 45 min walk/run

    pm 1 hour fast pace or Fartlek weights

Thursday am 45 min walk/run

    pm 2 hour moderate to slow pace; static stretching

Friday am 45 min walk/run

    pm 1½ hour high aerobic pace (as Thursday)

Saturday am 45 min walk/run

    pm 1 hour fast or Fartlek static stretching

During Phase I, the morning workouts are optional or can be done every day. Also a walker may choose to join for cross country during this period.

B. Phase II (October to Thanksgiving)

Sunday am Rest

    pm 2-3 hour walk

Monday am 45 min walk or run (aerobic)

    pm 10-12 miles aerobic (pulse 140-150/min.) weights

Tuesday am 45 min. walk/run

    pm 5-7 x 1000 "readiness" pace (pace one can maintain with moderate ease at this date)

Wednesday am 45 min walk/run

    pm 10-12 miles aerobic pace; weights

Thursday am 45 min walk/run

    pm 880 or mile repeats at goal pace (4-6 mile total); static stretching

Friday am 45 min walk/run

    pm 8-12 miles aerobic pace

Saturday am 45 min walk/run

    pm 8 miles high aerobic pace (150-155/min. pulse)

C. Phase III (Late November and December)

Sunday am 45 min. walk/run

    pm 1 hour + Fartlek weights date pace = P speed all out = S

Tuesday am 45 min. walk/run

    pm (indoors) 12 x 1000 or 12 x 400 (90 sec. rest between) P, P, P, S; P, P, S, S; P, S, S, S. 12 x 40-60 meters backward sprints; static stretching

Wednesday am 45 min. walk/run

    pm 2 hour high aerobic walk weights

Thursday am 45 min. walk/run

    pm repeat 880's for technique and individual problems at date pace; static stretching; 12 x 40-60 m backward sprints

Friday am 45 min walk/run

    pm 1 hour walk easy; weights

Saturday am rest

    pm competition - 2 miles OR 1.5 hours high aerobic walk; static stretching

D. Phase IV (January to March)

Sunday, Monday, Wednesday, Friday and Saturday - same as Phase III

Tuesday am same as above

    pm 1. 4-6 mile

       2. 1.5 mile, mile, 3/4 mile, 880, 2 x 440, 10 x 110

       3. 4 x 440, 1 x 880, 4 x 440 OR 4 x 880, mile, 4 x 880 2 x 880, 1 x 440, mile, 440, 2 x 880 (to meet challenger in a race): 880 slightly faster than race pace; 440 all out; mile race pace

Thursday pm 880's or combinations of 880-440 (880 pace; 440 speed)

E. Phase V (March)

Reestablish base conditioning for 3-4 weeks. See Phase I.

F. Phase VI (April-May)

Sunday	pm	3 hours aerobic walk (140-155 or higher pulse)
Monday	am	45 min. walk/run
	pm	6-9 x 1-1.25 miles OR 3-4 x 2 miles OR combination of 1 & 2 miles, weights
Tuesday	am	45 min. walk/run
	pm	2 hour walk; static stretching
Wednesday	am	45 min. walk/run
	pm	12-20 x 1000 OR fartlek for 1-1.25 hours, weights
Thursday	am	45 min. walk/run
	pm	2 hour walk
Friday	am	45 min. walk/run
	pm	1 hour easy and 4-8 x 220-440
Saturday	pm	Competition, 5000 up to 20 km (mainly 10 km)

G. Phase VII (Summer: June-July)

Training here depends upon what the athlete wants for the summer. Recommended are some races or active rest with slow to moderate pace distance work. The main emphasis is to build a larger base for the future.

One should work all year round on weight training, static stretching and stamina training.

V. RACEWALK JUDGING

Every walking race must have judges to enforce the rules of legal racewalking. Ideally, there should be at least three judges with one designated as the head or chief judge. Of course, ideal situations do not always exist, especially in local meets. Nevertheless, a knowledgeable, fair and mobile judge can handle a track race to the satisfaction of all.

The judge should carry an index card and immediately record the number of the athlete and the type of infraction. The symbol for violation of rule (1) above "lifting" is ⌣. The symbol for violation of rule (2) "creeping" is >. If a judge observes flagrant or intentional violation of either rule, immediate disqualification (DQ) should result. If a walker appears to be on the verge of an infraction, but is still within the rules, he/she should be given a caution. Any number of cautions may be received without DQ. When three judges rule for DQ, the athlete is out of the race. The chief judge only may issue the official DQ.

Juding Tips: Indications that a walker may be walking illegally.

1. Vigorous pushing off with the rear toes. This may push the entire body off the ground.
2. Coming down flat-footed with the lead foot. This method of landing is not illegal, but there is a tendancy for the lead foot not to touch the ground before the rear foot leaves.
3. Bouncing head and shoulders. Again, this is only a sign that a person **may** be off the ground. To get the best view to evaluate a walker for lifting, a judge should block out the upper body with the hand or a card and just observe the feet.
4. High, tensed shoulders and high arm action may bring the walker off the ground.
5. A sudden burst of speed. When a walker increases speed quickly to pass someone or avoid being overtaken at the finish he/she may start to lift.
6. Bending forward at the waist or shoulders. This posture often makes it difficult for the walker to straighten his/her leg at the knee, resulting in creeping.
7. A noticeable "limp" in the stride of the walker almost always indicates that the walker is not straightening one leg and therefore, throwing off his/her balance and rhythm.

The best position for judging is on the outside of the track, observing the walker from the side, approximately 50 feet before and after he/she passes the judge.